PICK®

Pocket Guide

5th Edition

JONATHAN E. SISK

McGraw-Hill, Inc.

New York St. Louis San Francisco Auckland Bogotá Caracas
Lisbon London Madrid Mexico City Milan Montreal New Delhi
Paris San Juan São Paulo Singapore Sydney Tokyo Toronto

Notices

Pick and Advanced Pick	Pick Systems, Inc.
MS-DOS	Microsoft Corporation
UNIX	Bell Laboratories

FIFTH EDITION
FIRST PRINTING

First edition, October, 1982
Second printing, January, 1983
Second edition, October, 1983
Third edition, June, 1986
Fourth edition, July, 1988
Second printing, March, 1989
Fourth edition – Desk Reference Edition (TAB Books), 1989
Fifth edition – Desk Reference Edition (McGraw-Hill), November, 1991
Printed in the USA.

Library of Congress Cataloging-in-Publication Data

Sisk, Jonathan E.
PICK pocket guide / by Jonathan E. Sisk.—5th ed.
p. cm.
Includes index.
ISBN 0-8306-3827-X (p)
1. Operating systems (Computers) 2. Pick (Computer program)
I. Title.
QA76.76.063S574 1990
005.4′46—dc20 91-11216
CIP

Questions regarding the content of this book should be directed to:
JES & Associates, Inc.
P.O. Box 19274
Irvine, CA 92713

Acquisitions Editor: Ron Powers
Technical Editor: Mark LeSuer
Production: Katherine G. Brown
Proofreaders: Linda King
Kelly Christman
Typesetting: Rhonda Baker
Book Design: Jaclyn J. Boone

Related Titles

Exploring the Pick Operating System, Second Edition
Jonathan E. Sisk and Steve VanArsdale

PICK/BASIC: A Programmer's Guide
Jonathan E. Sisk

The Pick Perspective
Ian J. Sandler

The Ultimate Pocket Guide, Version II
Jonathan E. Sisk

The CIES/Pick Pocket Guide
Jonathan E. Sisk

Pick for the IBM PC and Compatibles
John and Dale Winters

Pick for Professionals: Advanced Methods & Techniques
Harvey E. Rodstein

Programming with IBM PC BASIC and the Pick Database System
David Clark

Contents at a Glance

Contents

Dedication

This book is dedicated to the memory of Ken Simms, who, in addition to being my mentor, was a great friend, a warm and compassionate human being, and a rock & roll animal.

Acknowledgments

I would like to thank the following individuals who have contributed to this book over the years: Ken All, John Brandon, Mary Brooks, Jerry Burley, Henry Eggers, Manuel Goyenchea, Terri Hale, Toby Kraft, Tim Malnati, Dick Pick, Harvey Rodstein, Ian Sandler, Ken Simms, and John Treankler.

Preface

This edition of the *Pick Pocket Guide* is current through release 3.1 from Pick systems on the PC-AT.

With the printing of this edition, there are now more than sixty thousand copies of this book in print.

We will do our best to keep it as up to date as possible and will contact you when new versions become available. If you purchased this book through a dealer and would like to be notified of new editions, please contact us and we'll put your name on our book replacement list.

Your comments are welcome and should be directed to me in care of JES & Associates Inc., Post Office Box 19274, Irvine, California, 92713, (714) 553-8200 and by FAX at (714) 553-9779.

Foreword

The Pick market has enjoyed stellar growth in the last decade. Adding to the health of this marketplace is the fact that JES & Associates has also paralleled the same growth.

Jon and his organization have, through a series of significant contributions, benefited the most important component in the Pick world, the end user.

Tens of thousands of Pick users have gained technical expertise by taking advantage of Jon's education and training.

Now, as we all face new challenges with the coming of Open Systems, we look to Jon again to help lead the Pick world into unparalleled growth of software functionality.

DICK PICK
Pick Systems

About SMA standards

The Pick Spectrum Association (formerly SMA: Spectrum Manufacturers Association) has agreed to allow references to the "standard" Pick features as defined by the SMA standards documentation. Copies of the SMA standards documentation are available for a subscription price of $25.00 per copy and includes future updates. Please direct all inquiries for the SMA standards documentation to:

Spectrum Manufacturers Association
10675 Treena Street, Suite 103
San Diego, CA 92131
(619) 578-3152 FAX: (619)271-1032

SMA standards are designed to serve the public interest through eliminating misunderstandings between manufacturers and purchasers, facilitating interchangeability and improvement of products, and assisting the purchaser in selecting and obtaining, with minimum delay, the proper product for his particular need.

"Some material contained herein is designated as proprietary by individual member companies of SMA listed below. Any unauthorized use of such proprietary information is prohibited."

Documentation conventions

The following documentation conventions are used consistently throughout the Pick Pocket Guide:

Convention	*Meaning*
{ }	Braces indicate an optional parameter. Typically shown where it *must* be included in a command or statement. For example: `>POVF {(P)}`
{ }...	Braces followed by three ellipsis points indicate an optional parameter that may be repeated.
( )	Options parameter indicator. Unless otherwise indicated, options are always the very last argument in a command line, enclosed in parentheses.
lowercase italic	User-specified argument or parameter. For example: MSG *acctname text*
UPPERCASE	Either means a literal that must be entered exactly as shown or a literal displayed by a process. For example: `>CREATE-Account<cr>`
"	Double quotes are used to indicate a literal parameter.

1
Editor

Format of TCL commands related to the Editor

ED {DICT} *filename itemlist** {(*options*)}

-or-

EDIT {DICT} *filename itemlist** {(*options*)}

-or-

EDIT-LIST *listname*

Activates the editor process for entry or update of any file-resident item in the system (i.e., PICK/BASIC programs, PROCs, data items, etc.). The EDIT-LIST command also invokes the standard editor.

Options:

- A Activates the Assembly formatter. Equivalent to the AS editor command.
- M Activates the Macro expansion function. Equivalent to the M editor command.
- P Directs the output to the system printer via the spooler.
- S Suppresses the display of line numbers in normal edit mode, or suppresses object code display when the assembly formatter is "on." Equivalent to the S editor command.
- Z Suppresses the "Top" and EOI" messages.

RECOVER-FD
ITEM NAME: *itemname*

Used to recover an item deleted with the editor FD command. It must be executed immediately after the FD command, otherwise the item is lost. If a list of items is active, there is no chance of recovering the item. This does *not* work on a list deleted through the EDIT-LIST command.

About SMA standards

No standard document currently exists for the Editor. Being one of the oldest components of the system, however, most of these commands work on nearly all versions of Pick.

About Editor commands

All Editor commands can be issued in either upper or lowercase characters and *must* be followed by a carriage return or linefeed.

About delimiters

Some of the following commands might require multiple arguments. These arguments must be separated by a single character called a delimiter. The delimiter can be any nonnumeric character that does *not* appear in the string or strings being affected.

Delimiters are sometimes used in the following EDITOR commands:

DE, FI, FS, I, L, ME, and R.

As a documentation standard, throughout this section the "/" character has been used wherever a delimiter is required in one of these commands. This, of course, can be changed as needed.

Command glossary

Command	*Function/Description*
n	Go to line number "n" (Same as Gn)
<cr>	Advance to next line
^	Toggle "wildcard" function
?	Display filename, itemname, line#
A	Again (repeat last "Locate" command)
AS	Assembly formatter
B	Bottom
C	Column display
DE	Delete line(s)
EX	Exit current item
EXK	Exit item and return to TCL
F	Flip buffers
FD	Delete current item
FDK	Deletes item and return to TCL
FI	File current item
FIK	File item and return to TCL
FIL	File current item as "list"

FIO	File into new item and overwrite
FS	File "save" item and remain in item
FSL	File "save" current item as "list"
FSO	File "save" item and overwrite duplicate
Gn	Go to linenumber "n"
I	Insert
Ln	List "n" lines
L	Locate
M	Macro expansion
ME	Merge
N	Next (move lined pointer down)
Pn	Prestored command load/activate
PD	Display prestored commands
R	Replace (first occurrence in line)
RU	Replace (all occurrences in line)
S	Suppress line numbers
S?	Display size in bytes
T	Top
TB	Tabstop
X	Oops! Cancels effect of last command
XF	Uh oh! Cancels all changes since last "Flip"
Z	Zone column limits

Editor error messages

COL#?

Appears when a nonnumeric character appears in a syntax position that would ordinarily require a number.

CMND?

Short for "command?." The editor's equivalent for system error message 3.

EOI n

End of Item occurs at line "n."

L n

Indicates either the current line number (with the ? command), or the last line affected by an X (oops) command.

NOT ON FILE.

Can't find requested item with the ME (merge) command.

SEQN?

Sequence? Remember that changes *must* be made from the top down. Issue an "F" (flip) command and try again.

STRING?

Usually means that the second part of the replace string has been omitted or that the syntax for the merge command is incomplete. Also appears when a nonnumeric character appears in a syntax position that would ordinarily require a number.

TOP

Positioned at attribute 0, top of item.

Wrapup error messages:

'id' Deleted.	(Error Message item-id = 222)
'id' Exited.	(Error Message item-id = 220)
'id' Filed.	(Error Message item-id = 221)

Editor commands

<cr>

Advances line pointer to next line and displays line.

^

Toggles the function of the up-arrow "wildcard" search character used in Locate and Replace commands. Initially, this function is on.

?

Displays current itemname and line number.

A

Again. Repeats last Locate command.

AS

Assembly format. Toggles assembly format on or off.

B

Bottom. Positions line pointer to end (bottom) of item.

C

Column. Displays terminal columnar positions.

DE*#lines*{/}
-or-

DE#*lines/string*

-or-

DE#*lines/string/b − e*

Delete. Deletes specified number of lines starting at current position (line number). Note that line pointer is not incremented. If a string is specified, only the lines containing the string are deleted.

The "b" and "e" parameters respectively indicate the beginning and ending column ranges in which strings are eligible for deletion.

A delete command ending in a delimiter displays the lines as they are deleted.

Examples of the DE command:

DE	Deletes the current line.
DE10	Deletes the current and next nine lines.
DE10/	Deletes and displays the current and next nine lines.
DE10/ABC	Deletes lines containing the string, "ABC," in the current and next nine lines.
DE10/ABC/5−9	Deletes and displays the lines containing the string, "ABC," in column ranges 5 through 9, in the current and next nine lines.

EX

Exits current item without saving any changes. Control returns to the next item in the list or to the TCL if no more items are in the list. See also: EXK.

EXK

Exits item and kills active item list, if present, without saving any changes. Control returns directly to the TCL.

F

Flip. Toggles current editor buffer, allowing examination of all changes made in an item. Positions line pointer to beginning (top) of the item. Changes to items *must* be made from the "top down," which means that changes may *not* be made to lines above a line where a change has already been made *without* using the F command. As a general rule, use the F command whenever changes are required above the last line in which a change was made, or upon receiving a SEQN? error message.

FD

File Delete. Deletes current item from file. Control returns to next item in the list or to the TCL if no more items are in the list. To recover the item, use the TCL command RECOVER-FD. This command must immediately follow the FD command. It is documented near the beginning of this section.

FDK

File Delete. Deletes current item from file and "kills" active item list. Control returns directly to the TCL. To recover the item, use the TCL command RECOVER-FD. This command must immediately follow the FDK command, and is documented near the beginning of this section.

FI
-or-
FI *itemname*
-or-
FI(*filename*
-or-
FI(*filename itemname*

Files current item. Control returns to next item in the list or to the TCL if no more items are in the list. Note that a different filename and/or itemname may be specified prior to actually filing the item. See also: FIO.

Example of using a different itemname:

```
>ED BP PROGRAM1<cr>
TOP
.FI NEW.PROGRAM1<cr>
'NEW.PROGRAM1' FILED.
```

FIL

File item in "list" format. This command is used to convert an item from the standard (data) item format into a list-class format. Caution: Be careful with this command—use it only for text or PICK/BASIC source code programs. PICK/BASIC *cannot* read a "list class" item, yet. Also, changing the "D" pointer of the DATA section of the file to a "DC" might be necessary before this works properly.

FIO *itemname*
-or-
FIO(*filename*
-or-
FIO(*filename itemname*

Files current item and overwrites, when a duplicate itemname exists already on file. This form has to be used only when specifying an itemname other than the one originally requested. See also: FI.

Example:

```
>ED BP PROGRAM1<cr>
TOP
.FI NEW.PROGRAM1<cr>
CMND?
```

This example does not actually mean that the command was invalid; rather, the item, NEW.PROGRAM1, was already on file. It can be overwritten as follows:

```
.FIO NEW.PROGRAM1
'NEW.PROGRAM1' FILED.
```

FS
-or-
FS *itemname*
-or-
FS(*filename*
-or-
FS(*filename itemname*

File "Save" current item. Same as FI command, but edit session continues within the current item. Note: When editing large items, you should issue an FS command periodically to ensure an update to the file. A different filename and/or itemname can be specified prior to actually saving the item. See also: FSO.

Example of using a different itemname:

```
>ED BP MAIN.PROGRAM<cr>
TOP
.FS MAIN.PROGRAM.ORIGINAL<cr>
```

This command effectively makes a backup copy of "MAIN.PROGRAM," calling the new copy "MAIN.PROGRAM.ORIGINAL."

FSL

Files "Save" in "list" format. Used to convert an item from the standard (data) item format into a list-class format. Caution: be careful with this—use it only for text or PICK/BASIC source code programs. PICK/BASIC *cannot* read a "list-class" item, yet. Also, you might have to change the "D" pointer of the DATA section of the file to a "DC" before this works properly. See also: FS.

FSO *itemname*
-or-
FSO(*filename*
-or-
FSO(*filename itemname*

File "Saves" current item and overwrites, when a duplicate itemname exists already on the file. Note that this form has to be used only when specifying an itemname other than the one originally requested. See also: FS.

Example:

```
>ED BP MAIN.PROGRAM<cr>
TOP
.FS MAIN.PROGRAM.ORIGINAL<cr>
CMND?
```

This example means that the item, MAIN.PROGRAM.ORIGINAL, was already on file. It can be overwritten as follows:

```
.FSO MAIN.PROGRAM.ORIGINAL
```

No indication that the operation took place successfully is displayed. Have faith; it probably did.

G*linenumber*
-or-
linenumber

Go to *linenumber*. Positions the line pointer to a specified linenumber. A number, followed by a <cr>, positions the line pointer to the specified linenumber, hence, the G command is optional.

I

Insert. Places editor into insert mode for the addition of new attributes to the current item. To return to (editor) command mode, issue a at the first position of any line.

Inserting a single line:

.I *string*<cr>
-or-
.I<cr>
00*n* + *string*<cr>
00*n* + <cr>

Inserting a "Null" line:

.I<cr>

Note: the space following the command. Without it, this will not work.

Inserting multiple lines:

Multiple lines may be inserted, if each text string (new line) is delimited with an Attribute Mark (Control {shift} ^). The shift is only required when the up-arrow keyboard character is designed as a shifted character.

Example of Inserting Multiple Lines:

.I newline1^newline2^newline3

L*#lines*
-or-
L *#lines*

List. Displays specified number of lines. Here's a secret feature: a space may be substituted for the "L" command. While in the editor, press the space bar, enter the number of lines to list, and then press <cr>. Legend has it that some lazy programmer left this in the system and didn't mention it to anyone. It seems to have drifted to nearly all of the current Pick implementations.

L/*string*
-or-
L*#lines/string*
-or-

L#lines/string/b
-or-
L#lines/string/b – e

Locate. Searches optionally specified number of lines for any occurrence of the specified string. If no #lines is entered, the next occurrence is located, and displayed.

The ending delimiter is required when the string contains trailing blank characters.

If the #lines parameter is specified, the requested number of lines are searched, and those that match are displayed. The line pointer is incremented by the specified number and therefore cannot be positioned at the last line displayed.

The "b" and "e" parameters respectively specify the beginning and ending column ranges that strings are eligible for matching.

The up-arrow (^) character is used as a wildcard search character within the string parameter for locating or replacing variable strings within strings. It matches any character.

The colon (:) is a special delimiter that indicates a column-dependent correspondence. See the following examples.

Examples of the Locate command:

.L/ABC
Locates and displays the next occurrence of the string, "ABC."

.L99/ABC
Locates and displays the string, "ABC," in the next 99 lines.

.L99/ABC/1 – 5
Locates and displays, in the next 99 lines, the occurrence of the string, "ABC," in column ranges 1 through 5.

.L99/A^C
Locates and displays, in the next 99 lines, any line containing a string beginning with the letter "A," followed by any character, and ending with the letter "C."

.L:ABC:
Locates the next line containing the string, "ABC," followed by one blank character in the first four positions of the line.

M

Macro. Toggles macro expansion display on or off, for use in assembly listings.

ME{#lines}/{itemname}{/startline}}
-or-
ME{#lines}(filename{itemname{)startline}}

Merge. Merges specify the number of lines from a specified item, beginning with line number "startline" in itemname. Line(s) will be merged at the current position of the line pointer.

Any delimiter, except a left parenthesis, specifies that the following parameter is an itemname. A left parenthesis specifies a different filename.

Default specifications:

No #lines means to merge 1 line.
No itemname means the current itemname.
No itemname following filename means current itemname.
No beginning linenumber (startline) means to start the merge from the first line.

Examples of the Merge command:

.ME10//
Merges 10 lines from the current item, beginning with line number 1.

.ME10/ABC/3
Merges 10 lines from the item called "ABC," beginning with line number 3.

.ME22(APPDOC PROG.DOC)10
Merges 22 lines from the item called, "PROG.DOC," which resides in the file, "APPDOC," beginning with line number 10.

N{*#lines*}

Next. Positions line pointer down specified number of lines from current position. An N command, followed by a <cr>, redisplays the current line.

P{*rangenumber*} *command* {[*command*}

Prestore (load). Assigns editor command sequence to specified rangenumber (in the range 0–9). Each prestored command may contain up to 100 bytes.

When no rangenumber is specified, zero (0) is assumed. The default for "P0" (or "P") is "L22" (List 22 lines).

The "escape" key (which appears as "[on the screen) is used as the command delimiter to separate multiple editor commands.

Note: prestored editor command sequences must be reloaded each time the editor is initiated.

Examples of defining prestored commands:

.P1 B[U22[L22
Stores in prestored command P1 the following command sequence: Bottom of item, Up 22 lines, List 22 lines. Now, each time the command, "P1," is issued, the last 22 lines of the item are displayed.

.P2 RU9999.ABC.XYZ.[FI[P2
Stores in command P2 the following command sequence: replace, in the next 9999 lines, all occurrences of "ABC" with "XYZ." It then files the item, and repeats the process on the next item. If all items have been processed, the command falls out to TCL.

P{*rangenumber*}

Prestore (activate). Executes selected prestored editor command sequence. The "P" command, followed by a <cr>, executes the command sequence stored in "P0" (zero), which normally defaults to "L22" (List 22 lines).

PD

Displays the current prestored commands

R
-or-
R{***#lines***}***/oldstr/newstr/***{***/***}{***b***{***−e***}}
-or-
RU{***#lines***}***/oldstr/newstr***{***/***}{***b***{***−e***}}

Replace. Replaces, in specified number of lines, the first occurrence of the string referenced in "oldstr" with the string referenced in "newstr." The "RU" form replaces ALL occurrences. If the #lines parameter is specified, the line pointer is incremented accordingly.

An R command, followed by a <cr>, allows the replacement of an entire line. Entering a <cr> at the first position of the line returns control to the editor command prompt and the line remains unchanged.

The "b" and "e" parameters respectively indicate the beginning and ending column ranges where strings are eligible for replacement.

If the "oldstr" parameter is null, then the "newstr" parameter is inserted at the beginning of the line. If the "newstr" parameter is null and the "oldstr" parameter is found, the "oldstr" parameter is deleted from the line.

Note: multiple replaces may be performed on a line without flipping the buffers with the F command.

Using wildcards in a replace:

The "up-arrow" (^) character is used as a wildcard search character within the string parameter, for replacing known and sometimes unknown strings within strings. It matches any character. Note that the up-arrow character is a normal character, not a control character. For example:

```
.R/^^^//
```

See also: "^".

Using attribute marks in a replace:

The control {shift} up-arrow represents an attribute mark in the editor. Used with the replace command, it has the effect of terminating the line.
For example:

```
.R/ABC/^
```

Examples of the Replace command:

```
.R
```

Positions cursor at beginning of line for replacement of entire line. A subsequent <cr> leaves the line intact.

```
.R10
```

Positions cursor at beginning of each of the next ten lines for entire line replacement.

R/^^^//

Replaces the first 3 characters (wildcards, or "regular" up-arrows) of the current line with null (i.e., deletes first three characters).

.R/ABC/^

Replaces the first occurrence of the string, "ABC," with an attribute mark (control or control-shift up-arrow), terminating the line prior to the string, ABC.

.R10//ABC

Replaces the string, "ABC" at the beginning of the next ten lines.

.R10/ABC/XYZ

Replaces the first occurrence of the string, "ABC," with the string "XYZ" in the current and next nine lines.

.RU10/ABC/XYZ

Replaces all occurrences of the string, "ABC," with the string, "XYZ," in the current and next nine lines.

.R10/ABC/XYZ/5 – 9

Replaces the first occurrence of the string, "ABC," with the string, "XYZ," in the current and next nine lines, when the string is found in columns 5 through 9.

S

Suppress line numbers. Toggles the display of editor line numbers, in normal editor mode, and suppresses display of object code when the assembly formatter is on.

S?

Displays the size of an item in bytes.

T

Top. Positions the line pointer at the beginning (top) of an item, without flipping buffers. See also: F.

TB *tabstop*{*tabstop* . . .}

Sets one or more tabstops. Each argument is separated by a space. The maximum is 16 tabstops. When the TAB key (or <control> I) is issued during input, the cursor is positioned at the next defined tabstop. The TAB key has no effect when positioned beyond the last tabstop. See also: TCL

Example:

.TB 3 6 9 12 15 18 21

U#lines

UP. Positions the line pointer up a specified number of lines from the current position. The U command, followed by a <cr>, redisplays the current line.

X

Oops! Cancels effect of the last input, insert, delete, or replace command. The X command will not work after multiple replacements within the same line.

XF

Uh oh! Cancels the effect of all commands executed since the last F (flip) command was issued.

Z

-or-

Zb−e

Zone. Defines zone display limits to display only the data between the specified beginning (b) and ending (e) column ranges. If both parameters are omitted, the zone function is reset to display the entire line.

2
TCL: Terminal control language

About standard TCL commands and SMA compatibility

This guide covers the "generic" version of Pick, including the Pick PC-AT and XT versions through release 3.1. Most of the commands listed in this section will work on other Pick systems in production today. Some commands, however, might behave differently than described in this text.

There are currently no TCL SMA standards. Consequently, the only commands that contain a compatibility index are those that are unique to a specific release of the Pick system for the AT or XT. For example, many new verbs were added in releases 2.2, 3.0, and 3.1 for the AT and might not be available on earlier releases or for the XT version.

Standard TCL options

Options are special characters that alter the normal effect of a TCL command. With the exception of spooler options, they always appear at the end of a TCL command.

Options *must* be preceded by a left parenthesis character. The right parenthesis is optional, as are commas between the parameters. However, this rule does not apply to spooler options.

The following two options are available for use with most TCL commands:

N Activates the NOPAGE function on output to the terminal.
P Directs output to the system printer, via the spooler.

Note: Please refer to the Glossary section for definitions of the standard terms used in the PICK system, along with the special terms that were created during the writing of this guide.

Special cursor control functions

Control-{shift}-_<cr>

Line continuation character. Extends TCL command line by another 140 characters.

Control-H

Backspaces one character.

Control-I

Same as the TAB key.

Control-J

Same as a linefeed.

Control-Q

Issues an X-ON character, resuming the process previously suspended with an X-OFF (Control-S)

Control-R

Retypes last line.

Control-S

Issues an X-OFF character, which can be reversed with an X-ON (Control-Q)

Control-W

Backs up one word.

Control-X

Cancels current input line, or terminates a multipage display, returning control directly to TCL.

TCL Verb classes

TCL commands can be divided into three different categories according to how they are invoked:

TCL-I verbs

These verbs require only the verb and a <cr>. Most verbs, however, allow options. The Common denominator to TCL-I verbs is that they do not affect files. However, the CRE-

ATE-FILE, CLEAR-FILE, and DELETE-FILE verbs are considered TCL-I, even though they break the apparent rule of not affecting files.

Examples of TCL-I verbs:

```
>WHO
>TIME
>POVF
```

TCL-II verbs

TCL-II verbs require a filename and usually a list of one or more item-ids. The only time that they do not require a list of item-ids is when the verb follows a SELECT, SSELECT, QSELECT, or GET-LIST. To determine if a verb falls into this category, issue the LIST-VERBS command. Any verb with a "2" in the second column (attribute) is considered a TCL-II verb and must conform to this syntax.

Examples of TCL-II verbs:

```
>ED MD LIST
```

In this example, one item is requested from the file called MD.

```
>ED MD LIST SORT COUNT
```

Here, a multiple item-ids are requested. Note that each item-id is separated by a space.

```
>ED MD *
```

The "*" is a special symbol used to request all items in a file.

```
>SELECT MD = 'LIST]'
n ITEMS SELECTED.
>ED MD<cr>
```

In this final form, a select list is built with the SELECT verb. Note that the item-id list does not have to be specified.

ACCESS verbs

The third and final class of verbs are ACCESS verbs. These are, by far, the most sophisticated of all verbs and require at minimum a verb and a filename. See the ACCESS section for further information. To determine if a verb belongs in this category, issue the LIST-VERBS command. If the second column (attribute) contains a "35", it's an ACCESS verb.

Examples of ACCESS commands:

```
>SORT CUSTOMERS BY NAME NAME ADDRESS CSZ LPTR
>SSELECT INVOICES WITH NO PAYMENT.AMOUNT BY DATE
>SSELECT ORDER BY SHIP.DATE
```

TCL commands

:FILES

Initiates a full restore as an alternative to doing it from the "options" prompt. The proper media type must be indicated with the SET-FLOPPY or SET-SCT prior to using this command. As of release 3.1, this process now updates the SYSTEM-CONFIG, ACC file to indicate a controlled system shutdown.

Compatibility: **Pick 2.2** and higher

SET-DMA DMA-channel

Redefines the SCT DMA channel from its default value.

STARTSPOOLER {(*options*{*s*})}

Initializes spooler and returns to normal operation.

Options:

- n Starts spooler process on a specified portnumber. (Used primarily by developers to test the spooler code.)
- C Clears all but permanent file control blocks (hold files). Does *not* return space to overflow table.
- D Used in conjunction with the "n" option to enable the debugger on the line.
- I Initializes and DESTROYS all spooler queue entries. Does *not* return space to overflow table.
- L Links workspace for inactive lines.

:SWD *filename itemlist**

Switches E pointer{s} to D pointer{s}. Used for copying D-pointers.

:SWE *filename itemlist**

Switches D pointer{s} to E pointer{s}.

:SWX *filename itemlist**

Switches D pointer to DX pointer. Extreme care should be exercised when using this command.

:SWZ *filename itemlist**

Switches D pointer to DZ pointer.

:TASKINIT *n*{,*m*}

Used to pre-allocate extra workspaces for use by the EXECUTE statement in PICK/BASIC. The "n" parameter indicates the number of process workspaces to pre-assign per port. The optional "m" parameter indicates the maximum nesting depth. This command can be useful to recover a disk in the event of running out of disk space by using "0" (zero) as the number of workspaces. Any workspaces already assigned will be returned to the overflow table. Each workspace takes up about 400 frames.

Note: this verb might not exist in all versions of Pick, but the code for the verb does exist. The usual verb definition item contains a "P" in attribute 1, and "13C" in attribute 2.

ACCOUNT-RESTORE *acctname*{(*options*)}

Restores an individual account from either an ACCOUNT-SAVE tape/diskette or a FILE-SAVE tape/diskette.

The tape must be positioned at the beginning of the (data) files section, or at the beginning of the target account.

Process will prompt for name under which account was saved on the tape.

See also: RESTORE-ACCOUNTS, SEL-RESTORE, ACCOUNT-SAVE, and FILE-SAVE.

Options:

A Indicates that the tape is already positioned at the correct account.
S Ignores any tape label information.

ACCOUNT-SAVE {*acctname*}

Activates a PROC to save an individual account to magnetic tape. See also: SAVE.

As of release 2.2, Pick no longer writes a file mark at the beginning of the tape. As of release 3.1, the account name may be provided with the command.

ADDD *decnum decnum*

Adds two decimal numbers and displays the result in decimal.

ADDENDA

Activates a PROC to display information about Operating System enhancements made by Pick Systems.

Compatibility: **Pick XT** (no longer provided as of 3.1)

ADDENDUM *number*

Activates a PROC to display information about a specific feature related to Operating System enhancements made by Pick Systems. Use this command after the ADDENDA command.

Compatibility: **Pick AT/XT** (no longer provided as of 3.1)

ADDX *hexnum hexnum*

Adds two hexadecimal numbers and displays the result in hexadecimal.

B/ADD
B/DEL
B/UNLOCK

Three orphan verbs that still linger around the Pick System. For a historical note, these verbs were among the very first verbs added to the system. Fortunately, their use has almost disappeared entirely except for the SET-FILE and DELETE PROCs, both of which reside in the PROCLIB file.

BASIC *filename itemlist** {(*options*)}

Activates PICK/BASIC compiler for translation of source code into object code.

Options:

- A Displays object code generated by PICK/BASIC compiler.
- C Compiles object code without end of line characters, which makes the PICK/BASIC debugger completely useless for debugging the program. Some implementations have changed this to mean "backward compatible."
- E Outputs error lines only.
- I Shows line numbers for code placed in the program by an INSERT or INCLUDE statement when used in conjunction with the L option.
- L Lists program as it compiles.
- M Generates program map.
- N Activates NOPAGE function on output to the terminal.
- P Directs output to system printer, via the spooler.
- Q Activates PAGE mode on errors.
- S Suppresses symbol table generation.
- X Cross-references all variables and places entries in the BSYM file.
- Y Provides compilation statistics, including: the start clock time in milliseconds, the size of the code in bytes, the size of the descriptor table, the size of the symbol table in bytes, the number of symbol table entries, and the end clock time in milliseconds.

BATCH {*integer-number*}

Displays and/or changes the batch setting parameter for the current process. Advice: leave this command alone.

BEEP

Activates PICK/BASIC program to continuously beep on a CRT until someone reaches over and slams their fist down on any of the keys.

Compatibility: **Pick AT/XT**

BLIST *filename itemlist** {(*options*)}

Utility to format and list PICK/BASIC source code.

Options:

R Directs output to system printer, via the spooler.

U Updates source item(s). See the PROC called BLIST in the MD of your account. Attribute two contains a number that is used to control the number of spaces to indent from the left margin. The default setting is two.

Compatibility: **Pick 3.1**

BLOCK-PRINT *text* {(P)}

Outputs block letters of text string on the terminal screen, or directs output to system printer via the spooler when used with the P option. The characters in the text string are defined in the BLOCK-CONVERT file.

Example:

```
BLOCK-PRINT "JOE'S" BAR (P
```

BREAK-KEY-OFF

Disables BREAK key. Prevents the user from entering the PICK/BASIC or System Debuggers.

Compatibility: **Pick 3.1**

BREAK-KEY-ON

Enables BREAK key. Allows the user to enter the PICK/BASIC or System Debugger.

Compatibility: **Pick 3.1**

BUFFERS

Displays current system virtual buffer usage.

Compatibility: **Pick AT/XT release 3.1**

CAT {*filename*}

Activates a PROC to display information about the compile date/time for a PICK/BASIC Program file.

Compatibility: **Pick AT/XT**

CATALOG *filename itemlist**

Creates a "verb" from a compiled PICK/BASIC program, by placing an entry in the current accounts' Master Dictionary that allows execution of the program by entering the program name at TCL. It is required for any program defined as an external subroutine. This is not true on every Pick implementation. Some versions do no require the program to be CATALOGed if it exists in the same file as the CALLing program.) It is not necessary to

(re-) CATALOG a program each time it is compiled. As of release 3.1, a program may now be CATALOGed without the source code being present.
Activating a cataloged BASIC program:

programname {(*options*)}

A program does not need to be re-CATALOGed each time it is compiled.

CHARGE-TO *acctname*

Terminates charges accumulation on the current process. Subsequent activity usage statistics are accumulated to the specified subaccount.

CHARGES

Displays total time logged on and CPU activity statistics.

CHECK-ACCOUNT

Prompts for account name, then performs a "dummy" save of account.

Compatibility: **Pick 3.1**

CHECK-FILES

-or-

CHECKFILES

Performs a "dummy" file save.

Compatibility: **Pick 3.1**

CHECK-SUM *filename* {*itemlist*}{*attrname*}{*sellist*}{*modlist*}{(*options*)}

Calculates the hexadecimal checksum for either a specified attribute. If no attribute is specified, the entire item in the specified filename is calculated.

CHOO-CHOO

Entertainment for the bored.

CL *listname*

Synonym for COPY-LIST command. Provided for compatibility with Advanced Pick.

Compatibility: **Pick 3.1**

CLEAR-BASIC-LOCKS

Resets all the execution locks established by LOCK statements from PICK/BASIC.

CLEAR-FILE (DATA *filename*{,*filename*})

-or-

CLEAR-FILE (DICT *filename*)

Clears the specified file of all items and retains the primary file space area.

CLOCK

Activates a program to demonstrate operation of the real-time clock.

Compatibility: **Pick AT/XT**

COLDSTART

Activates the "COLDSTART" PROC (procedure). This command is usually the last step in the system coldstart procedure. COLDSTART was modified for release 3.1 to verify system integrity and to ensure that the system was properly shut down prior to proceeding with normal COLDSTART procedure.

COLOR {*foreground*}{*background*}{*/options*}

Sets foreground and/or background colors on the color graphics monitor. The options allow special visual attributes to be activated or deactivated. The command may only be used from port 0 (zero).

Valid color choices:

BLACK, BLUE, BROWN, CYAN, GREEN, MAGENTA, RED, and WHITE

Valid options for visual attributes:

/B or /BLINK	Activate blinking
/F or /FULL	Full intensity foreground
/H or /HALF	Half intensity foreground
/NB or /NOBLINK	Deactivate blinking
/NR or /NOREVERSE	Deactivate reverse video
/R or /REVERSE	Activate reverse video

Compatibility: **Pick AT/XT**

COMPARE *filename itemlist** {(*options*)} <cr>
WITH:{(*filename*}*itemlist*

Produces a comparative listing of a specified itemlist, indicating where differences occur among the source and the target item{s}.

Options:

A All elements on each attribute. Default is first three elements, delimited by blanks (assembler source code format).

N Activates NOPAGE function on output to the terminal.

P Directs output to the system printer via the spooler.
S Suppresses display of identical items.
T Uses tape as source file. Must be in T-DUMP format and positioned at the correct file.
Z Outputs errors only in assembly format.

Status characters:

D Indicates deleted line.
I Indicates inserted line.

COMPILE *filename itemlist** {(*options*)}

Activates BASIC compiler for translation of source code into object code. Synonym for BASIC verb. (Might not exist on all Pick Systems; use the BASIC verb instead.)

Options:

See the BASIC verb for valid options.

CONFIG

Displays system configuration.

Compatibility: **Pick 3.1**

COPY *filename itemlist** {(*options*)}
TO:{(*filename*}{*itemlist*}

Copies a specified filename and itemlist to a different filename and/or itemlist. Notes: the filename may refer to a dictionary level by preceding the filename with the word, "DICT," followed by a space; no itemlist* is required when the COPY follows a SELECT, SSELECT, GET-LIST, or QSELECT.

Options:

n Integer number. Specifies the number of items to copy. Typically used for copying data for test files.
A Activates assembly MLIST format.
D Deletes source item after copy.
F Outputs a form-feed between each item.
I Suppresses item-id list during a file copy.
L Changes item to list format if destination file is a "DC"-type file.
M Activates Macro (assembly) format on terminal or printer output only.
N Activates NOPAGE function on output to the terminal
N Inhibits new items on copies between files, which means that the item-id must already exist in order for an item to be copied.
O Overwrites existing items when duplicate item-ids exist.
P Directs output to system printer via the spooler.
S Suppresses display of line numbers on copy to terminal or printer.
S Suppresses error message output on a file copy.

T Directs output to the terminal.
X Outputs in hexadecimal.

COPY-LIST *itemlist** {(*options*)}
TO: {(*filename*} {*listname*}

Copies a previously saved listname to either a new name, a new filename, or the specified output device. Defaults to POINTER-FILE for filename.

Options:

D Deletes item from source file after copy.
N Activates NOPAGE function on output to terminal.
O Overwrites duplicate itemname{s}.
P Copies list to system printer via the spooler.
T Copies list to terminal.
X Outputs list in hexadecimal format.

COPYDOS *DOS.path* {(*options*)}

Copies data, in Pick storage format, from a DOS partition into the Pick partition.

Addressing the DOS path:

drive: \ *filename*
-or-
drive: \ *directory* \ *filename*
-or-
drive: \ *directory* \ *directory* \ *filename*

The pattern continues. Effectively, there could be many directories.

Options:

D Displays diagnostic information during translation.
F Flags characters. System prompts for further information.
L Creates list-type (indirect) item. (Release 2.2)
M Creates multiple (Pick) items.
O Overwrites (duplicate) Pick item{s}.
P Strips the most significant bit off characters as they are converted, except for flagged and/or translated characters. (Release 2.2)
R Indicates DOS data is in a random file.
S Indicates DOS data is in a sequential file.
T Translates characters. System prompts for further information.
X Creates hexadecimal image of DOS file.

When the file type (S or R) is omitted, the default is S. Note that when this is executed without the T and F options, DOS end-of-line characters (carriage returns or X'0D') are automatically converted to attribute marks (X'FE'). Line feeds (X'0A' and nulls X'00') are deleted.

Note: A verb called COPYPICK is now provided by Pick Systems. This verb allows the movement of Pick items into a DOS partition and must be executed from DOS. See chapter 7 "PC-AT," under the sub-heading "DOS Considerations" for more information on how to use this command.

Compatibility: **Pick AT/XT**

COUNT *filename* {*itemlist*}{*sellist*}{*modlist*}{(*options*)}

Outputs the number of items that meet the selection criteria as determined by the itemlist and sellist specifications.

CREATE-ACCOUNT {*acctname*}

Activates a PROC to create a new account and place an entry in the SYSTEM file. The command may be executed only from the SYSPROG account. After execution of the CREATE-ACCOUNT command, the following prompts appear:

ACCOUNT NAME?

The name of the new account. It must *not* already exist in the SYSTEM file. If you are unsure whether or not it already exists, end this procedure and issue the command:

SORT ONLY SYSTEM<cr>

L/RET CODES?
Retrieval code(s) for read-access to files. Typically left null.

L/UPD CODES?
Update code(s) for write-protection to files. Typically left null.

PASSWORD?
Optional logon password. See also the (TCL) PASSWORD command to change or remove passwords.

PRIVILEGES?
Privilege level. Must be either SYS0 (lowest), SYS1, or SYS2 (highest). As of release 2.2, SYS0 is now the default.

MOD, SEP?
Optional modulo and separation for new account MD. Typically, if omitted, this defaults to 29 for modulo and 1 for separation.

Upon answering this last prompt, the process copies all of the items from the NEWAC file into the new MD. The account is now ready for use. See also: LOGTO.

CREATE-BFILE *filename* modulo{,separation} modulo{,separation}

dictionary *data section*

-or-

CREATE-BFILE DICT *filename modulo*{*,separation*}

-or-

CREATE-BFILE DATA *filename*{*,filename*} *modulo*{*,separation*}

Similar to the CREATE-FILE command, but used for creating files for use with PICK/BASIC. After creation, the file D-pointer is changed to a "DC." The modulo should be a prime number and may be up to 32,267, provided that the separation is one (1).

Modulo is the number of groups to allocate for primary file space.

Separation is the number of frames per group. The default separation is one.

~~*Compatibility:* **Pick 3.1**~~

CREATE-FILE *filename* *modulo*{*,separation*} *modulo*{*,separation*}

(*modulo*{*,separation*} = ***dictionary***; *modulo*{*,separation*} = ***data section***)

-or-

CREATE-FILE DICT *filename modulo*{*,separation*}

-or-

CREATE-FILE DATA *filename*{*,filename*}*modulo*{*,separation*}

Reserves space for and creates a new filename placing the file pointer entry in the current accounts Master Dictionary (or dictionary when creating a DATA section on an existing dictionary). The modulo should be a prime number and may be up to 32,267 provided that the separation is one (1).

Modulo is the number of groups to allocate for primary file space.

Separation is the number of frames per group. The default separation is one.

Examples of the CREATE-FILE command:

```
CREATE-FILE CUSTOMERS 7,1 101,1
```

Creates both a new dictionary and data section.

```
CREATE-FILE DICT POINTER-FILE 31,1
```

Creates a dictionary-only file.

```
CREATE-FILE DATA CUSTOMERS,ARCHIVE 101,1
```

Creates a new data section called "ARCHIVE" and places a pointer to it in a dictionary of CUSTOMERS. The new data section can now "share" all the attribute-defining items in the CUSTOMERS dictionary.

CROSS-INDEX *filename itemlist** {*(options)*}

Produces cross-reference of assembly source code in specified filename. Requires the CSYM file. (May not exist on all systems. Usually provided with the Assembler account.)

Options:

F Prompts for filename. Default is CSYM.

O Scans operand field.

CS

Clears the terminal screen.

Compatibility: **Pick AT/XT**

CT *filename itemlist** {(*options*)}

Copies specified itemlist to terminal. See also: COPY.

CURRENCY

Activates program to demonstrate international currency conversions.

Compatibility: **Pick 3.1** and higher

DATE

Displays the current system date.

Compatibility: **Pick 3.1** and higher

DCD {*portnumber*}

Displays the current status of DCD (Data Carrier Detect) on a specified port, or for the current port if one is not specifically requested. DCD is used to sense changes in the signal being transmitted over the wire to the terminal; when it drops, the terminal is automatically logged off. Note: special cabling is required prior to enabling this feature on a line.

Compatibility: **Pick 2.2** and higher

DCD-OFF {*portnumber*}

Disables the monitoring of Data Carrier Detect on the specified portnumber. If the portnumber is omitted, the current port is affected. This command may not be issued on or against line 0 (zero). The default setting is off.

Compatibility: **Pick 2.2** and higher

DCD-ON {*portnumber*}

Enables the monitoring of Data Carrier Detect on the specified portnumber. If the portnumber is omitted, the current port is affected. This command may not be issued on or against line 0 (zero). The default setting is off.

Compatibility: **Pick 2.2** and higher

DECATALOG *filename itemlist**

Deletes object code and catalog pointer if one exists in the MD of the current account.

DED

Activates disk sector editor program.

Compatibility: **Pick 3.1**

DEFINE-CURSOR

See also: **DEFINE-TERMINAL**.

DEFINE-TERMINAL

-or-

DEFINE-CURSOR

Allows the addition or modification of term types for using different types of terminals on the system. All information needed for the process is requested from the menu presented upon issuing the command. See also: **TEST-CURSOR** and chapter 7 for additional terminal characteristic features added to this command in release 2.2. As of release 2.2, the following additional terminal characteristics have been added to DEFINE-TERMINAL. Note that each of these codes are preceded by an "at sign" (@), when used in PICK/BASIC or PROC.

Code	*Description*
(−11)	Activate screen protect
(−12)	Deactivate screen protect
(−13)	Activate reverse video
(−14)	Deactivate reverse video
(−15)	Activate underlining
(−16)	Deactivate underlining
(−17)	Activate slave printer
(−18)	Deactivate slave printer
(−19)	Move cursor right
(−20)	Move cursor down
(−21)	Activate graphic character set
(−22)	Deactivate graphic character set
(−23)	Keyboard lock
(−24)	Keyboard unlock
(−25)	Control character enable
(−26)	Control character disable
(−27)	Write status line
(−28)	Clear status line
(−29)	Initialize terminal mode
(−30)	Download function keys
(−31)	Nonembedded stand-out on
(−32)	Nonembedded stand-out off

(−99) Returns a 1 if the terminal uses embedded attributes or 0 (zero) if it does not. Returns null if not defined through DEFINE-TERMINAL.
(−100) Half-intensity (except on memory mapped monitor).
(−101) Full-intensity (except on memory mapped monitor).

Compatibility: **Pick AT/XT**

DEL-ACC

PICK/BASIC program used by the DELETE-ACCOUNT PROC.

DELETE *filename* {*itemlist**}

Deletes specified itemlist from specified file.

DELETE-ACCOUNT{({N{P}}}<cr>

Account Name?account name

-or-

DELETE-ACCOUNT *acctname* {({N{P}}}<cr>

Deletes all files in an account and removes the account name from the SYSTEM file. Should be executed from the SYSPROG account with all other users logged OFF.

After all of the files to be deleted have been listed, the user is asked if the account should still be deleted, which requires a "Y" or "N" response. As of release 3.1, the account name may be provided with the command.

DELETE-FILE *filename*

-or-

DELETE-FILE DICT *filename*

-or-

DELETE-FILE DATA *filename* {,*filename*}

Releases all frames used by specified file to overflow table, and removes filename from current account's Master Dictionary.

The DICT (dictionary) level cannot be deleted without first deleting any data sections that it might have pointers to.

DELETE-LIST *itemlist**

Removes the specified listname(s) from the POINTER-FILE. Note that the "*" is fitted as a listname and will delete all of your saved-lists! See also: DL.

DIR {\DOS.*path*{*subdirectory...*}}{(*options*)}

Displays file information from DOS floppy diskette.

Options

P Directs output to system printer, via spooler.
N Suppresses wait at end of page. (Opposite of NOPAGE).
W Displays in wide format, five files per line.

Compatibility: **Pick 3.1**

DISKCOMP {P}

Compares two floppy diskettes.

Compatibility: **Pick 3.1**

DISKCOPY {(*options*)}

Copies a floppy diskette.

Options

C Compares duplicate with original.
F Formats diskette before copying.
R Repeats duplication. The user is prompted for number of copies.

Compatibility: **Pick 3.1**

DISK-USAGE

Activates PICK/BASIC program to display disk usage statistical information.

Compatibility: **Pick 3.1**

DIVD *decnum decnum*

Divides two decimal numbers and displays the result in decimal.

DIVX *hexnum hexnum*

Divides two hexadecimal numbers and displays the result in hexadecimal.

DL *listname*

Synonym for DELETE-LIST command. Provided for compatibility with *Advanced Pick.*

Compatibility: **Pick 3.1**

DTR {*radix*} *value*

Converts decimal value to specified radix (base) and displays the result. If the radix is omitted, a radix of 16 is assumed. This command then behaves like the DTX command, converting decimal to hexadecimal.

Example:

```
DTR 2 8
1000
```

This command converts the decimal number 8 to its binary (base 2) equivalent.

DTX *decnum*

Converts decimal value to its equivalent hexadecimal value.

DUMP {.} *fid* {*-fid*} {*Spooler Options Handler*}

Outputs contents of specified fid{s}. A fid specification preceded by a period (.) indicates that the address format is in hexadecimal.

Options:

- n Specifies individual frame.id
- n-n Specifies beginning and ending frame.id range.
- A Displays output in EBCDIC format.
- C Dumps entire frame, beginning with byte zero.
- G Outputs each sequentially linked frame in a group.
- L Outputs forward frame linkages.
- N Activates the NOPAGE function on output to the terminal.
- P Directs output to system printer, via the spooler.
- U Outputs backward frame linkages.
- X Outputs in hexadecimal and character format.

ECHO

Toggles terminal echo. When terminal echo is off, characters entered from the keyboard are not displayed on the terminal screen.

ED *filename itemlist*{(*options*)}

-or-

EDIT *filename itemlist*{(*options*)}

-or-

EDIT-LIST *listname*

-or-

EL *listname*

Activates editor processor for entry or update of programs, PROCs, and data items.

Options:

- A Activates Assembly formatter. Equivalent to the AS command.
- M Activates Macro expansion function. Equivalent to the M command.
- P Directs output to system printer, via the spooler.

S Suppresses line numbers, in normal edit mode, or suppresses object code display when the assembly formatter is "on". Equivalent to the S command.

Z Suppresses "Top" and "EOI" messages.

EDIT-LIST *listname* {(Z)}

-or-

EL *listname* {(Z)}

Retrieves specified listname and enters editor processor. Refer to the EDITOR section for the available commands and syntax requirements.

Option:

Z Suppresses "TOP" and "EOI" messages.

EL *listname*

Synonym for EDIT-LIST command. Provided for compatibility with *Advanced Pick*.

Compatibility: **Pick 3.1**

EPSON

Activates PICK/BASIC program to change characteristics for an EPSON printer.

Compatibility: **Pick AT/XT**

EXCHANGE *filename itemname1 itemname2*

Activates PROC to switch the names of the two specified items.

EXPORT {*filename*} {*itemlist*} {(*options*)}

TO: DOS.file

Moves one or more items from a Pick file to a DOS diskette. Must be executed from the Pick partition.

Options:

A Appends segment mark at the end of Pick item(s). When used with the T option, Pick items are separated and DOS files are terminated with specified character.

C Concatenates Pick selected item(s) into one DOS file. Unless the A option is used, Pick files are not separated by any delimiter.

D Displays automatic information during transfer and can be combined with the P option.

I Includes (Pick) item-id(s) with the DOS file. Each item-id is preceded by a line-feed character.

N Sorts Pick item-ids numerically.

O Overwrites duplicate DOS file.

P Directs output to system printer, via the spooler.

S Creates DOS file using same name as the Pick item-id.
T Translates (replaces) specific characters during export. User is prompted for further information.

Compatibility: **Pick 3.1**

FC

Displays the current status of "flow control" or DSR (Data Set Ready) and X-ON/X-OFF protocol on a specified port. The current port is the default if one is not specifically requested. When the DSR signal is off or the X-OFF protocol is invoked, the output to the port is suspended.

Compatibility: **Pick 2.2** and higher

FC-OFF {*portnumber*}

Disables the flow control on the specified portnumber. If the portnumber is omitted, the current port is affected. This command may not be issued on or against line 0 (zero). The default setting is on. See also: FC-ON, MODEM-ON, and MODEM-OFF.

Compatibility: **Pick 2.2** and higher

FC-ON {*portnumber*}

Enables the flow control on the specified portnumber. If the portnumber is omitted, the current port is affected. This command may not be issued on or against line 0 (zero). The default setting is on. See also: FC-OFF, MODEM-ON, and MODEM-OFF. (Release 2.2).

Compatibility: **Pick 2.2** and higher

FDISK

Activates menu to allow any of the following functions:

- Change partition pointer, which affects the boot process next time it is used.
- Delete the Pick partition.
- Display partition information.
- Create a PICK partition.
- Select next fixed disk drive (release 2.2).
- Undo changes to partition data, leaving them the way they were prior to invoking FDISK. (Release 2.2)

This command may only be issued from the SYSPROG account while on port 0 (zero). See also: REBOOT.

FILE-SAVE

Activates PROC to save the entire contents of the system on magnetic tape, typically followed by a T-DUMP of the STAT-FILE and generation of the file statistics report. See also: ACCOUNT-SAVE, LIST-FILE-STATS, and SAVE.

As of release 2.2, Pick no longer writes a file mark at the beginning of the tape. As of release 3.1, this process displays a list of the accounts that will and will not be saved.

FILE-TEST *filename* {*itemlist*} {*sellist*} {(*options*)}

In the SMA standard document, this verb replaces the HASH-TEST and ISTAT verbs formerly used to analyze the statistics and distribution of items in a file.

The statistics that it produces include: the count of items, the total number of bytes, and the average bytes per item. Additionally, the SMA standards document indicates that the information *may* also include: a hashing structure illustrated with a histogram, the average number of items per group and standard deviation, and the average number of bytes per group.

Option:

S Suppresses detail; only shows statistical data.

Compatibility: **SMA**

FILECOMP

Activates PICK/BASIC program to compare and analyze the contents of two files.

Compatibility: **Pick 2.2** and higher

FIND

Activates PICK/BASIC program to search a file for the existence of one or more strings of characters in any attribute and to optionally save the items in a saved list.

Compatibility: **Pick AT/XT**

FKEYS

Activates PICK/BASIC program used for maintaining function key definition items. Pick Systems advises reviewing the program in the SYSPROG-BP file prior to using it.

Compatibility: **Pick 2.2** (no longer provided with 3.1)

FORMAT

Activates process to format floppy diskettes for use *only* with the Pick system. This command may only be issued from the SYSPROG account. As of release 2.2, the FORMAT command now supports $5^1/_4$ and $3^1/_2$ inch diskettes.

Options: (All added in Release 3.1)

D Formats for use with DOS.
F Formats diskette only.
V Verifies diskette only.

Compatibility: **Pick AT/XT**

GET-LIST {*filename*} *listname*

-or-

GL {*filename*} *listname*

Retrieves listname from specified file, or defaults to POINTER-FILE if no filename is specified. Note GL is only provided in release 3.1 and higher.

GROUP *filename* {(*options*)}

Outputs hashing information on specified filename. Output includes base fid, the item-id{s} in each group, each items' (hexadecimal) byte count field, a count of the total number of items in each group, the total number of bytes, the total number of "full" frames, and the number of bytes used in the "last" frame of each group."

Options:

- I Suppresses display of null groups.
- N Activates NOPAGE function on output to the terminal.
- P Directs output to system printer, via the spooler.
- S Suppresses output of item-id's.

HALT-SYSTEM

Immediately halts system without waiting for users or printers. As of release 3.3, this process now updates the SYSTEM-CONFIG.ACC file to indicate a controlled system shutdown.

Compatibility: **Pick 3.1**

HASH-TEST *filename* {*itemlist*} {*sellist*} {(*options*)}
TEST MODULO: modulo

Outputs a histogram showing the item hashing distribution of all items meeting the selection criteria with a test modulo, entered by the operator. See also: ISTAT.

Option:

- S Suppresses display of histogram.

HUSH

Toggles terminal output on or off. When this is activated, the output from any process will not appear on the screen.

IMPORT DOS.*path* {(*options*)}
TO: (*filename* {(*itemname*)}

Moves data from a DOS diskette or DOS hard partition into a file in the Pick partition.

The DOS.path must include the drive-id and the DOS directory, subdirectory (or subdirectories) and filename.

Example:

>IMPORT A: \AUTOEXEC.BAT<cr>
TO: (TEMP<cr>

Options:

D Displays diagnostic information during transfer.
F Flags characters. User prompted for further input.
L Creates list-class (indirect) item.
M Creates multiple items. User prompted for further input.
O Overwrites item if duplicate item-id exists.
P Parity strip. Characters converted to values 0-127. Flagged or translated characters are not stripped.
R DOS data is in random file mode.
S DOS data is in sequential file mode (default).
T Translates characters. User is prompted for further input.
X Creates hexadecimal image of DOS file.

Notes:

- If neither the R nor S option is specified, the S option is assumed.
- If neither the F nor T option is specified, IMPORT will automatically translate the DOS characters X'OD' (carriage return) to X'FE' (attribute mark). Also, X'OA' (linefeed) and X'00' (null) characters are deleted.
- If no PICK filename is provided at the "TO:(" prompt, the DOS filename is used as the PICK itemname.
- If the DOS file is larger than 25,000 bytes and the M option is not used, the process will break the DOS file into multiple items and append a sequential number to the end of each item-id. If the L option is used, a "list-class" item is created and the breaking up process does not take place.

Compatibility: **Pick 3.1**

INIT-ABS

Activates PICK/BASIC program for initializing ABS frames. User is prompted for range of frames.

Compatibility: **Pick 3.1**

INTER {*integer-number*}

Displays and/or changes the interactive setting parameter for the current process. Advice: leave this alone.

ISTAT *filename* {*itemlist*} {*modlist*} {(*options*)}

Outputs a histogram showing the item hashing distribution, based on specified filename's current modulo and the optionally specified selection criteria. See also: HASH-TEST.

Option:

S Suppresses display of histogram.

ITEM *filename itemlist* {options}*

Outputs the base fid of the group to which the specified item-id "hashes", and a list of all item-id's that are currently "hashed" to the same group. Also displayed is each item's (hexadecimal) byte count field, a count of the total number of items in the group, the total number of bytes, the total number of "full" frames, and the number of bytes used in the "last" frame of the group.

Options:

N Activates NOPAGE function on output to the terminal.
P Directs output to system printer, via the spooler.
S Suppresses output of item-id's.

LINK-WS

Relinks the process workspace for all lines. This event occurs automatically during a cold-start and normally is not required.

LIST *filename {itemlist} {sellist} {modlist} {outlist} {(options)}*

Outputs specified items, in order of appearance in the filename.

LIST-FILE-STATS

Activates PROC to print the file statistics report from the data placed in the STAT-FILE by the most recently executed FILE-SAVE or ACCOUNT-SAVE. See also: SAVE.

LIST-ITEM *filename {itemlist} {sellist} {modlist} {(options)}*

Outputs items, in COPY format.

LIST-LABEL *filename {itemlist} {sellist} {outlist} {modlist} {(options)}*

Outputs formatted labels from specified filename in order of item appearance in filename.

Upon pressing the carriage return the prompt character, ?, appears, which is for the entry of the following label parameters:

```
?columns,rows,skip,indent,size,space,C
```

Where:

columns = number of labels across page.
rows = number of lines requested to print on each label.
skip = number of lines (vertically) between labels.
indent = number of spaces from left margin to beginning output column.
size = number of print positions per label.

space = number of spaces (horizontally) between labels.
C = compresses null values.

Note: Each of the parameters must be separated by commas during input.

Following the entry of the above parameters, if the INDENT parameter is non-zero, the prompt character, ?, appears for the number of times indicated in the rows parameter (i.e., if rows was 4, expect 4 question marks).

These prompts (?'s) are for the entry of "headers" that print in the INDENT area to the left of the first row of labels.

Example:

```
LIST-LABEL VENDORS NAME ADDRESS CSZ (CI<cr>
?2,3,1,0,30,2,C
```

LIST-LOCKS {(*options*)}

Outputs base fid and line location of all current group locks, BASIC execution locks, and optionally, item locks (indicated by an asterisk "*").

Options:

n Displays item-lock status for the group starting at the specified frame-id (fid).
I Displays item-lock status.
P Directs output to system printer, via the spooler.

LIST-LISTS

Displays saved-lists from POINTER-FILE. See also: LL.

Compatibility: **Pick 3.1**

LIST-PORTS {(Z)}

Displays the baud rate, parity bits, stop bits, and word length for every connected port on the system. See also: SET-PORT.

Option:

Z Displays the status for all configured ports, connected or not.

Compatibility: **Pick 2.2** and higher

LISTABS {*options*}

Outputs current spooler assignment parameters for every port on the system. See the SP-ASSIGN command for interpretation of the displayed status codes.

LISTACC {*acctname*} {NOPAGE} {LPTR}

Outputs system usage statistics from ACC file for all accounts, or individually specified account.

LISTCONN {*filename*} {NOPAGE} {LPTR}

Outputs connectives in specified filename (default filename is MD).

LISTDICT {*filename*} {NOPAGE} {LPTR}

Outputs all dictionary item information in specified filename (default filename is MD).

LISTF

-or-

LISTFS

Displays dictionary and data files from current account in hierarchical format.

Compatibility: **Pick 3.1**

LISTFILES {*filename*} {LPTR}

Outputs all filenames in specified filename (default filename is MD).

LISTPEQS {*options*}

Outputs lists of spooled entries.

Options:

'acctname'	Displays spooler entries created by specified account name.
n	Integer number, in the range (0-600), indicating the spooler entry to display.
n-n	Specifies beginning and ending spooler entries to display.
A	Outputs the status of all reports created from current account.
C	Outputs count of spooled entries and total storage (frames) used.
E	Outputs print file absolute location.
F	Outputs status of jobs queued for output in queue order (0-125).
H	Outputs hold files only.
L	Outputs active and deleted reports.
P	Directs output to system printer, via spooler.

Status Codes:

A	Available	O	Currently being output
C	Closed	P	Printer
G	Align	R	Requested
H	Hold file	S	Spooled
I	Immediate	T	Tape
L	Locked	X	Aborted
N	No close		

LISTPROCS {*filename*} {NOPAGE} {LPTR}

Outputs all PROCs in specified filename (default filename is MD).

LISTPTR {(*options*)}

Outputs the printer control block status for all printers.

Options:

n-n Specifies beginning and ending printer numbers.
N Activates NOPAGE function on output to terminal.
P Directs output to system printer, via the spooler.

LISTU
-or-
LISTUSERS

Outputs portnumber, account name, PCB-FID, logon time, logon date, and location of every terminal currently logged onto system.

LISTVERBS {*filename*} {NOPAGE} {LPTR}

Outputs all verbs in specified filename (default filename is MD).

LL

Displays saved-lists from POINTER-FILE. See also: LIST-LISTS.

Compatibility: **Pick 3.1**

LOCK-FRAME (.) *fid*

Locks specified fid in memory. See also: UNLOCK-FRAME.

LOGOFF {(U)} <cr>
CHANNEL:*line#*

Logs off process on specified portnumber.

Option:

U Unconditional logoff. Prevents cleanup of work areas.

LOGON {(P)}<cr>
CHANNEL, NAME:*line#,acctname*

Logs on specified line# to specified account name.

As of release 2.2, a change has been made to the way the logon process is handled. After three unsuccessful logon attempts, the port is rendered *inactive*, preventing further attempts. To "*reactivate*" the port, press any key (other than the <cr>) followed by two <cr>'s.

Option:

P Starts process as a *phantom* line. Note this option does not have the same mean ing as what is often considered a phantom, where the process spawns a new process workspace. Rather, this option requires an existing unused port, just like any other port being used for a remote logon. In this context, phantom means that it is treated like a spooler process. The logon sequence is suppressed, which turns off the display of the time and date logged on, the "welcome message" and the automatic update of the ACC file.

LOGTO *acctname{password}*

-or-

TO *acctname{password}*

Terminates the current session, and starts a new session on the specified acctname. If the password is omitted and required, the system will prompt for it. See also: TO.

LOOP-ON *command*

Start an infinite repetition of the specified TCL command.

MESSAGE (or MSG) *acctname text*

-or-

MESSAGE (or MSG) * *text*

-or-

MESSAGE (or MSG) *!line#text*

-or-

MESSAGE (or MSG) *!*text*

Sends message to all users logged on to the specified acctname, or, if the literal, asterisk (*), is used, to all users currently logged on to system. The "!line#" form of the command sends a message to the specified linenumber. For example:

```
MESSAGE !0 ARE YOU THERE? <cr>
```

sends the message to port zero only.

The "!*" form sends the message to every terminal (and serial printer!) connected to the system, whether or not the device is logged on. The "receiver(s)" of the message see the time/date, account name/portnumber of the transmitter, and the text of the message. As of release 3.1, the message verb will check parameter ranges and unlock message frame when aborted.

MLIST *filename itemlist** {(*options*)} (Assembler Account Only)

Produces formatted assembly source code listing of specified itemlist.

Options:

n   Specifies line number to list.
n-n   Specifies beginning and ending line numbers of listing.

E Outputs error lines only.
M Outputs macro expansions.
N Activates NOPAGE function on output to the terminal.
P Directs output to system printer, via the spooler.
S Suppresses object code display.
Z Inhibits entry into editor when used with E option.

MLOAD *filename itemlist** {(*options*)}

Loads assembled object code into virtual memory address defined in routine.

Options:

N Returns item checksum data without actually loading item.
V Verifies mismatches and errors only.

MODEM-OFF

Disables the flow control on the current port. This command may not be issued on or against line 0 (zero). The default setting is on. See also: FC, FC-ON, FC-OFF, and MODEM-0N.

Compatibility: **Pick 2.2** and higher

MODEM-ON

Enables the flow control on the current port. This command may not be issued on or against line 0 (zero). The default setting is on. See also: FC, FC-ON, FC-OFF, and MODEM-OFF.

Compatibility: **Pick 2.2** and higher

MONO {(/*options*)}

Sets options for the monochrome display unit. The options allow special visual attributes to be activated or deactivated. This command may only be used from port 0 (zero).

Valid options for visual attributes:

/B or /BLINK	Activate blinking
/F or /FULL	Full intensity foreground
/H or /HALF	Half intensity foreground
/NB or /NOBLINK	Deactivate blinking
/NU	Deactivate underlining
/NOUNDERLINE	Deactivate underlining
/NR	Deactivate reverse video
/NOREVERSE	Deactivate reverse video
/R or /REVERSE	Activate reverse video
/U	Activate underlining
/UNDERLINE	Activate underlining

Compatibility: **Pick AT/XT**

MSG

See the MESSAGE command.

MULD *decnum decnum*

Multiplies two decimal numbers and displays result in decimal.

MULX *hexnum hexnum*

Multiplies two hexadecimal numbers and displays results in hexadecimal.

MVERIFY *filename itemlist** {(*options*)}

Compares assembled object code in virtual memory against corresponding itemlist in specified filename.

Options:

A Outputs columnar listing of all mismatches.
E Outputs error only.
P Directs output to system printer, via the spooler.

OFF

Terminates current session, logs current process off system.

OKIDATA

Activates a menu to allow changing the printer characteristics for an Okidata parallel printer. See also: the program **OKI-192** in SYSPROG BP.

Compatibility: **Pick AT/XT**

P

Toggles terminal output on or off. When this command is activated, the output from any process will not appear on the screen. Same as the HUSH command.

PACK

Activates PICK/BASIC program to compact multiple items into composite items for transmission. Pick Systems provide this program, but no support for it. See also: UNPACK.

Compatibility: **Pick 2.2** (No longer provided as of release 3.1)

PASSWORD

Allows adding, changing, or removing an existing account password. Must be issued from the SYSPROG account. The password is encrypted into an 8-byte hexadecimal string.

Knowing the old password is not necessary in order to change or remove it.

Compatibility: **Pick AT/XT**

PICK-SETUP

Activates a process to establish administrative guidelines for the system, including: selection of ABS frames, date format, monitor keyboard, system time and date, shutdown delay, restoring and update of accounts, creation of accounts, and assigning passwords. See also: SET-DATE-FORMAT, SET-KBRD, SET-SHUTDOWN-DELAY, SET-DATE, SET-TIME, RESTORE-ACCOUNTS, UPDATE-ACCOUNTS, CREATE-ACCOUNT, and PASSWORD.

Compatibility: **Pick 3.1**

POVF {(P)}

Outputs available linked and contiguous overflow space.

POWER-OFF

Brings the system to an "orderly shutdown" by flushing memory to disk, disabling all users, and parking the disk drive heads prior to halting the system. This command may only be executed from port 0 (zero) when all other users are logged off. As of release 2.2, this command will not work if any lines other than zero are active, which includes spooler-controlled lines (printers). As of release 3.1, this process now updates the SYSTEM-CONFIG, ACC file to indicate a controlled system shutdown.

Compatibility: **Pick AT/XT**

PRIME

Activates program to provide next higher prime number from the number provided. See also: PRIMES program in SYSPROG BP.

Compatibility: **Pick 3.1**

PRINT-ERR *filename itemlist**

Outputs text of specified error message number.

PRIO

Displays the batch, interactive, and the timeslice parameters for the entire system.

PVERIFY *filename itemlist**

Verifies integrity of PICK/BASIC object code. This command hasn't been needed since about 1980 (R80).

QSELECT *filename itemlist** *{(attr#)}*

Creates a select list item from the specified filename and itemname entered, and is similar to the GET-LIST command. If the optional attr# (attribute number) is specified, the list is created from the multivalues contained in the specified attribute number.

REBOOT

Causes the system to reinitialize, rather than using the CTRL-ALT-DEL keys. This command may only be issued from port 0 (zero), and disables all users and flushes memory prior to rebooting. See also: FDISK, POWER-OFF, and chapter 7 for more documentation on booting Pick. As of release 2.2, this command will not work if any lines other than zero are active, which includes spooler-controlled lines (printers). As of release 3.1, this process now updates the SYSTEM-CONFIG,ACC file to indicate a controlled system shutdown.

Compatibility: **Pick AT/XT**

RECOVER-FD <cr>
ITEM NAME *itemname <cr>*

Allows recovery of an item deleted via an FD command. It must be executed immediately after the FD command, otherwise the item is lost. If a list of items is active, there is no chance to recover the item.

REFORMAT *filename {itemlist} outlist {modlist} <cr>*
FILE NAME:*destination-file or TAPE*

Inserts data elements defined in specified filename into another filename, in the order of appearance in the outlist. Note the first entry in the outlist is used as the item-id for the destination file. Each subsequent entry in the outlist becomes an attribute in the destination item, in the order of specification in the outlist. Upon execution of this command, the prompt "FILE NAME:", appears on the screen. Either a filename may be entered, directing the output to the specified filename, or the literal, TAPE, which directs the output to the attached magnetic tape.

RESTORE-ACCOUNTS

Activates PROC to restore multiple accounts from a FILE-SAVE tape or diskette(s). See also: ACCOUNT-RESTORE. As of release 3.1, this command will restore all accounts on save media.

Compatibility: **Pick 2.2** and higher

ROBOT

Activates PICK/BASIC program on SYSPROG account to occupy time while waiting for the five o'clock whistle.

Compatibility: **Pick AT/XT**

RTD {*radix*}*value*

Converts radix (base) to its decimal equivalent and displays the result. If the radix is omitted, a radix of 16 is assumed, and behaves like the old XTD command, converting hexadecimal to decimal.

Example:

```
RTD 2 1000
8
```

This converts the (binary - base 2) number 1000 to its decimal equivalent.

RUN *filename itemname* {(*options*)}

Executes a PICK/BASIC program.

Options:

- A Prohibits entry into PICK/BASIC debugger; aborts on error conditions.
- D Enters PICK/BASIC debugger prior to execution.
- E Enters debugger on any error condition.
- I Inhibits variable initialization.
- N Activates NOPAGE function, on output to the terminal.
- P Directs output from PRINT statement to system printer, via the spooler.
- S Suppresses runtime warning messages. (Useful when demonstrating new programs).

RUNOFF *filename itemlist** {(*options*)}

Activates output function of RUNOFF text processor.

Options:

- n Any integer. Specifies the number of times to overstrike a character or characters designated as boldface.
- C Suppresses .CHAIN and .READ output.
- I Outputs next item name.
- J Suppresses highlighting function.
- N Activates NOPAGE function on output to the terminal.
- P Directs output to system printer, via the spooler.
- S Suppresses boldface and underline function.
- U Outputs in all uppercase.

S-DUMP *filename* {*itemlist*} {*seqlist*} {*sellist*} {*modlist*} {HEADING *"text"* {(*options*)}

Copies to tape all itemnames from the specified filename that meet the specified selection criteria, in order of the specified sort key{s}. The HEADING modifier specifies the tape label to write to the tape prior to the data.

Options:

H Suppresses the tape label.
I Suppresses the display of item-id's as they are dumped.

SAVE {*(options)*}

Activates the save (backup) processor for any of the following functions:

- Copy contents of entire system to magnetic tape
- Copy contents of a single account to magnetic tape
- Produce file statistics data

See also: ACCOUNT-SAVE, FILE-SAVE, and LIST-FILE-STATS.

Options:

D Saves data files.
F Outputs filenames. When omitted, only SYSTEM-level names are displayed.
G Handles GFE's encountered during SAVE. Rather than stopping and waiting for a response, it skips the rest of the current group and proceeds to the next group. Logs entries in STAT-FILE when the S option is used.
I Individual account (used in ACCOUNT-SAVE).
N No overflow space is required.
P Outputs filenames to the system printer.
S Creates file statistics in STAT-FILE.
T Outputs to magnetic media. Omitting this option is useful for regenerating system statistics and/or finding GFE's. Hint: don't use the G option when trying this.

As of release 3.1, the format for SAVE media is:

```
LABEL EOF LABEL DATA.
```

This was added because some tape units will not restore saved data in the format:

```
EOF LABEL EOF DATA
```

SAVE-LIST {*filename*} *listname*

-or-

SL {*filename*} *listname* (added in release 3.1)

Saves listname in specified filename. The default filename is POINTER-FILE.

SEL-RESTORE *filename itemlist** {*(options)*}
ACCOUNT-NAME ?:*acctname*
FILENAME ?:*filename*

Selectively restores items from either a FILE-SAVE tape or an ACCOUNT-SAVE tape. Tape must be positioned at the start of the file (data) section on a FILE-SAVE tape, or at the beginning of the account on an ACCOUNT-SAVE tape.

The specified acctname and filename must match exactly with the appropriate name on tape. The first file filename reference specifies the file where the items are to be restored. The latter reference to filename indicates the filename, as stored on the magnetic tape. Entering a <cr> at the latter filename reference specifies to restore the specified account's MD (Master Dictionary).

Note that the term, "tape," is used for a documentation convention only. The type of media is determined prior to using this command by the use of either the SET-FLOPPY, SET-SCT, or other media-attaching commands. After the media is attached, all of the normal tape-handling verbs can be used, with a few exceptions like T-RETEN and T-ERASE.

Options:

- A Indicates that tape is already positioned at the correct account.
- C Allows restoration of every item before next end-of-file, when used with the N option.
- F Displays filenames for all accounts. This option may not be used with the N option.
- I Suppresses display of item-id's.
- N Identifies file by location (order) number.
- O Overwrites items, when duplicate item-id's exist.
- S Suppresses "EXISTS ON FILE" messages when the target item-ids already exist and the O option is not being used.

SELECT *filename* {*itemlist*} {*sellist*} {*outlist*} {*modlist*}

Retrieves all items from a specified filename that meet selection criteria, in order of their appearance in the filename, and creates a list that either can be saved for future use or acted on immediately.

The outlist parameter specifies the attribute definition item(s) from which values are to be extracted for creation of the list.

SET-BAUD {*portnumber,*} *baud rate*

Allows changing the baud rate for lines 1 and 2 on the XT, and for 1 through 10 on the AT. The default baud rate for each line is 9600. When the line (port) number is not specified, the current line is affected. See also: SET-PORT.

The valid baud rate choices are:
110, 150, 300, 600, 1200, 2400, 4800, 9600 (and 19200 on release 2.2 and higher).

Compatibility: **Pick AT/XT**

SET-DATE *mm/dd/yy*{*yy*} {(*U*)}

Sets the system date to a specified setting. See also: SET-DATE-EUR and SET-DATE STD. Note that this is now a PROC that executes the verb called SET.DATE.

Option:

U Updates the hardware real-time clock, as well as the system (software clock).

Compatibility: **Pick AT/XT**

SET-DATE-EUR

Toggles the standard date format to European format: dd/mm/yy/. See also: SET-DATE-FORMAT.

Compatibility: **Pick AT/XT**

SET-DATE-STD

Toggles the European date format to North American format: mm/dd/yy. See also: SET-DATE-FORMAT.

Compatibility: **Pick AT/XT**

SET-DATE-FORMAT {*country.code*} {(*options*)}

Changes format of domestic date/time format from items in the DATE-FORMAT file.

Supported Country Codes:

US American
GR German
IT Italian
SP Spanish
UK English/United Kingdom

Options:

S Sets system date format using SYSTEM-CONFIG DATE-FORMAT item.
U Updates SYSTEM-CONFIG DATE-FORMAT item using specified country code.

Compatibility: **Pick 3.1**

SET-FILE {*acctname* {*filename*}}

Creates or updates the item called QFILE in the MD of the current account. Provides access to specified filename in specified acctname by using the filename, QFILE, in place of the filename parameter during any file-handling commands.

SET-FLOPPY {(*density,drive*)}

Used after the T-ATT command to designate the density to read/write diskettes and which floppy drive to use, when more than one is present. Drive choices are typically A or B. See also: FORMAT. Don't forget to "rewind" the diskette with the T-REW command prior to attempting any read or write operation. Usually, this doesn't take too long. The defaults are: drive A, High density. As of release 2.2, 3 1/2 inch floppies are supported.

Density choices:

S Standard density (360Kb for 5 1/4 inch, 720Kb for 3 1/2 inch)
H High density (1.2Mb for 5 1/4 inch, 1.44Mb for 3 1/2 inch)

Compatibility: **Pick AT/XT**

SET-FUNC *filename itemname*

Specifies name of item to use in assigning function keys for use only by port 0 (zero). Each function key may be assigned one character. See the file called FUNCKEYS on the SYSPROG account. The default when on booting is that the function keys are undefined. See the item called SET-KBRD.DOC in the DOC file in the SYSPROG account for more information on defining function keys.

Compatibility: **Pick AT/XT**

SET-KBRD *filename itemname*

Specifies name of item to use in assigning the type of keyboard for use only by port 0 (zero). The items available in the KEYBOARDS file on the SYSPROG account include: BRITISH (ENGLISH), DVORAK, FRENCH, FRENCH 2, GERMAN, ITALIAN, SPANISH, SPANISH 2 and USA (the default). See the item called KBRD.DOC, in the DOC file on the SYSPROG account. It contains a detailed explanation for constructing keyboard definition items. As of release 2.2, Pick Systems now provides support for 101/102 keyboards.

Compatibility: **Pick AT/XT**

SET-KEYS {*keyboard.name*}

Specifies name of item to use in assigning the type of keyboard for use only by port 0 (zero). The items available in the KEYBOARDS file on the SYSPROG account include: BRITISH (ENGLISH), DVORAK, FRENCH, FRENCH 2, GERMAN, ITALIAN, SPANISH, SPANISH 2, and USA (the default). See the item called KBRD.DOC, in the DOC file on the SYSPROG account. It contains a detailed explanation for constructing keyboard definition items. As of release 2.2, Pick Systems now provides support for 101/102 keyboards.

Compatibility: **Pick 3.1**

SET-LPTR

-or-

SET-LPTR *number*

-or-

SET-LPTR {*number*}, {*delay*}, {*burst*}, {*slice*}}

Used to display or change performance parameters on parallel printers. To obtain an optimum blend of printer and system performance, experiment with different settings. When no parameters are provided, the current settings are displayed. A printer number may be specified to display its current settings. Like the TERM command, existing parameters may be left intact by providing two successive commas where the parameter would normally appear.

The "number" parameter indicates the printer number in the range 0 to 3.

The "delay" parameter indicates the number of times to attempt to send a character to the printer. The higher the value, the slower the system performance, but faster printer performance. The default is 300, and the value must be in the range 1 to 4095.

The "burst" parameter indicates the number of characters to transmit to the printer in one packet, and relates to the size of the printer (RAM) buffer. The default is 200, and must be in the range 1 to 255. Pick Systems suggests that 15 provides good performance.

The "slice" parameter indicates the number of timeslices that the printer waits prior to receiving its next timeslice. The default is 1, and it must be in the range 1 to 15. Pick Systems advises using a number equal to or greater than the number of users on the system.

Compatibility: **Pick AT/XT**

SET-PORT {*portnumber*{*,baud,parity,stopbits,wordlength*}}

Activates program to display or change baud rate, parity bits, stop bits and word length for a port. When no portnumber is specified, the existing settings are displayed.

- The valid baud rates (as of release 2.2) are: 110, 150, 300, 600, 1200, 2400, 3800, 9600, and 19200. The default baud rate is 9600.
- To leave an existing parameter intact, use two successive commas (like the TERM command).
- Parity can be **N** for none, **O** for odd or **E** for even.
- Stop bits can be either 1 or 2.
- Word length can be either 7 or 8.

See also: LIST-PORT.

Compatibility: **Pick AT/XT**

SET-SCT (*blocksize*)

Used after the T-ATT command to designate that the Streaming Cartridge Tape should be used for any subsequent tape operations. If the blocksize is omitted, it will default to 16384. The blocksize must be between 2048 and 16384, and a multiple of 512.

Compatibility: **Pick XT** only

SET-SCT {*buffers*} {({*blocksize*} {*options*}}

Used after the T-ATT command to designate that the Streaming Cartridge Tape should be used for any subsequent tape operations.

The "buffers" parameter indicates the number of 512-byte buffers to assign for the tape buffer. The default (and minimum) is 128. The maximum is a function of how much memory is present on your system. Up to half of the memory may be allocated. For example, if your system has 640Kb of main memory, the maximum number of buffers is 640.

If the blocksize is omitted, it defaults to 16384. The blocksize must be between 512 and 32500, and a multiple of 512.

Options:

M Assigns number of buffers using the total of real memory minus 256K or 768 buffers, or 384K on a 640K system. Pick Systems strongly encourages the use of this option to increase tape streaming and decrease the number of stop/starts, which decrease tape reliability. This option was added in release 3.1.

R Indicates that the tape is in "old" format, meaning that it was created on a version prior to 2.2.

Compatibility: **Pick 2.2** and higher

SET-SHUTDOWN-DELAY *{delay}* *{(options)}*

Displays or alters the delay number of seconds prior to shutdown. For users with disk caching hard-disk controllers, the command allows time for the disk to flush. The delay may be a positive number between 1 and 65536. All by itself, the command displays the current setting. The default setting is 512.

Options:

S Sets monitor shutdown delay using SHUTDOWN-DELAY item in SYSTEM-CONFIG file.

U Updates SHUTDOWN-DELAY item in SYSTEM-CONFIG file with specified value.

Compatibility: **Pick 3.1**

SET-SYM *filename* *{(T)}*

Sets symbol file pointer for use by system debugger. Filename is typically PSYM.

Option:

T Sets secondary file pointer to TSYM file.

SET-TERM *termwidth, termdepth, lineskip, lfdelay, ffdelay, backspace, printwidth, printdepth, termtype* *{(R)}*

Specifies default terminal and printer characteristics for entire system. Any parameter may be left intact by entering a null (two consecutive commas). The termtype parameter may appear anywhere in the command. See also: DEFINE-TERMINAL, which is used to add or modify existing terminal types. It displays a list of the available types of terminals on your system.

Term definitions:

termwidth—number of print positions per line on terminal
termdepth—number of lines on terminal
lineskip—number of blank lines at the bottom of the screen
lfdelay—number of delay characters output after linefeed
ffdelay—number of delay characters output after a top-of-form is executed.
backspace—decimal number of ASCII character to echo to the terminal when the backspace key is pressed.
printwidth—number of print positions per line on printer output.
printdepth—number of lines per page on printer output
termtype—type of terminal (for BASIC and PROC cursor control)

Terminal Types Supported: (Consult documentation for additional types—these were compiled from the CURSOR file on a Pick AT release):

A	Adds 580	B	Ampex 210
C	C Itoh VT52	D	Datamedia
E	Esprit	F	Televideo 910
G	IBM 3161/3163	I	IBM Monochrome
J	VT 100	L	Lear Seagler
M	Ampex 80	N	Wyse 100
P	Pertec 701	Q	QVT 102
R	Adds Regent	S	Soroc
T	Televideo 910	V	ADDS Viewpoint
W	Wyse 50		

Option:

R Redisplays TERM parameters after entry.

About the ffdelay parameter: This parameter also determines when to eject a page (or clear the screen) between output pages. The following settings illustrate this concept:

Setting / Function

0 Suppresses page eject between output pages on both the terminal and the printer.

1 Suppresses page eject on the terminal only.

2 Normal mode. Any value greater than or equal to two will clear the screen (and eject a page on the printer) between each output page.

SET-TIME *hh:mm* {*:ss*} {(*U*)}

Sets the system to specified setting. Note that this is now a PROC that executes a verb called SET.TIME.

Option:

U Updates the hardware real-time clock, as well as the system (software clock).

Compatibility: **Pick AT/XT**

SETUP.SIO

This program was provided with release 2.0 to alter the parity, stop bits, and word length for a port. As of release 2.2, it has been renamed SET-PORT.

Compatibility: **Pick AT/XT**

SL *listname*

Synonym for SAVE-LIST command. Provided for compatibility with Advanced Pick.

Compatibility: **Pick 3.1**

SLEEP *numberseconds*

-or-

SLEEP *untiltime*

Suspends further processing until specified time is exhausted or reached.

Examples:

SLEEP 600<cr>

Puts the process to sleep for ten minutes.

SLEEP 23:59:59<cr>

Puts the process to sleep until one second before midnight. (It's as close as you can get.)

SLICE *timeslice*

Used to set the timeslice for all ports on the system. Timeslice must be in the range 1 to 255. This verb may or may not be on your system and is usually better left alone.

SNAKE

More entertainment for the hopelessly bored.

SORT *filename {itemlist} {seqlist} {sellist} {outlist} {(options)}*

Outputs specified filename, in order of specified sort key{s}.

SORT-ITEM *filename {itemlist} {seqlist} {sellist} {modlist} {(options)}*

Outputs items, in COPY format.

SORT-LABEL *filename {itemlist} {sellist} {seqlist} {outlist} {modlist} {(options)}*

Outputs formatted labels from specified filename in order of specified sort key{s}.

Upon pressing the carriage return the prompt character, ?, appears. This is for the entry of the following label parameters:

?columns,rows,skip,indent,size,space,C

Where:

columns = number of labels across page
rows = number of lines requested to print on each label
skip = number of lines (vertically) between labels
indent = number of spaces from left margin to beginning output column
size = number of print positions per label
space = number of spaces (horizontally) between labels
C = compresses null values

Note: each of the parameters must be separated by commas during input.

Following the entry of the above parameters, if the INDENT parameter is nonzero, the prompt character, ?, appears for the number of times indicated in the rows parameter. (i.e., if rows was 4, expect 4 question marks.

These prompts (?'s) are for the entry of headers that print in the INDENT area to the left of the first row of labels.

Example:

```
SORT-LABEL INVENTORY BY PART.# PART.# DESC PRICE (P
?3,4,1,0,30,2,C
```

SOUNDEX

Activates program to demonstrate SOUNDEX user exit conversion. Program resides in SYSPROG BP.

Compatibility: **Pick 3.1**

SP-ASSIGN {*options*}

Sets spooler output assignment for current process.

Note: an SP-ASSIGN command with *no* options resets the assignment back to the default state, which *must* be done prior to using the SP-EDIT command on hold files when attempting to de-spool.

Options:

- n Integer number in the range (1-125) indicating the number of copies. (Default = one).
- ? Outputs resulting setting, or current setting when entered alone.
- C Activates choke function. *Choke* means that the spooler will require no more than 20 frames to print the job, and will *recycle* the 20 frames. Must be used with an I option, and may not be used with H option.
- Fn Directs output to formqueue "n", where "n" is an integer number in the range (0-125).
- H Directs output to hold files{s}.
- I Instant print. Begins output (assuming device is ready) as soon as the first frame of output is completed.
- M Suppresses "Entry n" message.
- O Indicates to leave file open upon completion of process. This allows placing

multiple print jobs in one physical spooler entry. See also: SP-OPEN and SP-CLOSE. To close the entry, use the SP-ASSIGN command without any options.

Rn Initiates the print file, "n" where "n" is an integer number in the range (0-125), for use with BASIC "PRINT ON" statements.

S Suppressed printing on system printer. Normally used with H option.

T Attaches tape unit as output device.

Note: the "n", "Fn", "Rn", and "Qn", options *must* be separated by a blank from any other options present in the command line.

Examples of the SP-ASSIGN Command:

```
SP-ASSIGN HS?
SP-ASSIGN 13 F2 ?
```

SP-CLOSE

Closes the currently open spooler entry. See also: SP-OPEN. Entries are automatically closed if a LOGTO, OFF, or SP-ASSIGN (without an R option) is issued.

SP-EDIT {*options*}

Accesses spooler entries for processing or deletion. When options are omitted, allows access to all entries generated from current account.

Options:

'acctname'	Accesses entries generated from the specified account.
n{-n}	Integer number, in the range (0-600), of spooler entry, or beginning and ending hold spooler entries.
D	Deletes{s} hold file{s}.
F{b{-e}}	Integer number, in the range (0-125), specifying the beginning and ending form queue{s} to access.
H	Suppresses tape label when directing output to tape.
L	Activates "look" function, and displays first 500 bytes of spooler entries.
MD	Manager (also called "magic" priority). Delete{s} spooler entries.
MS	Manager priority. Spool{s} spooler entries.
N	Activates NOPAGE function when spooling to terminal.
O	When used with the L option, allows looking at spooler entries already being output.
P	Directs hold file to currently assigned printer.
R	Changes output parameter settings to currently assigned parameter{s}.
T{W}	Directs output to tape. W indicates to wait for tape to be readied, if not already.
U	Accesses all spooled entries generated from current process.
V	Converts hold file to data file, without trimming blanks and blank lines.

Examples:

```
SP-EDIT MSP
```

```
SP-EDIT MSP1-5
SP-EDIT MD1-10
SP-EDIT MUD
```

SP-KILL {*options*}

Stops output of currently active spooler entry on specified printer.

Options:

n{-n}	Integer number, in the range (0-19) indicating which printer to stop.
A	Stops spooler entry or entries created from current account.
B	All spooler entries.
Dn{-n}	Deletes printer{s}. The beginning and ending printer number{s} must be in the range (0-19). Note: the maximum number of printers can vary between various PICK-class systems.
F{b{-e}}	Returns spooler entries to available hold file status. The beginning and ending parameter{s} must be in the range (0-600).
N	Suppresses abort message on output when directed to a printer.
O	Unlinks spooler entry already being output.

Examples:

```
SP-KILL 1
SP-KILL OF7
```

SP-OPEN

Specifies that the spooler is to leave the spooler entry open upon completion of process. See also: SP-CLOSE, and SP-ASSIGN O.

SP-STATUS {*options*}

Displays status of all spooler controlled devices.

Options:

n{-n}	Integer number indicating the beginning and ending printer number{s} to display.
B	Outputs status of all printers.
P	Directs output to system printer, via the spooler.

SP-TAPEOUT {*options*}

Retrieves reports previously spooled to magnetic tape, and outputs to current device assignment.

Options:

A	Converts EBCDIC format to ASCII format.
L	Allows output of tapes created with each line being treated as a tape record.
U	Converts all lowercase characters to uppercase.

SREFORMAT *filename {itemlist} {outlist} {seqlist} {modlist}* FILE NAME:destination-file or TAPE

Inserts data elements defined from the specified filename into another filename, in the order of the appearance in the outlist, after sorting the data by the specified sort key{s}. Note: the first entry in the outlist is used as the item-id for the destination file. Each subsequent entry in the outlist becomes an attribute in the destination item, in the order of specification in the outlist.

After execution of this command, the prompt "FILE NAME:", appears on the screen. Either a filename can be entered, which directs the output to the specified filename, or the literal, TAPE, which directs the output to the attached magnetic tape.

SSELECT *filename {itemlist} {sellist} {seqlist} {outlist} {modlist}*

Retrieves all items from specified filename that meet selection criteria, in order of the specified sort key{s} and creates a list that can be saved for future use or acted on immediately.

The outlist parameter specifies the attribute definition item{s} from which values are to be extracted for creation of the list.

STARTPTR *printer#,formqueue#,#ejectpages,printer specification, {A} {(S{Xlinecount} {(D)}*

Activates and initializes parallel or serial printer.

The printer specification is composed of two parameters; the type (P or S), and the address or location of the device.

The letter A may follow the printer specification. When used, it allows for forms alignment on the newly started printer.

Printer Types:

- P Parallel. This requires special hardware. Consult your vendor to find out if more than one parallel printer is supported.
- S Serial. Can go in any serial I/O port.

Examples of Printer Specifications:

- P0 Parallel printer 0.
- S12 Serial printer on port 12.

Options:

- D Enables debugger on line. (Used primarily by developers to test spooler code.)
- S Suppresses first from feed on serial printer.
- Xn Specifies the number of lines per page for serial printers.

Examples:

```
STARTPTR 0,0,0,P0
STARTPTR 1,1,0,S12
```

STARTREK

Activates the program originally written by Ken Simms on Pick XT/AT releases only.

STAT *filename {itemlist} {sellist} {modlist} {attrname} {(options)}*

Outputs item count and an average value of all items that meet the specified selection criteria.

STOPPTR *{(options)}*

Stops the specified printer at the end of the current print job. The default printer is printer zero (0).

Options:

n Integer number of printer to stop, in the range (0-19).

B Stops all printers.

STRIP-SOURCE *filename itemlist** {(O)}
DESTINATION FILE: *filename*

Removes assembled object code from itemlist in source filename, moving only object code to specified destination file.

SUBD *decnum decnum*

Subtracts two decimal numbers and displays the result in decimal.

SUBX *hexnum hexnum*

Subtracts two hexadecimal numbers and displays the result in hexadecimal.

SUM *filename {itemlist} attrname {sellist} {modlist} {(options)}*

Outputs total of the specified attrname for all itemnames meeting specified selection criteria. The default attrname is zero (0) (item-id), if the attrname is omitted.

T-ATT *{blocksize}* {(U)}

Attaches tape unit and assigns blocksize to tape I/O buffer. If no parameters are specified and the tape is already attached, this command outputs the current attachment status. The default blocksize varies between Pick systems. See also: SET-FLOPPY and SET-SCT.

Option:

U Unconditionally attaches the tape unit. Not a good way to win friends and influence people.

T-BCK *{number tape records}*

Moves tape backwards over specified number of tape records. When the number of tape records is omitted, the tape moves back over the last EOF mark and requires a T-FWD command. Note: this command is not supported on Streaming Cartridge Tapes (SCT's).

T-CHK {(*options*)}

Checks magnetic tape file for parity errors. When the "A" option is omitted, only the current tape file is checked.

Options:

A Checks to end of data.
L Displays label data if one is found after an end-of-file mark (release 2.2) and higher).
P Directs output to system printer, via the spooler.

T-DET {(U)}

Detaches tape unit from current process.

Option:

U Unconditionally detaches tape unit. This requires a SYS2 privilege level.

T-DUMP *filename* {*itemlist*} {*sellist*} {*modlist*} {HEADING "text"/*options*} {(*options*)}

Copies to tape all itemnames that meet specified selection criteria. The HEADING modifier allows specifying the contents of the tape label written to the tape prior to the dump.

Options:

H Suppresses the tape label.
I Suppresses the display of item-id's as they are dumped.

T-EOD {(*options*)}

Moves tape forward to end of data.

Options:

L Displays label data if one is found after an end-of-file mark (release 2.2 and higher). If the tape record size is different, it will change automatically.
P Directs output to system printer, via the spooler.

T-ERASE

Performs a retension and erases a Streaming Cartridge Tape.

Compatibility: **Pick AT/XT**

T-FWD (*number tape records*)

Moves tape forward to next end-of-file, or the specified number of tape records.

T-LOAD *filename* {*itemlist*} {*sellist*} {*modlist*} {(*options*)}

Copies from tape to specified filename all items that meet specified selection criteria.

Options:

I Suppresses listing itemnames to terminal.
O Overwrites existing items, when duplicate item-id{'s} exist.
V Verifies T-DUMP media without reloading. (Added in release 3.1)

T-RDLBL {(*reelnumber*)}

Reads tape label number from optionally specified (hexadecimal) reel number.

T-READ {(*options*)}

Reads a block of data from the magnetic tape unit attached to current process.

Options:

A Converts EBCDIC format to ASCII.
P Directs output to system printer, via the spooler.
n Indicates to read block "n".
n-n Specifies beginning and ending block from current position.
X Outputs in hexadecimal.

T-RETEN

Retensions Streaming Cartridge Tape by moving all the way to the end of the tape, then rewinding. Recommended prior to using tape for any purpose. Automatically performed during FILE-SAVE and ACCOUNT-SAVE.

Compatibility: **Pick AT/XT**

T-REW

Rewinds magnetic tape to load point.

T-SPACE {*number tape records*}

Moves tape forward specified number of tape records, displaying each tape label as it is encountered.

T-STATUS

Indicates the type and drive number of the currently attached off-line storage device.

Compatibility: **Pick AT/XT**

T-VERIFY {(*options*)}

-or-

T-VERIFY *acctname* {(*options*)}

Verifies integrity of FILE-SAVE or ACCOUNT-SAVE media.

In default mode, when no options are provided, only the account names are displayed, and the media is compared with the file system. All errors found are displayed.

Items are displayed in file hierarchy format as follows:

Account > Dictionary Level > Data Level > Item-ID {Errors}

Options:

- A Verifies and displays all accounts on media, until an "end-of-save" occurs. This option *must* be used if no account name is provided.
- D Suppresses duplicated item-id's in a group.
- E Displays errors only.
- F Sequentially displays only files found on media, in hierarchy format. When used with I option, items are also displayed.
- G Suppresses group hash testing on all items. Ignores errors if items are in the wrong group.
- I Displays items from media in file hierarchy format. Items display continuously in place, unless this option is combined with the F option, which displays each item on a separate line.
- L Logs errors to user-specified log file. Attribute 1 of items written in log file will contain the error message from the ERRMSG file. Attribute 2 will be the element that caused the error, in hierarchical format.
- N Activates the NOPAGE function on output to the terminal.
- P Directs output to system printer, via the spooler.
- Q Queries user on each error found. User has option to continue, quit, or skip file system comparisons for the current file.
- V Verifies contents of media only, without comparing to file system. When this option is used, the F, I, and Q options must also be used.

T-WEOF

Writes an EOF (End of File) mark on magnetic tape.

T-WTLBL

Writes a tape label on the attached media.

TA {*portnumber*}

Displays status of type-ahead buffer on specified portnumber, or current port if omitted. See also: TA-OFF and TA-ON.

Compatibility: **Pick 2.2** and higher

TA-OFF {*portnumber*}

Disables type-ahead buffer on specified portnumber, or current port if omitted. See also: TA and TA-ON.

Compatibility: **Pick 2.2** and higher

TA-ON {*portnumber*}

Enables type-ahead buffer on specified portnumber, or current port if omitted. See also: TA and TA-OFF.

Compatibility: **Pick 2.2** and higher

TABS

-or-

TABS {I} {*tabstop*{*,tabstop...*}

-or-

TABS I {S}

-or-

TABS {O} {tabstop{,tabstop...}

-or-

TABS O {S}

Displays tabstops previously set during the Editor process or assigns new tabstop positions for input (I) or output (O). Note that output tabstop positions are useful only on printing terminals that have a physical tab facility. Don't use output tabstops on normal CRT's.

Input tabstops can be disabled by issuing the command TABS I<cr>. Similarly, output tabstops can be disabled by issuing the command TABS O<cr>.

The S parameter indicates that the previous tabstop settings are to be used.

TERM *termwidth, termdepth, lineskip, lfdelay, ffdelay, backspace, printwidth, printdepth, termtype* {(R)}

Specifies terminal and printer characteristics for the current process. Any parameter can be left intact by entering a null (two consecutive commas). The termtype parameter can appear anywhere in the command.

See also: TERM-TYPE and DEFINE-TERMINAL, which is used to add or modify existing terminal types and displays a list of the available types of terminals on your system.

Term definitions:

termwidth—number of print positions per line on terminal
termdepth—number of lines on terminal
lineskip—number of blank lines at bottom of screen
lfdelay—number of delay characters output after linefeed
ffdelay—number of delay characters output after a top-of-form is executed.
backspace—decimal number of ASCII character to echo to the terminal when the backspace key is pressed.
printwidth—number of print positions per line on printer output
printdepth—number of lines per page on printer output
termtype—type of terminal (for BASIC and PROC cursor control)

Terminal Types Supported: (Consult documentation for additional types—these were compiled from the CURSOR file on a Pick AT release):

A	Adds 580	B	Ampex 210
C	C Itoh VT52	D	Datamedia
E	Esprit	F	Televideo 910
G	IBM 3161/3163	I	IBM Monochrome
J	VT 100	L	Lear Seagler
M	Ampex 80	N	Wyse 100
P	Pertec 701	Q	QVT 102
R	Adds Regent	S	Soroc
T	Televideo 910	V	ADDS Viewpoint
W	Wyse 50		

Option:

R Redisplays TERM parameters after entry.

About the ffdelay parameter: This parameter also determines when to eject a page (or clear the screen) between output pages. The following settings illustrate this concept:

Setting/Function

0 Suppresses page eject between output pages on both the terminal and the printer
1 Suppresses page eject on the terminal only
2 Normal mode; any value greater than or equal to two will clear the screen (and eject a page on the printer) between each output page.

TERM-TYPE

Activates PICK/BASIC program to automatically set the terminal characteristics for the current line. The item read in to set the characteristics is found in the DICT of the ACC file. The item-id is the 2-digit portnumber. The editor is used to maintain individual port characteristics. For example, to change the terminal characteristics for line 0, you could enter:

```
ED DICT ACC 00<cr>
TOP
.L2<cr>
001 Memory Mapped Monitor
002 79,24,1,0,2,8,80,60,I
```

Compatibility: **Pick AT/XT**

TEST-CURSOR

Activates a program to test the various terminal capabilities such as clear screen, clear to end of line, "X,Y" addressing, reverse video, etc. See also: DEFINE-TERMINAL.

Compatibility: **Pick 2.2** and higher

TIME

Displays current system time and date.

TO *acctname {,password}*

Synonym for the LOGTO command.

Compatibility: **Pick 3.1**

UNLOCK-FRAME {.}fid

Removes previously locked frame from memory. See also: LOCK-FRAME.

UNPACK

Activates PICK/BASIC program to convert composite items back into the smaller, multiple items created with the PACK command. Pick Systems provides this program, but no support for it. See also: PACK.

Compatibility: **Pick 2.2** (No longer provided as of 3.1)

UPDATE-ACCOUNT *acctname {acctname...}*

-or-

UPDATE-ACCOUNTS *acctname {acctname...}*

Activates process to update MD verb definitions to new release for one or more accounts. Any conflicts found will be logged in the CLASHES file, with a new data section being added for each account. For example, if the account called "DUMMY" was run through this process, the clashes would be stored in CLASHES, DUMMY. To see the existing data sections, use: LISTFILES DUMMY.

Compatibility: **Pick 3.1**

VERIFY-SYSTEM {(O)}

Verifies the integrity of the Pick System software by comparing each attribute in the item called CHECK-SUM in the ERRMSG file against its corresponding virtual memory address. When differences occur, a message displays indicating that mismatches occur in one or more of the ABS frames. These can usually be corrected by performing an ABS restore from your sys-gen media.

Option:

O Generates new checksum item in ERRMSG file.

VIDEO.DEMO

Activates program to demonstrate line 0 video functions.

Compatibility: **Pick 3.1**

WHAT *{options}*

Outputs system status (normally produced by the WHERE command), configuration information, group and execution lock status (LIST-LOCKS), and the current status of the spooler (SP-STATUS).

Options:

'account name'	Outputs WHERE status for only the users of the specified account name.
n	Outputs WHERE status for line "n" only.
n-n	Outputs WHERE status for lines "n" through "n".
L	Suppresses display of lock status.
P	Directs output to system printer, via the spooler.
S	Suppresses display of SP-STATUS.
W	Suppresses display of WHERE command.
Z	Displays WHERE status for all lines.

WHERE *{(options)}*

Outputs current execution information on processes currently logged on to the system. The information displayed usually includes the portnumber, the PIB status, the process's PCB address, and the virtual return stack.

Options:

n	Displays information on line "n".
n-n	Displays information on lines "n" through "n".
'account name'	Outputs status for accounts logged onto specified account name.
P	Routes output to system printer, via the spooler.
Z	Displays status of all lines.

WHICH

Provides current release level.

Compatibility: **Pick AT/XT**

WHO *{line#{-line#}}*

-or-

WHO *{*}*

-or-

WHO *'acctname'*

Outputs account name being used on specified linenumber, range of linenumbers, or the current account name when no linenumber is specified. The asterisk (*) displays the current account name for all lines, whether or not they are logged on. An account name may also be specified to determine the ports logged on to that account.

X-REF

Assembler cross-reference verb used in XREF proc.

XCS {*portnumber*}

Displays status of Extended Character Set for specified portnumber or current port if omitted. When XCS is enabled, the high-order bit is *not* stripped from input. This allows characters in the (decimal) range 128 to 239 to be used. See also: XCS-OFF and XCS-ON.

Compatibility: **Pick 2.2** and higher

XCS-OFF {*portnumber*}

Disables extended character set on specified portnumber or current port if omitted. See also: XCS and XCS-ON.

Compatibility: **Pick 2.2** and higher

XCS-ON {*portnumber*}

Enables extended character set on specified portnumber or current port if omitted. See also: XCS and XCS-OFF.

Compatibility: **Pick 2.2** and higher

XREF

Activates PROC to produce a cross-reference listing in the XSYM file of the most current CSYM file. Usually, this file only resides in the ASSEMBLER account.

XTD *hexnum*

Converts hexadecimal value to its equivalent decimal value.

3
ACCESS

General information

This chapter is divided into four subsections:

- The first section covers the general form of ACCESS commands and notes about related issues such as using quotes and logical operators.
- The second section is an alphabetic listing of ACCESS verbs.
- The third section provides an alphabetic listing of all ACCESS modifiers and connectives.
- The fourth and final section provides an alphabetic listing of all the correlative and conversion codes.

About compatibility with SMA standards

Some instructions in this section might not conform to the SMA standard. Those that are unique to the Pick AT/XT versions are indicated with a compatibility index following the instruction. If no index is provided, the instruction conforms to SMA standards.

General format of ACCESS sentences

```
verb filename {itemlist} {seqlist} {sellist} {outlist} {modlist} {options}
```

Where:
verb is any of the verbs listed in this chapter (e.g., LIST, SORT, etc.)
filename is the name of the file (e.g., STAFF, DICT STAFF, etc.)
itemlist is the specific list of item-ids (e.g., '101,' '102'...)
seqlist is the list of sort keys (e.g., BY STATE BY ZIP...)
sellist is the list of selection criteria (e.g., WITH NAME, WITH BAL > "0"...)
outlist is the specific list of fields to output (e.g., NAME STATE...)
modlist is the list of modifiers (ID-SUPP, LPTR, etc.)
options are any of the standard options listed below or additional unique verb options (e.g., (PI...))

Standard ACCESS verb options

The following options generally work with every ACCESS verb. Some verbs, however, may use the same option with a different meaning than listed below. Where there are differences in "standard" options, they are listed with the verb.

- B Suppresses linefeed after compile phase. Doesn't really have much function. The automatic linefeed indicates that the sentence compiled properly, but it doesn't necessarily mean that it will work.
- C Same as COL-HDR-SUPP modifier. Turns off column and page headings, and "number of items" message.
- D Same as DET-SUPP modifier. Suppresses detail lines in sorted reports using BREAK-ON's.
- F Issues form-feed on each new item. Used with LIST-ITEM and SORT-ITEM verbs.
- H Same as HDR-SUPP (or SUPP) modifier. Turns off page heading and "number of items" message (in releases prior to 3.1).
- H Same as HDR-SUPP (or SUPP) modifier. Turns off page heading only (changed in release 3.1).
- I Same as ID-SUPP modifier. Suppresses display of item-ids.
- N Same as NOPAGE modifier. Causes output to CRT to not pause at the end of each page of output. For Evelyn Woods graduates.
- P Same as the LPTR modifier. Directs output to system printer, via the spooler.
- S Suppresses "number of items"message (new in release 3.1).
- Y Shows ACCESS compiled string to the terminal, even if the P option is in effect. The compiled string contains information about the attributes to display on the report in a sort of internal format. If any fields to output contain A correlatives, each is translated into an F correlative prior to processing and the F correlative form is displayed.
- Z Shows ACCESS compiled string to the printer, even if the P option is *not* in effect.

General rules about ACCESS sentences

- ACCESS verbs may be issued from TCL, PROC, or PICK/BASIC (using EXECUTE).
- The ACCESS verb *must* be the first word in the command.
- Exactly one filename must be specified in the command, unless the USING modifier is present, in which case, two filenames are needed.
- Any number of Attribute-Defining-Items may be requested for output by the command, provided they all are defined in the dictionary of the file being accessed.
- Any number of modifiers and relational operators may be used in an ACCESS sentence, provided they all are defined in the Master Dictionary, Note: only nine AND clauses are allowed in any ACCESS sentence.

- Each word or character in an ACCESS sentence must be delimited with a blank, unless it is a quoted string.
- Multiple sort keys are processed left to right.

Rules on using quotes in ACCESS sentences

The use of single or double quote marks depends on the nature of the command. For referencing values (data elements), the string should be enclosed in double quotes:

```
LIST CUSTOMERS WITH NAME = "JES]"
```

For referencing item-ids, the (item-id) string should be enclosed in single quotes:

```
LIST CUSTOMERS '100"101"102'
```

Both item-id strings and value strings may be included in an ACCESS statement:

```
LIST CUSTOMERS '100"101"102' WITH CONTACT = "[JON]"
```

The last case is the only time that Pick enforces the rules about single quotes surrounding item-ids and double quotes surrounding value strings.

The backslash (\ ) character may also be used as a string delimiter, which is useful when the string being searched contains both single and double quotes.

Logical operators

Logical operators are used in the selection criteria process:...WITH attribute-name **operator** "valuestring"

Examples:

```
WITH STATE = "CA"
WITH AMOUNT.DUE #"O"
WITH BIRTHDAY > "1/1/62"
WITH AGE > "21"
```

Note: each operator has an "english" equivalent which may be used interchangeably with the "symbol" form.

When no operator is present, the default assumed is an "equal to" (=).

Examples:

```
WITH STATE EQ "CA"
WITH AMOUNT.DUE NOT "O"
WITH BIRTHDAY BEFORE "1/2/62"
WITH AGE GT "21"
```

Relational operators

Symbol/Word	*Meaning*
= , EQ	Equal to
#, NE, NO, NOT	Not equal to
>, GT, AFTER	Greater than
<, LT, BEFORE	Less than
> =,GE	Greater than or equal to
< =,LE	Less than or equal to
&, AND	Logical Boolean connectives

Logical connectives: AND and OR

Logical connectives are Boolean operators used to connect two or more selection criteria phases in an ACCESS sentence. When two phases are connected with an OR, either phase may be true for data to be selected for processing.

WITH CITY = "HOLLYWOOD" **OR** WITH STATE "CA"

When an AND clause connects two phases, both phases have to be true for data to be affected.

WITH CITY "HOLLYWOOD" **AND** WITH STATE "CA"

When the connective between two phases is omitted, the default connective is OR.

WITH CITY "HOLLYWOOD" WITH STATE "CA"

The AND clauses take precedence over OR clauses, and a maximum of nine AND clauses may be specified.

Throwaway connectives

Throwaway connectives are words that used to provide continuity to a report, but are actually ignored by the ACCESS language. These words reside in your MD and the normal set includes the following:

A, AN, ANY, ARE, FILE, FOR, IN, ITEMS, OF, THE

This list of available throwaway connectives can easily be expanded by copying any one of the above items in the MD to new items, as in the following example:

>COPY MD A A A A<cr>
TO: DISPLAYING SHOWING FIELD ATTRIBUTE <cr>

After adding the new items, the following sentence is now possible:

SORT THE CUSTOMER FILE SHOWING THE NAME FIELD

where THE, FILE, SHOWING, and FIELD are all ignored, but would provide for a more grammatically correct sentence, which makes it easier for tailoring user vocabularies to foreign languages, like Texan, for example.

The USING connective

The USING connective allows using the dictionary from one file on the data section of another.

General form:

USING DICT *filename*

Specifies the file dictionary to access for attribute definition items.

Example:

LIST CUSTOMERS **USING** DICT SUPPLIERS

String searching

When used in conjunction with the WITH modifier, data elements may be searched for the occurrence of a string of characters, as shown in the following examples:

...WITH *attribute operator* "[value]"

searches entire element for occurrence of "value". Any string of characters may precede or follow "value".

...WITH *attribute operator* "[value"

Only returns data when the element being searched *ends* with "value", that is, any string of characters may precede "value", but the element must end with "value".

...WITH *attribute operator* "value]"

Only returns data when the element being searched *begins* with "value", that is, any string of characters may follow "value", but the element must begin with"value".

Wildcards

Wildcards are used in the selection criteria to exclude one or more specific characters in a string search.

...WITH *attribute operator* "[...^...]"

Example:

...WITH NAME = "[SM^TH]"

This command will retrieve any item containing at least five characters, the first two of which begin with "SM", followed by any character, and ending with "TH". In other words, this would retrieve "SMITH", "SMYTH," and "SMOTHERS".

Examples of wildcard searches:

```
LIST CUSTOMERS WITH NAME = "I^M"
```

searches the file for items whose attribute, defined by NAME, contains a string beginning with "I", followed by any character, and ending with "M".

```
LIST CUSTOMERS WITH NAME = "A^ ^"
```

searches attribute for values containing a string beginning with "A" and followed by two characters. Any two characters following the "A" will meet the selection criteria.

Multiple string searches in ACCESS sentences

When applying multiple selections against a single attribute value, building a separate selection criteria phase for each selection is not necessary, as in the following examples:

```
LIST CUSTOMERS WITH STATE = "CA" WITH STATE = "AZ"
```

This could also be stated as:

```
LIST CUSTOMERS WITH STATE "CA""AZ"
```

ACCESS verbs

CHECK-SUM *filename* {*itemlist*} {*attrname*} {*sellist*} {*modlist*} {(*options*)}

Calculates the hexadecimal checksum for either a specified attribute, or if no attribute is specified, the entire item in the specified filename.

COPY-LIST *itemlist* {(*options*)}
TO: {*filename*} {*listname*}

-or-

CL *itemlist* {(*options*)}
TO: {*filename*} {*listname*}

Copies a previously saved listname to either a new name, a new filename, or the specified output device. Defaults to POINTER-FILE for filename. Note: the "CL" form was added to the PC-AT version of Pick in release 3.1.

Options:

D Deletes item from source file after copy.
N Activates NOPAGE function on output to terminal.
O Overwrites duplicate itemname{s}.
P Copies list to system printer, via the spooler.
T Copies list to terminal.
X Outputs list in hexadecimal format.

COUNT *filename* {*itemlist*} {*sellist*} {*modlist*} {(*options*)}

Outputs the number of items that meet the selection criteria as determined by the itemlist and sellist specifications.

DELETE-LIST *itemlist**

-or-

DL *itemlist**

Removes the specified listname{s} from the POINTER-FILE. **The * (asterisk) is permitted as a listname! This will delete all of your saved lists!** Also note: the "DL" form was added to the PC-AT version of Pick in release 3.1.

EDIT-LIST *listname* {(Z)}

-or-

EL *listname* {(Z)}

Retrieves specified listname and enters editor processor. Refer to the EDITOR section for the available commands and syntax requirements. Note: the "EL" form was added to the PC-AT version of Pick in release 3.1.

Option:

Z Suppresses the "Top" and "EOI" messages.

FILE-TEST *filename* {*itemlist*} {*sellist*} {(*options*)}

In the SMA standard document, this verb replaces the HASH-TEST and ISTAT verbs formerly used to analyze the statistic and distribution of items in a file.

The statistics that it produces include: the count of items, the total number of bytes, and the average bytes per item. Additionally, the SMA standards document indicates that the information may also include: a hashing structure illustrated with a histogram, the average number of items per group and standard deviation, and the average number of bytes per group.

Option:

S Suppresses detail; only shows statistical data.

Compatibility: **SMA**

GET-LIST {*filename*} *listname*

-or-

GL {*filename*} *listname*

Retrieves listname from specified file, or defaults to POINTER-FILE if no filename is specified. Note: the "GL" form was added to the PC-AT version of Pick in release 3.1.

HASH-TEST *filename {itemlist} {sellist} {(options)}*

TEST MODULO:modulo

Outputs a histogram showing the item hashing distribution of all items meeting the selection criteria with a test modulo, entered by the operator. See also: ISTAT.

Option:

S Suppresses display of histogram.

ISTAT *filename {itemlist} {modlist} {(options)}*

Outputs a histogram showing the item hashing distribution, based on specified filename's current modulo and the optionally specified selection criteria. See also: HASH-TEST.

Option:

S Suppresses display of histogram.

LIST *filename {itemlist} {sellist} {modlist} {outlist} {(options)}*

Outputs specified items, in order of appearance in the filename.

LIST-ITEM *filename {itemlist} {sellist} {modlist} {(options)}*

Outputs items, in COPY format.

LIST-LABEL *filename {itemlist} {sellist} {outlist} {modlist} {(options)}*

Outputs formatted labels from specified filename in order of item appearance in filename.

Upon pressing the carriage return the prompt character, ?, appears, which is for the entry of the following label parameters:

?columns,rows,skip,indent,size,space,C

Where:

columns = number of labels across page
rows = number of lines requested to print on each label
skip = number of lines (vertically) between labels
indent = number of spaces from left margin to beginning output column
size = number of print positions per label
space = number of spaces (horizontally) between labels
C = compresses null values

Note: each of the parameters must be separated by commas during input.

Following the entry of the parameters, if the INDENT parameter is nonzero, the prompt character, ?, appears for the number of times indicated in the rows parameter (i.e., if rows was 4, expect 4 question marks).

These prompts (?'s) are for the entry of "headers" that print in the INDENT area to the left of the first row of labels.

Example:

```
LIST-LABEL VENDORS NAME ADDRESS CSZ (CI
?2,3,1,0,30,2,C
```

QSELECT *filename itemlist* {(attrnum)}*

Creates a select list item from the specified filename and itemname entered, similar to the GET-LIST command.

If the optional "attrnum" (attribute number) is specified, the list is created from the multivalues contained in the specified attribute number.

Note: this is actually a TCL II command, but is included here for its use in building lists.

REFORMAT *filename {itemlist} outlist {modlist} <cr>* *FILE NAME:destination-file or TAPE*

Inserts data elements defined in specified filename into another filename, in the order of appearance in the outlist. Note: the first entry in the outlist is used as the item-id for the destination file. Each subsequent entry in the outlist becomes an attribute in the destination item, in the order of specification in the outlist.

Upon execution of this command, the prompt, "FILE NAME:", appears on the screen. Either a filename may be entered, directing the output to the specified filename, or the literal, TAPE, which directs the output to the attached magnetic tape.

S-DUMP *filename {itemlist} {seqlist} {sellist}* *{modlist} {HEADING "text"} {(options)}*

Copies to tape all itemnames from the specified filename that meet the specified selection criteria, in order of the specified sort key{s}. The HEADING modifier specifies the tape label to write to the tape prior to the data.

Options:

H Suppresses the tape label.
I Suppresses the display of item-id's as they are dumped.

SAVE-LIST *{filename} listname*

-or-

SL *{filename} listname*

Saves listname in specified filename. The default filename is POINTER-FILE. Note: the "SL" form was added to the PC-AT version of Pick in release 3.1.

SELECT *filename {itemlist} {sellist} {outlist} {modlist}*

Retrieves all items from specified filename that meet selection criteria, in order of their appearance in the filename, and creates a list that either can be saved for future use or acted on immediately. The outlist parameter specifies the attribute definition item{s} from which values are to be extracted for creation of the list.

SORT *filename* {*itemlist*} {*seqlist*} {*sellist*} {*outlist*} {(*options*)}

Outputs specified filename, in order of specified sort key{s}.

SORT-ITEM *filename* {*itemlist*} {*seqlist*} {*sellist*} {*modlist*} {(*options*)}

Outputs items, in COPY format.

SORT-LABEL *filename* {*itemlist*} {*sellist*} {*seqlist*} {*outlist*} {*modlist*} {(*options*}

Outputs formatted labels from specified filename in order of specified sort key{s}.

Upon pressing the carriage return the prompt character, ?, appears. This is for the entry of the following label parameters:

```
?columns rows,skip,indent,size,space,C
```

Where:

columns = number of labels across page
rows = number of lines requested to print on each label
skip = number of lines (vertically) between labels
indent = number of spaces from left margin to beginning output column
size = number of print positions per label
space = number of spaces (horizontally) between labels
C = compresses null values

Note: each of the parameters must be separated by commas during input.

Following the entry of the above parameters, if the INDENT parameter is nonzero, the prompt character, ?, appears for the number of times indicated in the rows parameter (i.e., if rows was 4, expect 4 question marks).

These prompts (?'s) are for the entry of headers that print in the INDENT area to the left of the first row of labels.

Example:

```
SORT-LABEL INVENTORY BY PART.# PART.# DESC PRICE (P
?3,4,1,0,2,C
```

SREFORMAT *filename* {itemlist} {outlist} {seqlist} {modlist} FILE NAME:*destination-file* or TAPE

Inserts data elements defined from the specified filename into another filename, in the order of the appearance in the outlist, after sorting the data by the specified sort key{s}. Note: the first entry in the outlist is used as the item-id for the destination file. Each subsequent entry in the outlist becomes an attribute in the destination item, in the order of specification in the outlist.

Upon execution of this command, the prompt, "FILE NAME:", appears on the screen. Either a filename may be entered, which directs the output to the specified filename, or the literal, TAPE, which directs the output to the attached magnetic tape.

SSELECT *filename {itemlist} {sellist} {seqlist} {outlist} {modlist}*

Retrieves all items from specified filename that meet selection criteria, in order of the specified sort key{s} and creates a list that can be saved for future use or acted on immediately.

The outlist parameter specifies the attribute definition item{s} from which values are to be extracted for creation of the list.

STAT *filename {itemlist} {sellist} {modlist} {attrname} {(options)}*

Outputs item count and an average value of all items that meet the specified selection criteria.

SUM *filename {itemlist} attrname {sellist} {modlist} {(options)}*

Outputs total of the specified attrname for all itemnames meeting specified selection criteria. The default attrname is zero (0) (item-id), if the attrname is omitted.

T-DUMP *filename {itemlist} {sellist} {modlist} {HEADING "text"} {(options)}*

Copies to tape all itemnames that meet specified selection criteria. The HEADING modifier allows specifying the contents of the tape label written to the tape prior to the dump.

Options:

H Suppresses the tape label.
I Suppresses the display of item-id's as they are dumped.

T-LOAD *filename {itemlist} {sellist} {modlist} {(options)}*

Copies from tape to specified filename all items that meet specified selection criteria.

Options:

I Suppresses listing itemnames to terminal.
O Overwrites existing items, when duplicate item-id{'s} exist.

Modifiers and connectives

Modifiers alter the normal operation of an ACCESS sentence and add special functions. A list of modifiers can be produced with the LISTCONN command.

BREAK-ON *attrname {" {text} {'options'}... "}*

Specifies creation of a logical and visual *break* in output data when the value in the current output field is different from the previous value. If the TOTAL modifier is specified, subtotals are also output. The text parameter, if specified, becomes a label that replaces the default "***" literal normally output in the column in which the control break occurs.

Options:

- B Outputs the value causing the break in either the HEADING or FOOTING output field where the B option is found in the HEADING or FOOTING option string.
- D Suppresses the break data line if only one detail line has been output since the last control break.
- L Suppresses a blank line preceding break data line.
- N Resets the page counter to one.
- P Forces a form feed after output of data that caused control break.
- R Outputs any occurrence of one or more control break lines at the end of the page, rather than at the top of the next page.
- U Underlines all TOTAL fields.
- V Outputs the value causing the control break in the BREAK-ON label.
- " Inserts a single quote in text.

Examples:

SORT INVOICES BY DATE **BREAK-ON** DATE...

SORT SALES BY SALESMAN **BREAK-ON** SALESMAN " 'BP' " TOTAL INVOICE.AMOUNT TOTAL QUANTITY.ORDERED PRODUCT HEADING " 'LC'DETAIL SALES FOR 'B' PAGE 'PNL' "

BY *attrname*

Specifies attrname as sort key.

BY-DSND *attrname*

Specifies attrname as sort key, in descending sequence.

BY-EXP *attrname {"explosion limiter"}*

Specifies multivalue attrname as sort key.
The "explosion limiter" specifies that output only occurs on data elements meeting the print limiting criteria.

Example:

SORT CUSTOMERS **BY-EXP** INV.ID

-or-

SORT CUSTOMERS **BY-EXP** INV.ID = "S100101"

BY-EXP-DSND *attrname {"explosion limiter"}*

Specifies multivalue attrname as sort key, in descending sequence.

The "explosion limiter" specifies that output only occurs on data elements meeting the print limiting criteria.

COL-HDR-SUPP (or C option)

Identical to HDR-SUPP, but also suppresses column headings above output columns.

DBL-SPC

Outputs data on page with double spacing.

DET-SUPP (or D option)

Suppresses display of detail data. Typically used in conjunction with the TOTAL or BREAK-ON modifiers.

DICT

Causes ACCESS to reference dictionary level of specified filename.

Example:

```
SORT-ITEM DICT CUSTOMERS WITH *A2 = "A""S""X" BY *A2
```

EACH *attrname {operator} {"value"}*

Specifies that each value in a multivalued attribute must meet the specified selection criteria in order to be eligible for processing. Same as EVERY modifier.

Used in the form: WITH {NOT} EACH...

EVERY *attrname {operator} {"value"}*

Specifies that each value in a multivalued attribute must meet the specified selection criteria in order to be eligible for processing. Same as EACH modifier.

Used in the form: WITH {NOT} EVERY...

FOOTING *"{{text} {'options'}...}"*

Specifies text to output at the bottom of each output page. Multiple options may be enclosed in the same set of single quotes.

Example:

```
FOOTING "LC'Page'PN' Printed at " 'TL'"
```

Options:

- B Inserts value that caused break condition in FOOTING text. The B option must be included in the BREAK-ON specification.
- C Centers output according to current page width.
- D Outputs (external) system date.
- F Outputs filename.
- Fn Outputs filename left justified in a field of "n" blanks.
- L Performs linefeed/carriage return.

P Outputs page number, right justified in a field of four blanks.
PN Outputs page number, left justified.
Pn Outputs page number, left justified in a field of "n" blanks.
T Outputs (external) system time and date.
'' Outputs one single quote.

GRAND-TOTAL *"{{text} {'options'}...}"*

Outputs specified text in place of the standard "***" literal string normally output on the last total line.

Options:

L Suppresses blank line preceding break data line.
P Forces form feed after output of data that caused control break.
U Underlines all TOTAL fields.
'' Inserts single quote in text.

HDR-SUPP (or H option)

Suppresses display of the default Top of Page heading (system time/date and page number) and the "number ITEMS LISTED" message on output. Also the same as the "SUPP" modifier.

HEADING *"{{text} {'options'}...}"*

Specifies text to output at the top of each output page. Multiple options may be enclosed in the same set of single quotes.

Example:

```
HEADING "'LC'Page 'PN' Printed at '' 'TL'"
```

Options:

B Inserts value that caused break condition in FOOTING text. The B option must be included in the BREAK-ON specification.
C Centers output according to current page width.
D Outputs (external) system date.
F Outputs filename.
Fn Outputs filename left justified in a field of "n" blanks.
L Performs linefeed/carriage return.
P Outputs page number, right justified in a field of four blanks.
PN Outputs page number, left justified.
Pn Outputs page number, left-justified in a field of "n" blanks.
T Outputs (external) system time and date.
'' Outputs one single quote.

ID-SUPP (or I option)

Suppresses the output of item-ids.

IF {*NOT*} {*EACH*} *attrname* {*operator*} {*"value"*}

Specifies the selection criteria must be present and true for data to be accepted for processing. Same as WITH modifier.

The NOT modifier indicates to test for the absence of attrname value.

The value string may be preceded by a logical operator and must be enclosed within double quotes.

LPTR (or P option)

Directs output to system printer, via the spooler.

NOPAGE (or N option)

Activates NOPAGE function on output to terminal, indicating that no carriage return is required between pages of display.

ONLY *filename*

Suppresses the output of implicit attribute definition items, and outputs only a list of item-id's. The ONLY modifier must precede the filename specification.

SUPP (or H option)

Suppresses display of the default Top of Page heading (system time/date and page number) and the "number ITEMS LISTED" message on output. Also the same as the "HDR-SUPP" modifier.

TAPE

Indicates data that will be retrieved from the currently attached magnetic tape or diskette, rather than the actual data level of the file. The tape must have been created in a T-DUMP format and must be positioned to the beginning of the appropriate (tape) file. The attribute definition items specified in the sentence are retrieved from the dictionary level of the specified filename.

This modifier may be used only with ACCESS verbs that do not sort prior to output, which includes the following:

COUNT, ISTAT, LIST, LIST-LABEL, REFORMAT, SELECT, STAT, SUM

TOTAL *attrname* {*"total-limiter"*}

Accumulates columnar total for specified attribute definition item. The optional total limiter functions like the "value string" portion of the selection criteria process, limiting totals to values that pass the specified selection criteria.

USING {DICT} *filename*

Specifies the file dictionary or data section to access for attribute definition items or data

Example:

LIST CUSTOMERS **USING** DICT SUPPLIERS NAME PHONE

WITH {NOT} {EACH} *attrname* {*operator*} {*"value"*}

Specifies the selection criteria must be present and true for data to be accepted for processing. Same as **IF** modifier.

The **NOT** modifier indicates to test for the absence of attrname value.

The value string may be preceded by a logical operator and must be enclosed within double quotes.

LIST WITHIN *filename 'item-id'* {*(options)*}

-or-

COUNT WITHIN *filename 'item-id'*{*(options)*}

Retrieves a list of all the items which are subitems of a specified item. This command is used to explode one attribute containing one or more multivalues that are item-ids within the same file, like in Bill Of Material explosions. The file definition item (D-pointer) must contain a V code in attribute 8 in the form: V;;n where "n" indicates the AMC to explode.

WITHOUT *attrname*

Same as WITH NOT or WITH NO.

Correlatives and conversions

Correlatives are special processing codes used to define an action to be taken on a specified attribute or set of attributes during the pre-processing phase of an ACCESS process, which is before data is selected and/or sorted.

Conversions are also special processing codes used to define an action to be taken on a specified attribute or the results of a correlative during the post-processing phase of an ACCESS process, which is just before the data is output, printed or displayed.

General format of attribute-defining items:

Attribute Number	*Attribute*	*Description*
000	item-id	The name of the item
001	type	Attribute definition type: A Attribute S "Synonym" X "Protected"
002	amc	Attribute Mark Count
003	header	Optional column header
004	associative	Associated attribute(s)

Attribute Number	*Attribute*	*Description*
005	not used	________
006	not used	________
007	conversion	Any valid conversion handled at post processing phase (print time)
008	correlative	Any valid correlative handled at pre-processing phase (select/sort time)
009	justify	Output column justification L Left justified (used on text fields) R Right justified (used on numeric fields) T Left with wraparound on blank U Unconditional left
010	width	Output column width maximum length

Attr	*NAME (in MD)*	*Function/Description*
1	D/CODE	Pointer (A,S,X)
2	A/AMC	Attribute Mark Count
3	S/NAME	Column Heading
4	S/AMC	Associated attributes
5	L/RET	Reserved for file pointers
6	L/UPD	Reserved for file pointers
7	V/CONV	Conversion
8	V/CORR	Correlative
9	V/TYP	Justification (L,R,T,U)
10	V/MAX	Maximum output width

Correlative and Conversion Glossary		*Attribute{s}:*
A	Algebraic expression	7,8
C	Controlling attribute	4
C	Concatenation	7,8
D	Dependent Attribute	4
D	Date conversion	7,8
F	Function	7,8
G	Group Extract	7,8
L	Length	7,8
M	Mask function	7,8
MC	Mask Characters	7,8
MD	Mask decimal (same as MR)	7,8
ML	Mask, left-justified	7,8
MP	Mask Packed Decimal	7,8
MR	Mask, right-justified	7,8
MS	Mask Sequence	8
MT	Mask Time	7,8
MX	Mask Hexadecimal	7,8

Correlative and Conversion Glossary		*Attribute{s}:*
MY	Mask Hex compression	7,8
P	Pattern match	7,8
R	Range	7,8
S	Substitution	7,8
T	Text Extraction	7,8
T	File Translation	7,8
U	User Mode Exit	7,8
V	WITHIN sublist code	7

About SMA standards

Most of the correlatives and conversion codes contained in this section remain compatible with the SMA standard. Those that do not are specifically noted.

A{*n*}{;} *expression* {*s*}

Recursive algebraic function for performing arithmetic and relational operations on specified operands. A correlatives are parsed into F correlatives by the ACCESS compiler. The functional operators and operands for the A correlative are the same as that of the F correlative, except as noted.

The "n" argument is optionally used to indicate the number of decimal digits (in the range 0–4) to retain during calculations involving a mixture of whole numbers and numbers with implied decimals, along with MR conversions in the body of the function.

The expressions formed are like BASIC expressions and consist of operands, operators, conditional statements, and special functions combined to yield a single value.

Operands of the A-correlative

n

An integer reference to an Attribute Mark Count.

Example:

```
A3*5
```

Multiplies the value in attribute 3 by the value in attribute 5.

n(corr/conv {]corr/conv...})

An integer reference to an AMC, which may be immediately passed through any other valid conversion or correlative, except another A or F correlative. Multiple correlatives or conversions may be used when each is delimited by a value mark.

Example:

```
A1(T1,40]MCT)
```

Retrieves attribute 1 of the current item, extracts the first forty characters, and converts each word to upper- and lowercase.

9998

Used as an AMC specification. Returns the sequential item counter.

9999

Used as an AMC specification. Returns the size of the item in bytes.

"alphanumeric string"

Any quoted text or numeric string, which is treated as a literal.

Example of Literal:

```
A"Attention: ":1
```

Concatenates the literal, "Attention: ", to the contents of attribute 1 of the current item.

Example of Numeric Constant:

```
A3*"12"
```

Multiplies the value of attribute three of the current item by the constant "12",

N (*attrname*){*corr/conv...*)}

Allows a reference to any valid attribute defining item in the dictionary of the file being accessed. Note: the string returned with this operand may subsequently be passed through one or more other valid conversions or correlatives (except another A or F correlative) as long as each is separated by a value mark. This conversion is where recursion occurs, as the attrname being referenced in the correlative might in fact reference an item which also contains an A correlative.

Examples:

```
AN (CITY):", ":N(STATE):" ":N(ZIP)
```

Concatenates the contents of the attribute referred to by the item, "CITY", with a comma and a blank, then joins the value of the attribute referred to by the item "STATE" with a blank and then appends the value of the attribute referred to by "ZIP"to the end of the string.

```
AN(CITY):", ":N(STATE) (TSTATES;C;;1):" ":N(ZIP)
```

Like before, but this time the value in the "STATE" attribute is "translated"to the STATES file, returning attribute 1 of the corresponding item.

D

Returns the system date in internal form.

Example:

```
A(D – N(INVOICE.DATE))
```

Subtracts the VALUE of INVOICE.DATE from the current system date, which determines the number of days that have elapsed since the date of the invoice.

NB

Returns the number of the break level. Note: there is a maximum of 255 break levels and the 255th level is reserved for the grand total.

ND

Returns the number of detail lines. Used only on line 7 (conversion). Note: this command might abort if the file contains more than 65,000 (about 64K) items. On some versions, it might crash with 32K items.

NI

Returns the number of the item being processed.

NV

Returns the number of the multivalue being processed.

NS

Returns the number of the subvalue being processed.

T

Returns the system time in internal format, meaning the number of seconds past midnight.

Operators

Arithmetic Operators:

+	add
*	multiply
–	subtract
/	divide

Concatenation Operator:

: (colon)

Arithmetic functions / operands

R(expression1,expression2)

Returns the remainder of expression1 divided by expression2.

S(expression)

Sums multivalued results.

Substring referencing

strexp [begexp,lenexp]

Substring function. Used to extract a fixed number of characters from a string expression. The "begexp" (beginning position expression) specifies the beginning character position and the "lenexp" (length expression) specifies the length, or number, of characters to retrieve. The begexp and lenexp may be quoted numbers or any expressions which derive numeric results.

Example:

```
A"(":N(PHONE)["1","3"]:") "-":N(PHONE) ["4","3"]:N(PHONE) ["7","4"]
```

This example take a phone number stored as "7145551212" and outputs it as "(714) 555-1212".

Relational operators and effects

Relational operators produce a numeric result. These results are either 1 (one) for a true condition or 0 (zero) for a false condition:

Symbol	*Meaning*
=	equal to if operand1 = operand2 then 1, else 0
#	not equal if operand1 # operand2 then 1, else 0
<	less than if operand1 <# operand2 then 1, else 0
>	greater than if operand1 > operand2 then 1, else 0
<=	less than or equal to if operand1 <= operand2 then 1, else 0
>=	greater than or equal to if operand1 >= operand2 then 1, else 0

Celement {;element...}

-or-

Celement{/}*

Concatenates any combination of elements. Each element may be delimited by a character to appear on output. The semicolon (;) has a special meaning; it does *not* appear on output.

Elements may be:

- Numeric constants, enclosed in quotes
- Attribute number reference by its numeric Attribute Mark Count
- Alphanumeric character strings. When delimited by semicolons, strings must be enclosed in quotes. Otherwise, alphanumeric strings are not separated from the other entries by semicolons (;).

The asterisk (*) is a special character used to concatenate the current data value.

Example:

```
C;3;", ";4;" ";5
```

Concatenates the value of attribute three of the current item with a comma and a blank, followed by attribute four, another blank, then attribute five.

C;*attrnum*{;*attrnum...*}

Controlling attribute function. Defines the control portion of a Control-Dependent attribute pair. Each attribute number specified in the "attrnum" parameters{s} must contain the dependent (D)code and attribute number of the controlling attribute. Note: this function belongs in attribute 4 of the item.

Example:

C;4;5;6

Indicates that the current attribute "controls" the values in attributes four, five, and six. Note: each of these three attributes will need to indicate in the attribute defining item that they are dependent upon this attribute.

D; *attrnum*

Dependent attribute function. Defines the dependent portion of a Control-Dependent attribute pair. The attribute number specified in the "attrnum" parameter must contain the controlling (C) code and attribute number of the controlling attribute. Note: this function belongs in attribute 4 of the item.

D {*year.length*}{*skipdel#skips*}{*outsep*}

Date conversion function. Converts value from internal to external date format.

The "year.length" parameter specifies the length of the year field. It must be between 0 and 4. The default length is the 4-digit year format.

The parameters specified in "skipdel" and "#skips"are functionally equivalent to the G (Group extract) correlative. They define the position of the date value portion in a multipart data value and for the most part, are unused.

If included, the "outsep" (output separation character) parameter specifies the character that delimits the month, day, and year values. The output order is 2-digit month, 2-digit day, and the year. The number of year digits depends on the "year.length" parameter.

If the "outsep" parameter is omitted, the format is 2-digit day, 3-digit month abbreviation, and year. Again, the number of year digits depends on the "yr length" parameter.

Output formats of date conversions:

Conversion	*Format of Output*	*Sample*
D	dd mmm yyyy	26 MAY 1999
D2-	mm-dd-yy	05-26-1999
D-	mm-dd-yyyy	05-26-1999
D0	dd mmm	26 MAY
D0	mm-dd	05-26
DD	dd (numeric day of month)	26
DI	nnnn (internal format)	11469
DJ	nnn (Julian date)	146

Conversion	*Format of Output*	*Sample*
DM	mm (numeric month)	5
DMA	xxxx (alphabetic month)	MAY
DQ	n (numeric quarter)	2
DW	n (numeric day of week)	3
DWA	xxxx (alpha. day of week)	WEDNESDAY
DY	YYYY (four-digit year)	1999
D2Y	YY (two-digit year)	99

Note: the "DI" conversion listed does the reverse of normal date conversions. It is used in those rare cases where a date is actually stored in external format. This conversion may be used to convert the date to internal format prior to sorting or selecting, then passed back through a legal date conversion to display or print it in external format.

F{n};*element*{;*element...*}

Mathematical function for performing arithmetic and relational operations on specified operands. The F correlative is a stack-oriented function, requiring the statement syntax to adhere to a classic Reverse Polish Notation format. The push-down stack has 7 possible entries. Unless otherwise noted, all of the operands and operators of the F-correlative are compatible with the SMA standard FS correlative.

Example:

```
F;3;4;*
```

This example instructs ACCESS to take the value of attribute three and multiply it by the value of attribute four.

All operands push a specific value on the top of the stack (STACK1). A push repositions all stack entries 1 position down. The entry in STACK7 is lost on an operand push.

Compatibility: **Pick**

See also: "FS" correlative

Operands of the F-correlative

n {R}{(*conversion*)}

Numeric reference to an Attribute Mark Count to push on the stack. The "conversion" represents any legal ACCESS conversion.

"*alphanumeric string*"

Any quoted text or numeric string, which is treated as a literal.

Example:

```
F;"Attention: ";1;:
```

Concatenates the literal, "Attention:", to the contents of attribute 1 of the current item.

Example:

F;3;"12;"*

Multiplies the value of attribute three of the current item by the constant "12".

nR{R}

Optional repeat code for multivalues. The "n" indicates an AMC reference. The optional R parameter specifies repeat code for subvalues.

Cn

Constant (alternate method). The "n" parameter may be any numeric string, or an alphanumeric string enclosed in quotes.

D

Returns the system date in internal form.

T

Returns the system time in internal form.

Operators

Most operators act on the first two entries in the stack (STACK1 and STACK2). These entries are both popped off the stack, following execution. The result is then pushed back on top of STACK1.

Mathematical operators and effects

Addition:	STACK1 = STACK2 + STACK1
Subtraction:	STACK1 = STACK2 − STACK1
Multiplication:	STACK1 = STACK2 *n STACK1
Division:	STACK1 = STACK2 / STACK1

Note: On the multiply operator, the "n" parameter specifies the descaling factor to apply to the result. (It doesn't work, but is supposed to).

Concatenation operator

: (colon)

STACK1 = STACK2 : STACK1

Relational operators and effects

Symbol	*Meaning*
=	Equal to If STACK2 = STACK1 then STACK1 = 1, else STACK 1 = 0
#	Not equal If STACK2 # STACK1 then STACK1 = 1, else STACK 1 = 0
<	Less than If STACK1 < STACK2 then STACK1 = 1, else STACK 1 = 0
>	Greater than If STACK1 > STACK2 then STACK1 = 1, else STACK 1 = 0

[Less than or equal to
If STACK1 < = STACK2 then STACK1 = 1, else STACK 1 = 0

] Greater than or equal to
If STACK1 > = STACK2 then STACK1 = 1, else STACK 1 = 0

Functional operators

R
Remainder
STACK1 = **R**(STACK2/STACK1)

S
Sum
STACK1 = Summation of multivalues into STACK1

P
Duplicate. Pushes a copy of STACK2 into STACK1. All stack positions push one position.

_
Exchanges the values of STACK1 and STACK2.

[ ]
Extract:
STACK1 = STACK3 [STACK2, STACK1], where STACK3 contains the string, STACK2 has the starting position, and STACK1 has the length. Result goes in STACK1.

:
Concatenation:
STACK1 = STACK2 : STACK1.

?
Mystery Operator. This operator is actually part of the code. We don't know, however, what it does.

(conversion)
Any ACCESS conversion may be used as an operator. The top entry of the stack is used as the source value for the conversion, which must be enclosed in parentheses.

Special operands

LPV
Loads result of last conversion on top of stack.

NA
Loads the number of attributes contained in the item on top of the stack.

Compatibility: **SMA**

NB
Number of break level.

ND
Returns the number of detail lines. Used only on line 7 (conversion).

NI
Returns the number of the item being processed.

NL
Loads the length of item on top of stack.

Compatibility: **SMA**

NV
Returns the number of the multivalue being processed.

NS
Returns the number of the subvalue being processed.

FS *{n};element{;element...}*

The SMA standard form of the F correlative differs from the generic Pick form. First, the letter "S" follows the F to indicate that this is the standard form. The other difference between the SMA standard and the generic Pick version is in the handling of relational operators:

Symbol	*Meaning*
<	Less than If STACK2 < STACK1 then STACK1 = 1, else STACK1 = 0
>	Greater than If STACK2 > STACK1 then STACK1 = 1, else STACK1 = 0
[	Less than or equal to If STACK2 <= STACK1 then STACK1 = 1, else STACK1 = 0
]	Greater than or equal to If STACK2 >= STACK1 then STACK1 = 1, else STACK1 = 0

Note: the references to STACK1 and STACK2 are reversed.

It's worth the time to test this function on your system with tests of the conditionals. For example:

```
F;C2;C1;<
```

Compatibility: **SMA**

G *{skipsegments} delimiter getsegments*

Group extract. Retrieves data elements from a string containing user specified (non-reserved) delimiters.

Note: the implied spaces between the arguments in this correlative are not part of the syntax, thus, they are not allowed. They were included there just to provide visual relief for the reader.

Example:

The "skipsegments" argument indicates the number of value segments to skip over. It must be numeric. If omitted, zero is used.

The "delimiter" may be any single nonreserved and nonnumeric character that delimits part of a stored value. The reserved characters are attribute, value, subvalue, and segment marks.

The "getsegments" argument determines the number of groups to retrieve from the data value.

Examples: (Using the stored data string = CA*92714*1000

Conversion	*Result*
G*1	CA
G0*1	CA
G1*1	92714
G2*1	1000
G1*2	92714*1000

L{*maxlength,* {*maxvalue*}}
-or-
L0

Length function. Specifies output length restrictions on data fields. The "maxlength" parameter indicates that the value will be output only if the length of the string is less than the "maxlength" parameter, otherwise a null is returned.

The L command, followed by a 0 (zero), returns the length of the data field.

Examples:

L0	Returns the length of field.
L9	Outputs data if field length is less than nine characters.
L3,9	Outputs data if field length is greater than three characters and less than nine characters.

M {*just*} {{*precision*} {*scalefactor*}} {Z} {,}{*signcode*} {$} {*formatmask*}

Mask (Decimal) function. Performs output conversions, literal insertions, and currency formatting on an input converted attribute.

The **just**ification specified in the "just" parameter may be either an **L** (left) or an **R** (right).

The **precision** parameter specifies the number of decimal positions to print after the decimal point. It must be between 0 (zero) and 9.

The **scaling factor** specified in the scalefactor parameter indicates the power to which the value is to be descaled. It must be between 0 (zero) and 9.

The **Z** parameter suppresses zero balance fields. The "," (comma) inserts commas in the thousands and millions position on output.

Signcodes:

The signcode parameter alters the normal handling of negative numbers, with the exception of the "D" signcode. Their functions are as follows on the next page:

C Negative values are followed by the literal, "CR".
D Positive values are followed by the literal "DB".
E Negative values are enclosed in angle brackets: <value>
M Negative numbers are followed by a – (minus) sign.
N Suppresses (leading) minus sign on negative numbers.

The **$** parameter appends a dollar sign to the value prior to justification.
The format mask may be any combination of literals and format operators:

Format, (Masking) Operators:

#n Fills with "n" blanks
*n Fills with "n" asterisks
%n Fills with "n" zeros

Examples:

Internal (Stored) Data	*Conversion*	*External Format*
12345	MR2	123.45
123456	MR2,$	$1,234.56
123456	MR4,$	$12.3456
–123456	MR2,$	–$1,234.56
–123456	MR2,E$	$<1,234.56>
–123456	MR2,C$	$1,234.56CR
123456	MR2,$*12	$***1,234.56

MC {/} *code*

Mask character function. Performs various string conversions, such as upper to lowercase and vice versa.

Additional Mask Character Codes:

MCA Retrieves all alphabetic characters from data value.
MC/A Retrieves all nonalphabetic characters and ignores alphabetic characters.
MCDX Converts decimal data value to its hexadecimal equivalent.
MCL Converts all uppercase characters to lowercase and ignores lowercase characters.
MCN Retrieves all numeric characters from data value.
MC/N Retrieves all nonnumeric characters from data value.
MCP Converts all nonprintable characters to periods. Nonprintable characters are those between the hexadecimal values X'OO'–X'1F' and those between X'7F'–X'FB'. Note: the characters above X'7F' display, but actually have different character meanings as their high order bit is lost.

Compatability: **Pick**

MCT Converts uppercase characters to lowercase, starting with the second character in each word. (Capitalizes the first character of each word after a nonalphabetic character).

MCU Converts all lowercase characters to uppercase and ignores uppercase characters.

MCXD Converts hexadecimal data value to its decimal equivalent.

MS

Mask sequence function. Used to sort an attribute in a sequence specified by the item called "SEQ" in the ERRMSG file. Only used on an attribute defined as a sort key, thus, this code must be applied as a correlative (attribute 8). Not available for use in PICK/BASIC. The SEQ item must be manually added to the ERRMSG file, which is the suggested format for the item:

```
SEQ (Item-id)
001 AaBbCcDdEeFfGgHhIiJjKkLlMmNnOoPpQqRrSsTtUuVv
    WwXxYyZz01234567890,.?!"';: + - */^=( )[ ]{ }< >@#$%&'~ \ |
```

Compatibility: **Pick 2.2** and higher.

MT{ {H} {S} }

Mask time conversion. Converts internal time to a formatted external output.

Options:

H Specifies a 12-hour clock. Default is (military) 24-hour clock.

S Includes seconds in output value.

Examples:

Internal (Stored) Data	*Conversion*	*External Format*
3600	MT	01:00
46800	MT	13:00
3600	MTH	01:00AM
46800	MTH	01:00PM
3630	MTS	01:00:30
46800	MTHS	01:00:00PM

MX

Mask hexadecimal function. Converts any decimal or ASCII character string to its hexadecimal equivalent.

MY

Mask hexadecimal compression. Converts a hexadecimal string, two bytes at a time, into the corresponding ASCII one-byte representation.

Compatibility: **SMA**

P (*matchstring*){;(*matchstring*)...}

Pattern matching function. The matchstring may be a composite of literals and/or match operators, appended to length specifications. To be accepted for processing, the value must be the exact length of the length parameter.

Matchstring Operators:

nA	"n" alphabetic characters only.
nN	"n" numeric characters only.
nX	"n" alphanumeric characters.
"text"	Any quoted text string.

A length of 0 (zero) allows any length of the following match operator. Multiple matchstring parameters will accept the data if any of the matchstrings are met.

R*minrange,maxrange*{*;minrange,maxrange...*}

Range function. Outputs data field only if data value falls between the ranges specified in "minrange" (minimum) and "maxrange" (maximum) parameters.

Multiple range specifications allow display of the data value if the data value falls between any of the range pair sets.

In using multiple range set specifications on negative values, the ranges should be in ascending sequence, beginning with the lowest.

S;*attrnum;attrnum*

-or-

S;*'text';'text'*

-or-

S;*;*'text'*

Substitution function. Substitutes data value from the attribute referenced in attrnum if current data value is null or zero, else the string specified in the text is displayed.

The "*" is used to display the original data value if it is not null or zero. Otherwise, the second argument is displayed.

This feature may be embedded within an F correlative in the following form:

```
Fattrnum(S;*;'text')
```

It also may be embedded within an A-correlative.

T{*startcolumn,*} *length*

-or-

T{*startcolumn*}

Text extraction (substring) function. Retrieves any number of characters from an attribute, starting at the position specified in "startcolumn", for a length of "length". Both parameters must be numeric.

If the length parameter is not specified, the extraction begins from the same end of the string as the justification attribute (9), either L (left) or R (right).

T{*DICT*} *filename;code*{*vmc*}*;inamc;outamc*{*;breakamc*}

File translation function. Allows an attribute value to translate through another file. The attribute referenced in line 2 of the dictionary definition item is assumed to be an item-id in the specified filename.

To retrieve a specific value within the attribute, the optional value mark count may be specified in the "vmc" parameter.

The translate code determines the action to take with unsuccessful translate values.

Translate Sub-Codes:

- C Displays original value, if the value does not exist in the translate file.
- Cn Functions like the "C" code. The "n"represents a value mark count of the value to retrieve.
- I Input verify only. Same functions as V code on input and C code on output.
- O Output verify only. Same functions as C code on input and V code on output.
- V Conversion item must exist and the specified attribute must have a value, otherwise an error message will display.
- X Displays a null, if value does not exist on translate file.

The "inamc"parameter specifies the Attribute Mark Count to use for input conversion. The default is null.

The "outamc" parameter specifies the Attribute Mark Count of the attribute in the translate file that contains the value{s} to output. The Attribute Mark Count referenced in the "breakamc" specifies to use this attribute for the BREAK-ON and TOTAL lines, rather than the "outamc".

User Exits:

User exits are special functions that make direct references to assembler routines known as "modes". They were added to the system to fulfill needs outside the standard boundaries of the PICK System prior to being replaced by extensions to the system. User exits have always been dangerous, and as long as they remain, will continue to be. EXTREME caution is advised in using them. *Caveat Emptor.*

Note: the topic of user exits was omitted from the SMA standards. The general form of user-exits in an Attribute-Defining Item:

```
item-id
001  pointer type
002  AMC
003  column heading
004
005
006
007  {user exit}
```

008 {user exit}
009 justification
010 column width

User exits are generally interchangeable with the standard conversions and correlatives.

The Structure of User Exits:

Uefff

where "e" is the (decimal) entry point, and "fff" is the (hexadecimal) frame-id.

User Exit Glossary:

User Exit	*Description*
U201E	Returns the number of attributes in the current item.
U0070	Performs correlated match on a multivalued set using the format: U0070, Dl, D2 where D1 is a match and D2 is the result to display.
U1070	Returns checksum value for current item.
U2070	Returns checksum value for specified frame.
U3070	Returns PCB-FID as four hexadecimal characters.
U4070	{Re-} enable output (print on).
U5070	Converts string abcdef to the form abc-000. If string is less than 3 characters, only the string is returned.
U6070	Inputs up to 100 characters. A <cr> is output before and after the input. The prompt character is used.
U7070	Inputs up to 100 characters. The prompt character is used, and there is no other output.
U9070	Toggles the page format flag (NOPAGE).
UA070	Returns the specified value from a multivalued set. The value number is obtained from the valuestring portion of the selection criteria in the ACCESS sentence.
UC070;n	Returns value number "n"from a multivalued set.
U508E	Activates the COPY processor from ACCESS. The HEADING and FOOTING modifiers are subsequently available. See also: LIST-ITEM and SORT-ITEM.

V;;n

Code used by the WITHIN connective and placed in attribute 8 of the D-pointer to the DATA section of the file.See also: WITHIN connective.

4
PICK/BASIC

This edition of the *Pick Pocket Guide* includes the new features added in release 3.1 for the PC-AT. New features are indicated with a compatibility index.

About compatibility with SMA standards

Some instructions in this section do not conform to the SMA standard. Those that are unique to the Pick AT/XT versions are indicated with a compatibility index following the instruction. If no index is provided, the instruction conforms to the SMA standard.

Format of PICK/BASIC processing commands

BASIC *filename itemlist* {(*options*)}

-or-

COMPILE *filename itemlist* {(*options*)

Activates PICK/BASIC compiler for translation of source code into object code. Note: the COMPILE verb may not exist on all systems.

Options:

- A Displays object code generated by PICK/BASIC compiler.
- C Compiles object code without end of line characters, which makes the PICK/BASIC debugger completely useless for debugging the program. Some Pick implementations have changed this to mean "backward compatible."
- E Outputs error lines only.
- I Shows line numbers for code placed in the program by an INSERT or INCLUDE statement, when used in conjunction with the L option.
- L Lists program as it compiles.
- M Displays program map of descriptor table and correlates source code lines to generated object code frames.
- N Activates NOPAGE function on output to the terminal.

P Directs output to systems printer, via the spooler.
Q Activates PAGE mode on errors.
S Suppresses symbol table generation.
X Cross-references all variables and places entries in the BSYM file.
Y Provides compilation statistics including: the start clock time in milliseconds, the size of the code in bytes, the size of the descriptor table, the size of the symbol table in bytes, the number of symbol table entries, and the end clock time in milliseconds.

BLIST *filename itemlist* {(*options*)}

Utility to format and list PICK/BASIC source code.

Options:

P Directs output to system printer, via the spooler.
U Updates source item(s). See the PROC called BLIST in the MD of your account. Attribute two contains a number that is used to control the number of spaces to indent from the left margin. The default setting is two.

Compatibility: **Pick 3.1**

CATALOG *filename itemlist**

Creates a *verb* from a compiled PICK/BASIC program, by placing an entry in the current accounts' Master Dictionary that allows execution of the program by entering the program name at TCL. It is required for any program defined as an external subroutine. (Although this is not true on every Pick implementation. Some versions do not require the program to be CATALOGED if it exists in the same file as the CALLing program.) A program does not need to be CATALOGED each time it is compiled. As of release 3.1, a program may be CATALOGED without the source code being present.

Activating cataloged PICK/BASIC programs
>programname {(options)}

The program name may be entered at the TCL prompt character. All options explained under the RUN command are available.

DECATALOG *filename itemlist**

Deletes object code and catalog pointer if one exists in the MD of the current account.

RUN *filename itemname* {(*options*)}

Executes a compiled PICK/BASIC program.

Options:

A Prohibits entry into PICK/BASIC debugger; aborts on error conditions.

- D Enters PICK/BASIC debugger prior to execution. Important when parameters are passed in a CALL statement.
- E Enters debugger on any error condition.
- I Inhibits variable initialization. Not recommended due to reliability, transportability, and data integrity reasons.
- N Activates NOPAGE function on output to terminal.
- P Directs output from PRINT statements to system printer, via the spooler.
- S Suppresses run-time warning messages. (Very useful for demonstrations, but likely to generate lawsuits when included in live applications.)

About PICK/BASIC source code files

The file containing PICK/BASIC source code must be defined as a two-level file, that is, it must have both a DICTionary and DATA section. The (D-pointer) entry in the MD defining the location of the dictionary *must* have a "DC" in attribute one, which defines the file as an object code file. This does *not* apply to *all* Pick system implementations, so you may need to check your system documentation to see if it applies.

In release 3.1, a new verb was added to create files for use with PICK/BASIC. This new verb, CREATE-BFILE, works just like the standard CREATE-FILE verb, except that it changes the D-pointer to a DC-pointer after creation.

About object pointers

After a program has been compiled with the BASIC verb, a *pointer item* is placed in the dictionary of the file that contains the source code. This pointer item defines the virtual location where the object code is actually stored. The name of the pointer item is the same as that of the source program itself. It has the following format:

Attribute	*Description*
1 CC	Object pointer identifier.
2 fid	First frame-id of object.
3 frames	Number of object frames.
4	(null)
5	hh:mm:ss dd mmm yyyy Time/date of compile.

The Pick system prevents the use of the Editor on these object pointers. Use the LIST-ITEM or SORT-ITEM command on the DICT of the source file to examine them.

Listing object code by date

Here's a handy trick to list the object code in order of compile date. It can also be used on the POINTER-FILE to show when lists were saved. Add the item on the following page to your MD:

```
        PF.DATE
001     A
002     5
003     PF.DATE
004
005
006
007     D2/
008     T11,11] DI        Note: ] is a value mark
009     R
010     8
```

The ACCESS sentence to display the report is:

```
>SORT DICT BP BY PF.DATE PF.DATE
```

POINTER-FILE may be substituted for BP.

Reserved characters

The following characters have special functions. Avoid their use in variable definitions:

: (Colon)

Concatenation operator and PRINT statement argument delimiter.

Example of concatenation:

```
X = "THIS IS"
Y = "CONCATENATION"
Z = X:"  " :Y
PRINT Z
```

Example of use in PRINT statement:

```
PRINT "THIS IS": "  ": "CONCATENATION"
```

; (Semicolon)

Program source line delimiter. Each semicolon *must* be followed by a legal PICK/BASIC instruction or remark.

Example:

```
X = 10;Y= 15; Z = X * Y;PRINTZ
```

@ (The "at" sign)

Cursor control (intrinsic) function. Documented at the beginning of PICK/BASIC statements and functions.

Example:

```
PRINT @(-1) : @(20,0) : "MAIN MENU":
```

, (Comma)

Tab function. Used in a PRINT statement between arguments to output 18 spaces.

```
PRINT "HELLO", "THERE"
```

! (Exclamation point)

Logical "or" statement. Also used to define user-specified remarks. See also: Logical Expressions.

Example of use as an "OR":

```
IFX<0!X>10 THEN...
```

Which reads: If X is less than 0 or X is greater than 10 then...

Example of use as a remark:

```
100 ! Mainline....
```

When used as a remark, the entire line is ignored by the compiler.

& (Ampersand)

Logical "and" statement. See also: Logical Expressions.

Example of use as an "AND":

```
IFX>0&X<10 THEN...
```

Which reads: IF X is greater than 0 and X is less than 10 then...

= (Equal sign)

Logical "equal" operator.

("Pound" sign)

Logical "not equal" operator.

− (Minus sign)

Mathematical operator (subtract). Also unary minus.

+ (Plus sign)

Mathematical operator (add). Also unary plus.

/ (Forward slash)

Mathematical operator (divide).

* (Asterisk)

Mathematical operator (multiply). Also used to define user-specified remarks.

Example of use in multiplication:

```
GROSS.WAGES = HOURS.WORKED*HOURLY.RATE
```

Example of use as a remark:

```
100 * Mainline...
```

When used as a remark, the entire line is ignored by the compiler.

^ (Up-arrow)

Mathematical operator (exponent). See also the PWR function.

Example of use in exponentiation:

```
PRINT X^3
```

Cubes the value of X.

< (Left angle bracket)

Logical operator for "less than." Also used as a dynamic array reference character.

Example of use as a "less than":

```
IF X < 0 THEN...
```

Example of use in a dynamic array:

```
CUSTOMER.ITEM<1> = NAME
```

> (Right angle bracket)

Logical operator for "greater than." Also used as a dynamic array reference character.

Example of use as a "greater than":

```
IF X > Y THEN...
```

Example of use in a dynamic array:

```
CUSTOMER. ITEM <1> = NAME
```

' (Apostrophe or single quote)

String delimiter. Generally, it does not matter which types of quotes are used on literals (strings). Some instructions, such as HEADING and FOOTING, do impose certain restrictions on their use.

" (Double quote)

String delimiter. Just like single quotes, it does not matter which types of quotes are used on literals (strings). Some instructions, such as HEADING and FOOTING, do impose certain restrictions on their use.

\ (Backslash)

String delimiter. Generally, it does not matter which types of quotes are used on literals (strings). Some instructions, such as HEADING and FOOTING, do impose certain restrictions on their use. See also: EXECUTE.

[(Left bracket)

Used in text string extraction. See also: Substring.

Example:

```
IF RESPONSE[1,1] = "Y" THEN PRINTER ON
```

] (Right bracket)

Used in text extraction. See also: Substring.

Example:

```
IF RESPONSE [1,1] = "Y" THEN PRINTER ON
```

(and) (Left and right parentheses)

Used in three ways:

1. as a function delimiter
2. to reference array elements in a dimensioned array
3. to change the order of precedence in mathematical calculations

See also: Precedence.

Example as function delimiter and dimensioned array reference:

```
PRINT OCONV(CUST.ITEM(TOTAL.SALES), "MR2,$")
```

In this illustration, the OCONV function is the function which acts upon the dimensioned array, CUST.ITEM, referring to the amc derived from the variable, TOTAL.SALES.

Example of changing precedence:

```
AGE = (TODAY - BIRTHDAY)/ "365"
```

Without the parentheses in the above calculation, an inaccurate result would be obtained due to the fact that division occurs at a higher level of precedence than subtraction.

Reserved words

The following words and symbols should not, and sometimes cannot be used as variable names in PICK/BASIC:

!
*
=
@
ABORT
ABS
ALPHA
AND
ASCII
BEGIN
BREAK
CALL
CASE
CAT
CHAIN
CHAR
CLEAR
CLEARFILE
CLOSE
COL1
COL2
COM
COMMON
COS
COUNT
CRT
DATA
DATE
DCOUNT
DEBUG
DELETE
DIM
DIMENSION
DO
DTX
EBCDIC
ECHO
ELSE
END
ENTER
EQ
EQU
EQUATE
EXECUTE
EXP
EXTRACT
FIELD
FOOTING
FOR
GE
GOSUB
GOTO
GT
HEADING
ICONV
IF
IN
INCLUDE
INDEX
INPUT
INPUTERR
INPUTNULL
INPUTTRAP
INSERT
INT
LE
LEN
LN
LOCATE
LOCK
LOCKED
LOOP
LT
MAT
MATCH
MATCHES
MATREAD
MATREADU
MATWRITE
MATWRITEU
MOD
NEXT
NE
NOT
NULL
NUM
OCONV
OFF
ON
OPEN
OR
OUT
PAGE
PRECISION
PRINT
PRINTER
PROCREAD
PROCWRITE
PROMPT
PWR
READ
READNEXT
READT
READU
READV
READVU
RELEASE
REM
REPEAT
REPLACE
RETURN
REWIND
RND
RQM
SELECT
SEQ
SIN
SLEEP
SPACE
SQRT
STEP
STOP
STR
SUBROUTINE
SYSTEM
TAN
THEN
TIME
TIMEDATE
TO
TRIM
UNLOCK
UNTIL
WEOF
WHILE
WRITE
WRITET
WRITEU
WRITEV
WRITEVU
XTD

Precedence and mathematical expressions

Symbols	*Precedence*	*Operation*
	0 (highest)	Function evaluation
[ ]	0	Substring extraction
< >	0	Dynamic array extraction
^	1	Exponentiation
*	2	Multiplication

Symbols	*Precedence*	*Operation*
/	2	Division
+	3	Addition
–	3	Subtraction
	4	Masking
:	5	Concatenation
	6	Relational operators
&	7	Logical AND
!	7	Logical OR

Notes on precedence

For program clarity, use parentheses in complex mathematical operations, rather than relying on the precedence of the operator.

Expressions are evaluated in order of precedence unless placed within parentheses. Expressions within the innermost parentheses are evaluated first.

Logical (Boolean) expressions

AND or **&**
-or-
OR or **!**

Boolean operators are used to connect conditional expressions. When an AND is present, *both* conditions must evaluate to be true. The OR accepts either condition as true.

Examples:

```
IF X = 1 OR X = "Y" THEN...
```

-or-

```
IF X > 1 AND X < 10 THEN...
```

The search for truth

This short explanation of the meaning of true and false might be important in saving you a lot of time in the future. Traditionally, the result of a logical or Boolean expression is considered true if it evaluates to 1 and 0 if false.

In the Pick system, expressions that depend on a result of true or false also will evaluate other values as true or false. This tendency varies somewhat between implementations.

In generic Pick, any nonzero integer that is positive or negative, evaluates to true. For example:

```
X = 5
IF X THEN STOP
```

Because X is a nonzero integer, the program takes the THEN branch and stops. In generic Pick, any zero or null value evaluates to false. See example on following page:

```
Y = ""
IF Y THEN STOP ELSE PRINT "YUP"
```

This condition prints "YUP" because Y is evaluated as false.

Some implementations additionally evaluate any negative numbers as false, and positive numbers as true.

You will have to take the *truth test* with your system to determine how it handles true and false. This program will accomplish the test:

```
LOOP
        PRINT "Value to test":
        INPUT VALUE
UNTIL VALUE = "QUIT" DO
        IF VALUE THEN PRINT "TRUE" ELSE PRINT "FALSE"
REPEAT
```

Try it with negative numbers, null (<cr>), positive numbers, letters, and whatever else you can think of.

Substring expressions

variable[begexp, lengthexp]

Allows the extraction of a "fixed" string from within another string. The "begexp" (beginning position expression) evaluates to a number indicating the starting position within the string, and the "lengthexp" (length expression) evaluates to a number indicating the number of characters to be retrieved.

Example:

```
PRINT "PRINT REPORT? (Y/N)":
INPUT RESPONSE
IF RESPONSE [1,1] = "Y" THEN PRINTER ON
```

Array reference expressions

Dimensioned array reference:

arrayvar (attrexp)
-or-
arrayvar (numexp,numexp)

Dimensioned arrays have a maximum of two dimensions and must first be defined with a DIM or DIMENSION statement. See also: DIM, MAT (assignment), MATREAD, and MATWRITE.

Dynamic array reference:

variable<attrexp>
-or-

arrayvar<attrexp,valexp>
-or-
arrayvar<attrexp,valexp,subvalexp>

See also: DEL, DELETE, EXTRACT, INS, INSERT, LOCATE, REPLACE, READ, and WRITE.

Pattern matching expression

expression **MATCH** *matchexpression*
-or-
expression **MATCHES** *matchexpression*

See also: MATCH or MATCHES.

Relational operators

Used to construct conditional expressions.

< or LT	Less than
> or GT	Greater than
<= or LE	Less than or equal to
>= or GE	Greater than or equal to
= or EQ	Equal to
# or NE	Not equal to
< > or > <	Not equal to

Concatenation operators

Joins two string expressions together.

string.expression **CAT** string.expression
-or-
string.expression: string.expression

Masking function

Performs formatting of output data values. General Format:

variable mask.expression

Special uses of masking

Any ACCESS conversion that begins with an "M" can be used as mask expression by dropping off the letter "M." For example, the ACCESS conversion "MCU" converts a string to all uppercase characters. Masking can be used in a PICK/BASIC program as follows:

```
PRINT NAME "CU"
```

Mask expression elements

Justification...
{number of digits after decimal}..
{scaling factor}..
{Z (suppresses leading zeros)}..
{, (inserts commas where appropriate)}..
{signcode}..
{$ (appends dollar sign)}..
fill character..
{length}

The scaling factor defaults to the PRECISION statement of the program. If the length of the mask is omitted, the actual length of the field is used.

Justifications:

R = Right justified L = Left justified

Signcodes:

C Outputs CR after negative values.
D Outputs DB after positive values.
E Outputs "<" before and ">" after negative values.
M Outputs "–" after negative values.
N Suppresses leading "–" sign on negative values.

Special fill characters:

%n Fills with "n" zeros
#n Fills with "n" blanks
*n Fills with "n" asterisks
Any other character may be substituted as a fill character.

Examples of masking:

```
PRINT X "R#12"
PRINT Y "L#15"
PRINT Z "R#12Z,E$*12'"
```

Default file variables

The following group of statements makes use of a feature known as default file variables:

CLEARFILE, DELETE, MATREAD, MATREADU, OPEN, READ, READU, READV, READVU, RELEASE, SELECT, WRITE, WRITEV, and WRITEVU

Most experts agree that this feature is best when it is not used, but here is a quick discussion of how default file variables work.

When a file is opened with an OPEN statement, it is usually assigned to a file variable for referencing the file later in the program with any of these statements. This takes the general form:

```
OPEN "CUSTOMERS" TO CUSTOMER.FILE ELSE...
```

The operative word here is "TO." It assigns the actual location (represented internally as a base, modulo, and separation) to the variable called CUSTOMER.FILE in this case. Later in the program, when an item is read from the file, the file variable appears in the appropriate form of a "read" statement, as in the form:

```
READ CUSTOMER.ITEM FROM CUSTOMER.FILE ELSE..
```

Here, the operative word is "FROM." With *default* file variables, nothing is explicitly assigned during the OPEN statement, as in the form:

```
OPEN "CUSTOMERS" ELSE..
```

Hence, a subsequent attempt to read from or write to the file does not require the file variable reference, as illustrated in the form:

```
READ CUSTOMER.ITEM ELSE...
```

Naturally, there may be only one default file variable in a PICK/BASIC program. Any subsequent file needed for input or output would have to have an explicitly assigned file variable during the OPEN statement. Using the default file variable form simply is not advised because it makes programs harder to maintain. By spending the few extra seconds to provide the file variable, you can save countless minutes (maybe hours) later in figuring out exactly what the program is intended to do.

Statement labels

Any PICK BASIC statement may include an optional statement label prior to the statement. It should be separated from the statement by one or more spaces. Currently, the SMA standards only provide for numeric statement labels. As of release 3.1, Pick now supports alphanumeric statement labels. When using alphabetic labels, the label must be terminated with a colon (:).

Variable replacement statements

There are at least five valid methods of replacing the contents of a variable:

1. *variable = expression*
2. MAT *array.variable = array.variable*
3. MAT *array.variable = expression*
4. MAT *array.variable = MAT array.variable*
5. *dynamic.array.variable < {,numexp{,numexp}} > = strexp*

About PICK/BASIC statements and functions

The difference between PICK/BASIC statements and functions is relatively simple; If the syntax requires that the instruction be followed by a set of parentheses (optionally containing an argument or arguments), then it is a FUNCTION. For example, the following are functions:

```
ABS(numexp)
RND(numexp)
ICONV(strexp,convexp)
```

Any instruction that does *not* have to be followed by a set of parentheses is most often a STATEMENT. For example:

```
PRINT X
INPUT Y
EXECUTE SENTENCE
```

There is at least one peculiar exception to the above rule: one variant of the LOCATE instruction is considered a statement, even though its syntax looks like it should be a function.

PICK/BASIC statements and functions

@ (function)

The @ function generates a string of control characters used for cursor positioning or other terminal or printer control features. These are usually routed to the terminal or printer with the PRINT or CRT statements. The @ is normally followed by a set of parentheses containing one or two numeric expressions.

Two numeric expressions, each being separated by a comma, evaluates to a column and row coordinate for addressing a specific terminal location.

When only one numeric expression appears, and its value is positive, it evaluates to a column-only terminal coordinate, which does not work consistently on all terminals.

The following table lists the "minus" functions, which are special intrinsic functions for performing various features and effects on a terminal.

(−1) Clears the screen and positions the cursor to home position (0,0)
(−2) Positions the cursor to the home position (0,0)
(−3) Clears to the end of screen from the current cursor position
(−4) Clears to the end of the line from the current cursor position

Compatibility of above Functions: **Pick SMA**

Note: the "At minus" function is perhaps the most nonstandardized of all features in this language between various Pick implementations. Rumor has it that at least one Pick licensee now has "At minus" functions through (−732).

The following functions are compatible only with generic Pick systems:

(−5) Enables blink function
(−6) Disables blink function
(−7) Enables protect function
(−8) Disables protect function

(−9) Moves the cursor position back one position
(−10) Moves the cursor up one line

If problems are experienced when attempting any of the above functions, make sure that the "termtype" parameter is correctly set for the type of terminal being used. See also: TERM in the TCL section.

The following additional control functions are specifically for the Pick PC-AT and XT releases:

(−11) Activate screen protect
(−12) Deactivate screen protect
(−13) Activate reverse video
(−14) Deactivate reverse video
(−15) Activate underlining
(−16) Deactivate underlining
(−17) Activate slave printer
(−18) Deactivate slave printer
(−19) Move cursor right
(−20) Move cursor down
(−21) Activate graphic character set
(−22) Deactivate graphic character set
(−23) Keyboard lock
(−24) Keyboard unlock
(−25) Control character enable
(−26) Control character disable
(−27) Write status line
(−28) Clear status line
(−29) Initialize terminal mode
(−30) Download function keys
(−31) Nonembedded stand-out on
(−32) Nonembedded stand-out off

The following background color control functions may only be used on Port 0 (zero), equipped with a color graphics display on the Pick AT/XT:

(−33)	White	(−34)	Brown
(−35)	Magenta	(−36)	Red
(−37)	Cyan	(−38)	Green
(−39)	Blue	(−40)	Black

Foreground Color Controls (Full Intensity):

(−41)	White	(−42)	Brown
(−43)	Magneta	(−44)	Red
(−45)	Cyan	(−46)	Green
(−47)	Blue	(−48)	Black

Foreground Color Controls (Half Intensity):

(−57)	White	(−58)	Brown
(−59)	Magenta	(−60)	Red
(−61)	Cyan	(−62)	Green
(−63)	Blue	(−64)	Black

Additional Control Functions:

(−89)	Activates monochrome display unit in 80 by 25 black and white mode.
(−93)	Activates color graphics monitor in 80 by 25 color mode
(−94)	Activates color graphics monitor in 80 by 25 black and white mode
(−99)	Returns a 1 if the terminal uses embedded attributes, a 0 (zero) if it does not, and null if not defined through DEFINE-TERMINAL
(−100)	Half-intensity (except on memory mapped monitor)
(−101)	Full-intensity (except on memory mapped monitor)

ABORT {*errmsg#*}

-or-

ABORT {*errmsg#, "parameter"* {, *"parameter"..*}}

Terminates program and PROC{s}. The parameter{s} are passed to the error messsage handler and displayed with the message stored in the message number indicated by "errmsg#." The ABORT statement automatically generates error message "[B1] Run-Time Abort at line n." See also: STOP and ERRMSG for available messages.

ABS (*numexp*)

Returns the absolute value of the numeric expression in parentheses.

ALPHA (*exp*)

Returns a 1 (true), if the expression contains only alphabetic characters, or 0 (false), if it contains any nonalphabetic characters. See section called "The search for truth" on p. 109.

ASCII (*exp*)

Converts an EBCDIC expression to its ASCII equivalent. The inverse of EBCDIC.

BEGIN CASE

Initiates the CASE statement. See also: CASE.

General Form:

```
BEGIN CASE
      {comment]
      CASE condexp
            statement{s}
```

```
  CASE condexp
       statement{s}
  .
  .
END CASE
```

BREAK OFF
-or-
BREAK *expression*

Disables the break key on the CRT. In the expression form, the break key is disabled when the expression evaluates to false. See the section called "The search for truth" near the beginning of this chapter.

BREAK ON
-or-
BREAK *expression*

Enables the break key on the CRT. In the expression form, the break key is enabled when the expression evaluates to true. See the section called "The search for truth" near the beginning of this chapter.

CALL *cataloged-program-name*
-or-
CALL *cataloged-program-name* (*arguments*{*s*})

Transfers program control, either directly or indirectly, to an external subroutine, passing all arguments in list. Arguments must be separated by commas (,). When passing arguments, the same number must occur in the CALL statement that is declared in the SUBROUTINE statement. There is a maximum of about 200 arguments. See also: SUBROUTINE.

Direct CALL:

```
CALL PROCESS.LINES(ID,ORDER.ITEM(1))
```
-or-
```
CALL "PROCESS.LINES"(ID,ORDER.ITEM(1))
```

With or without quotes, this example still calls PROCESS.LINES subroutine.

Indirect CALL:

```
PROGRAM.VARIABLE = "PROCESS.LINES"
CALL @PROGRAM.VARIABLE(ID,ORDER.ITEM(1))
```

Avoid using this form if you want to write maintainable, efficient programs.

CASE *condexp*

-or-

CASE *condexp;statement{;statement...}*

Conditional execution function, based on whether the value being tested meets the criteria defined in the conditional expression.

```
BEGIN CASE
      {comment}
      CASE condexp
            statement{s}
            .
            .
      CASE condexp
            statement(s)
            .
            .
      CASE 1
            statement{s}
            .
            .
END CASE
```

CASE 1 is often used at the end of a set of CASE statements as the condition to perform if none of the other CASE statements are executed.

CAT or :

Concatenation operator. Used to join strings.

CHAIN *exp*

Transfers control to TCL, which interprets and executes the command defined in the expression. Control does not return to the program. See also: EXECUTE.

CHAR (*numexp*)

Returns the ASCII character equivalent of a numeric value. The inverse of SEQ. See section 13 for the available ASCII codes.

CLEAR

Initializes all variables to zero. Avoid using this statement. It makes debugging programs nearly impossible.

CLEARFILE {*filevar*}

Deletes all items in specified file variable, just like the TCL CLEAR-FILE command.

The default file variable is cleared if no file variable is specified. See the section called "About Default File Variables" near the beginning of this section.

Be careful with this command. On some implementations, if you clear the dictionary level of a file, it also wipes out the data file's D-pointers.

COL1( )

Returns the numeric column position of the character preceding the substring retrieved in the most recently executed FIELD function. The parentheses following the function are required, and never contain any arguments.

COL2( )

Returns the numeric column positions of the character following the substring retrieved in the most recently executed FIELD function. The parentheses following the function are required, and never contain any arguments.

COM *variable* {,*variable...*}

-or-

Common *variable* {,*variable...*}

Specifies data elements to share among programs executed by a CHAIN ENTER, or CALL statement, and defines the storage order for variables. When using a CHAIN or ENTER statement to initiate another runtime PICK/BASIC program, the "I" option must be used with the RUN command (at TCL) to prevent the reinitialization of variables in workspace and to keep the COMMON area intact (Most experts agree that there is actually no way to keep the COMMON space intact when using the "I" option.) Suggestion: don't use COMMON in conjunction with CHAIN OR ENTER. The only justification for using COMMON is when it can be INCLUDEd or INSERTed into code. Otherwise, it make maintaining programs a real nuisance.

COS (*numexp*)

Calculates the cosine of the angle specified in the numeric expression, and returns the results in degrees.

COUNT (*strexp1,trexp2*)

Returns the number of occurrences of strexp2 within strexp1. See also: DCOUNT for counting delimiters.

CRT

-or-

CRT *exp*

Directs output unconditionally to the terminal. This command functions like the PRINT command, but is not affected by any items on the following page:

1. the (P) option used with the RUN command at TCL
2. the "PRINTER ON" statement
3. a HEADING, FOOTING, or PAGE statement.

All of the "@" functions are allowed. See also: @.

DATA *exp{exp,...}*

Holds value(s) for use by subsequent input requests initiated from CHAIN, ENTER, EXECUTE, or INPUT statements. Multiple DATA statements are permitted, which is preferable to stacking all the data in one long statement.

DATE ( )

Returns current system date in internal format (an integer value indicating the number of days since December 31, 1967). The parentheses following the function are required, and never contain any arguments.

DCOUNT *(strexp1,strexp2)*

Returns the number of occurrences of the delimiter specified in strexp2 within strexp1. The strexp2 parameter may be a reserved system delimiter, such as a value mark. The difference between this statement and the COUNT statement is that one is added to the result unless the string referenced in strexp1 is null.

DEBUG

Transfers control to PICK/BASIC symbolic debugger. See also: D and E options with the RUN command.

DELETE *(arrayvar,attrexp)*

-or-

DELETE *(arrayvar,attrexp,valexp)*

-or-

DELETE *(arrayvar,attrexp,valexp,subvalexp)*

Deletes a value at any point in a dynamic array. In this form, the DELETE is always on the right side of an equal (=) sign.

DELETE *idexp*

-or-

DELETE *filevar,idexp*

Deletes specified item-id expression from optionally-specified file variable. See the section called "About Default File Variables" near the beginning of this section.

DIM *variable (dimension)* {*,variable(dimension)...*}

-or-

DIM *variable (dimension1,dimension2)*

Defines dimensioned array. In the first form, a single-dimensional vector is established. In the second form, a two-dimensional array or matrix is established. The two-dimensional array has *nothing* to do with the handling of multivalues or subvalues in conjunction with the MATREAD or MATREADU statements.

DO

Initiator for the REPEAT portion of the LOOP statement. See also: LOOP..WHILE and LOOP..UNTIL.

DTX *(exp)*

Converts decimal value to its equivalent hexadecimal value. See also: XTD. As of release 3.1, this function now returns a 0 (zero) instead of a null value.

EBCDIC *(exp)*

Converts an ASCII expression to its EBCDIC equivalent. The inverse of ASCII.

ECHO OFF

-or-

ECHO *expression*

Disables terminal character echo mode. All characters entered on the keyboard are *not* displayed on the terminal. In the latter form, echo is disabled when the expression evaluates to false. See the section called "The search for truth" near the beginning of this chapter.

ECHO ON

-or-

ECHO *expression*

Enables terminal character echo mode. All characters entered on the keyboard are displayed on the terminal. In the latter form, echo is enabled when the expression evaluates to true. See the section called "The search for truth" near the beginning of this chapter. As of release 2.2, control characters entered while ECHO is off are not echoed.

ELSE

Precedes statements to execute when the IF clause evaluates to false. See the section on the THEN/ELSE construct and the section called "The search for truth" near the beginning of this chapter.

```
IF condexp {THEN statement{s}} {ELSE statement{s}}
```

END

Used as a compiler directive in two ways:

1. physical program end (optional)

```
......statements......
...body of program....
......statements......
END
```

(The trailing END statement is not required on PICK/BASIC source code, but is helpful for program readability.)

2. logical end of a multiline IF

```
IF exp THEN
        statement{s}
        .
        .
END
```

Multiline THEN/ELSE statements *must* have terminating END statements. See the section on THEN/ELSE construct at the end of PICK/BASIC.

END CASE

Terminates the CASE statement.

General Form:

```
BEGIN CASE
     CASE condexp
          statement{s}
          .
          .
END CASE
```

ENTER *cataloged-program-name*

-or-

ENTER *@programname.variable*

Transfers control to specified cataloged program. See also: COMMON. Must *not* be used from a subroutine. Control does not return to the program.

EQU{ATE} *symbol* TO *constant*{,*symbol* TO *constant...*}

-or-

EQU{ATE} *variable* TO *variable*

Performs constant or variable assignment at compile time. A symbol is similar to a variable name, with the exception that it may not be modified by placing it to the left of the equal sign in an assignment expression. As of release 3.1, the EQUATE statement now allows negative numbers.

Examples:

```
EQU CLEAR.SCREEN TO CHAR (12)
EQU RING.BELL TO CHAR (7)
EQU ATTRIBUTE.MARK TO CHAR (254)
EQU CUSTOMER.NAME.ATTRIBUTE TO 1
EQU INVOICE.NUMBER TO CUSTOMER.ITEM (13)
EQU TITLE TO "PICK POCKET GUIDE"
```

EXECUTE TCL.*exp* {RETURNING *return.var*} {CAPTURING *capture.var*}

Issues any valid TCL expression, and continues execution of the program at the next line after completion. The TCL expression may be any valid TCL command, including ACCESS sentences, verbs, PROCs, or other cataloged PICK/BASIC programs.

Any input that might be needed by the EXECUTE statement may be provided with the DATA statement.

The optional RETURNING clause is used to direct any error message numbers generated as a result of the EXECUTE statement into a variable. Each ERRMSG item-id is separated by a space. See also: SYSTEM function, parameter 17.

The optional CAPTURING clause is used to direct the output from a process into a variable. Carriage return/linefeed combinations are converted to attribute marks, which allows the variable to be treated like a dynamic array. Clear screens are converted to nulls.

Important Notes about EXECUTE:

The SMA standard provides an EXECUTE statement. It is not as technically elaborate as the generic Pick form, and does not provide for the RETURNING or the CAPTURING clauses. Most licensees, however, support these extensions.

Control does *not* return from an EXECUTE that issues an OFF or LOGTO command.

Each level of EXECUTE builds a new process workspace area. As the number of levels increase, so do disk space requirements. The maximum number of workspaces is currently five on most systems. It may be changed with the :TASKINIT verb.

Examples of the EXECUTE statement:

1. Issuing a simple TCL command:
   ```
   EXECUTE "SORT STAFF BY NAME NAME TOTAL SALARY (P)"
   ```
2. Passing input from the DATA statement:
   ```
   DATA "(QFILE"
   EXECUTE "COPY NEWAC*"
   ```
3. Capturing output:
   ```
   EXECUTE "LISTU" CAPTURING OUTPUT
   ```
4. Capturing error message numbers:
   ```
   EXECUTE "SSELECT INVOICES" RETURNING ERRNUM
   ```

5. Using all 3 types of string delimiters:
```
EXECUTE /SORT ORDERS = 'S]' WITH DATE GE "1/1/92"\
```
6. Processing Lists:
```
EXECUTE "SSELECT STAFF BY HIRE.DATE BY NAME"
EXECUTE "SAVE-LIST STAFF.LIST"
```

EXP (*numexp*)

Returns the exponential of the numexp, that is, e raised to the power of the numeric expression, 2.7177. (e^ numexp). The inverse of LN.

EXTRACT (*arrayvar,attrexp*)

-or-

EXTRACT (*arrayvar,attrexp,valexp*)

-or-

EXTRACT (*arrayvar,attrexp,valexp,subvalexp*)

Retrieves a specific element from a dynamic array.

Alternate Method (using dynamic array reference symbols):

arrayvar<attrexp>

-or-

arrayvar<attrexp,valexp>

-or-

arrayvar<attrexp,valexp,subvalexp>

Examples:

```
PRINT EXTRACT(CUSTOMER.ITEM,1,0,0)
```
-or-
```
PRINT CUSTOMER.ITEM<1>
```

Both of these examples retrieve the entire first attribute from the dynamic array, CUSTOMER.ITEM.

```
PRINT EXTRACT(CUSTOMER.ITEM(1),1,2,0)
```
-or-
```
PRINT CUSTOMER.ITEM(1)<1,2>
```

Both of these examples retrieve the second (multi-) value from the first attribute of the dimensioned array, CUSTOMER.ITEM.

FIELD (*strexp,search.delimiter,numexp*)

Returns a substring from a string expression by specifying a delimiter and the desired occurrence. The search delimiter may not be a reserved system delimiter (Attribute Mark, Value Mark, or Sub-Value Mark). See also: COL1( ) and COL2( ).

Examples:

```
GL.ACCOUNT = "02*4000*11"
COMPANY.CODE = FIELD(GL.ACCOUNT,"*",1)
```

This function indicates that everything up to the first asterisk in GL.ACCOUNT should be assigned to the variable "COMPANY.CODE." As a result, afterward, COMPANY.CODE contains the value "02."

```
ACCT.NUMBER = FIELD(GL.ACCOUNT,"*",2)
```

This function indicates that everything from the first to the second asterisk should be stored in the variable, "ACCT.NUMBER." Thus, "ACCT.NUMBER" would contain the value, "4000."

FOOTING *exp*

-or-

FOOTING *"{{text} {'options'}...}"*

Designates text to output at the bottom of each page. Options must be enclosed within single quotes to distinguish them from text. Multiple options may be enclosed in the same set of single quotes. See also: PAGE.

Example:

```
FOOTING "'LC'Page 'PN' Printed at 'TLC' This end into shredder first.'L'"
```

This function issues a blank line prior to the centered footing, which includes the text, "Page," followed by the left-justified page number. On the same centered line the text, "Printed at," appears and is subsequently followed by the system time and date. After the time and date, the "L" issues a linefeed and the "c" centers the text "This end into shredder first" on the next line. The final "L" issues an extra blank line at the end of the page or screen.

Standard Pick Options:

- '' Outputs (one) single quote
- C Centers output line
- D Current date (Format dd mmm yyyy)
- L Carriage return and linefeed
- P Current page number, right justified in a field of four blanks
- PN Current page number, left justified
- T Current time and date (Format hh:mm:ss dd mm yyyy)

SMA Standard Option (in addition to the above):

- P{n} Current page number, right justified in field of n blanks; the default for n is four.

FOR..NEXT

Incremental loop function.

General Form:

For *variable* = *exp* TO *exp* {STEP *exp*}

```
    statement{s}
    .
    .
NEXT variable
```

The STEP function indicates the value to increment the counter variable on each pass. The default step is one.

FOR..NEXT..UNTIL

Conditional incremental loop function. Executes until expression following the UNTIL clause evaluates to true. When used, the UNTIL clause *must* appear in the first line of the FOR..NEXT loop. See the section called "The search for truth" near the beginning of this chapter.

General Form:

```
For variable = exp TO exp {STEP exp} UNTIL exp
    statement{s}
    .
    .
NEXT variable
```

FOR..NEXT..WHILE

Conditional incremental loop function. Executes while the WHILE value clause evaluates to true. When being used, the WHILE statement *must* appear in the first line of the FOR..NEXT loop. See the section called "The search for truth" near the beginning of this chapter.

General Form:

```
FOR variable = exp TO exp {STEP exp} WHILE exp
    statement{s}
    .
    .
NEXT variable
```

GOSUB *statement.label*

Transfers control to specified local subroutine. See also: RETURN. As of release 3.1, Pick now supports alphanumeric statement labels. When using alphabetic labels, the label must be terminated with a colon (:).

GOTO *statement.label*

-or-

GO TO *statement.label*

Transfers control to specified statement label. As of release 3.1, Pick now supports alphanumeric labels. When using alphabetic labels, the label must be terminated with a colon (:).

HEADING *exp*

-or-

HEADING *"{{text}{'options'}...}"*

Designates text to output at the top of each page. Options must be enclosed within single quotes, to distinguish them from text. Multiple options may be enclosed in the same set of single quotes. See also: PAGE.

Example:

```
HEADING "'LC' Accounts Receivable 'LC' Aged Trail Balance 'L'"
```

This command issues a blank line at the top of the screen or page, then centers the text, "Accounts Receivable." The next 'L' option issues a linefeed and then centers the text "Aged Trail Balance" on the next line, which is followed by a blank line. See also: FOOTING.

Standard Pick Options:

- " Outputs (one) single quote
- C Centers output line
- D Current date (Format dd mmm yyyy)
- L Carriage return and linefeed
- P Current page number, right justified in a field of four blanks
- PN Current page number, left justified
- T Current time and date (Format: hh:mm:ss dd mmm yyyy)

SMA Standard Option (in addition to the above):

- P{n} Current page number, right justified in a field of n blanks, the default for n is four.

ICONV *(exp,convexp)*

Converts expression to internal format, according to conversion code specified in conversion expression.

Examples:

```
INPUT CHECK.AMOUNT
CHECK.AMOUNT = ICONV(CHECK.AMOUNT,"MR2")
INPUT CHECK.DATE
CHECK.DATE = ICONV (CHECK.DATE,"D")
```

The ACCESS chapter contains information on the various conversion codes that are available to the ICONV function.

IF *condexp* THEN *statement{s}* {ELSE statement{s}}

Performs conditional execution of one or more statements. See the section on the THEN/ ELSE construct and the section called "The search for truth" near the beginning of this chapter.

IN *variable*

Accepts a single character of input. No prompt character is displayed and no carriage return is required. The character is stored in its ASCII (decimal) format in the variable. The majority of Pick implementations have implemented this differently than the generic Pick form. The others tend to use the form: INPUT X,**0**.

Compatibility: **Pick 2.2** and higher

INCLUDE {*filename*} *itemname*

Inserts compiled object code from specified itemname in the program. When the filename is omitted, the current file is assumed. (Some Pick implementations use **$INCLUDE** rather than **INCLUDE**)

Examples:

```
INCLUDE STANDARD.EQUATES
INCLUDE FILE.DEFS CUSTOMER.FILE.EQUATES
INCLUDE FILE.DEFS INVOICE.FILE.EQUATES
```

Compatibility: **Pick 2.0** and higher   SMA

INDEX (*strexp,substring,numexp*)

Searches a string expression for the occurrence of the specified substring indicated in the numeric expression. Returns the starting column position of the matched substring. If the specified substring is not found, then 0 is returned.

Example:

```
TEST = INDEX("ABCDEFG","D",1)
```

This example returns the value, 4, to the variable called TEST because the first occurrence of "D" was found in the fourth position of the string.

INPUT {@(x,y)} {:}*variable*{*,lenexp*}{:}{*maskexp*}

Prompts for the input of data from the terminal, using the default prompt character (?), or the character previously defined by a PROMPT statement. (Some Pick implementations now support an ELSE clause on the INPUT statement. Check your system documentation for this feature.) The "at sign" (@) form of INPUT prompts for the input of data from the terminal, at the coordinates specified in the "x" (column) and "y" (row) parameters. Assigns input to specified variable after performing optional mask function.

The optional colon (:) preceding the input variable indicates to display the "old" value of the variable being input. The length expression indicates the length of input to accept. A linefeed is performed when the length of the argument is satisfied. The optional colon (:) character following the "lenexp" inhibits the automatic carriage return and linefeed when completing the input. The cursor remains positioned after the entered value. If the input data value does not match the optionally-specified mask expression, then the statement reprompts for input. Mask functions may be any combination of conversions, pattern-matching operators, or text justification. See the section on the masking function.

INPUTERR *strexp*

Outputs message, defined in string expression, on status (bottom) line of terminal. Used in conjunction with the INPUT@ statement.

INPUTNULL *character*

Defines null default character as a specified character. This character is recognized as a null on subsequent INPUT statements. Used in conjunction with INPUT@ statements.

INPUTTRAP *strexp* GOSUB *statement.label* {*,statement.label*}...

Tests value of last executed INPUT@ statement. Upon execution, branches to statement label address of local subroutine that corresponds with location in the statement label list. As of release 3.1, Pick now supports alphanumeric statement labels. When using alphabetic labels, the label must be terminated with a colon (:).

Example:

```
INPUTTRAP "ABC" GOSUB 1,2,3
```

INPUTTRAP strexp GOTO statement.label {,statement.label}...

Tests value of last executed INPUT@ statement. Upon evaluation, branches to statement label address that corresponds with location in the statement label list. As of release 3.1, Pick now supports alphanumeric statement labels. When using alphabetic labels, the label must be terminated with a colon (:).

INSERT (*arrayvar,attrexp;exp*)

-or-

INSERT(*arrayvar,attrexp,valexp;exp*)

-or-

INSERT (*arrayvar,attrexp,valexp,subvalexp,exp*)

Inserts the element referenced by "exp" into a specific location in a dynamic array. A "−1" may be specified as the attrexp, valexp, or subvalexp, which causes the exp to be inserted as the last element in the respective location. Only the last form shown is acknowledged by the SMA standard.

INT (*numexp*)

Returns the integer value of the numeric expression, that is, all the numbers to the left of the decimal point.

LEN (*strexp*)

Returns the length of the string in the string expression.

LN (*numexp*)

Returns the natural logarithin (base e, which is 2.7183) of the numeric expression. Inverse of EXP.

LOCATE (*exp,arrayvar*{*,attrexp,*{*valexp*}}*;setvar*{*;'sequence'*}) {THEN *statement*{*s*}} ELSE *statement*{*s*}

Locates string expression (exp) in array referenced by arrayvar, returning the positional value into setvar. If the string expression is not found, the value returned in setvar contains the position where the element should be inserted using the INSERT function. See the section on the THEN/ELSE construct.

Sequence parameters: (the single quotes around parameters are required)

'AL' Ascending, left-justified.
'AR' Ascending, right-justified.
'DL' Descending, left-justified.
'DR' Descending, right-justified.

If no sequence parameter is specified, setvar position defaults to end of array element.

The use of the optional attrexp and valexp indicate whether the value returned into setvar is a Value Mark Count or a Subvalue Mark Count. If both are omitted, the value returned into setvar is an Attribute Mark Count.

Compatibility: **Pick 2.0** and lower

The SMA and Pick 2.1 form of LOCATE:

LOCATE *exp* IN *arrayvar* {*attrexp*{*,valexp*}}*,numexp* BY *strexp* SETTING *setvar* {THEN *statement*{*s*}} ELSE *statement*{*s*}

The parameters included in the syntax for the SMA standards are the same as those of the standard Pick form, except for the one called "numexp." This numeric expression is not optional and it indicates the starting position within the specified item, attribute, or value to begin. In other words, if you were searching attribute 2 for a value and the numexp was 3, the LOCATE would begin at the third value of the attribute.

Compatibility: **Pick 2.1** and higher SMA

LOCK *lock-number* {THEN/ELSE *statement*{*s*}}

Sets an execution (lock) flag in the range, (0-63). This command is used to prevent program re-entrancy, such that only one process may run this program at any given time. If the lock-number expression evaluates to greater than 63, then the result is divided by 64, and the lock-number is equal to the remainder of the equation. See the section on the THEN/ELSE construct. There are only 48 execution locks in Pick 2.0 and lower releases. Many implementations now provide up to 128 execution locks.

LOOP...{UNTIL}

Conditional loop function. Performs specified operations until the UNTIL clause evaluates to true. See the section called "The search for truth" near the beginning of this chapter.

General Forms:

```
LOOP {statement{s}} UNTIL condexp DO {statement{s}} REPEAT
LOOP {statement{s}} UNTIL condexp DO
    statement{s}
  .
  .
REPEAT
LOOP
    {statements}
  UNTIL condexp DO
    {statements}
  .
  .
REPEAT
```

LOOP...{WHILE}

Conditional loop function. Performs specified operations as long as the WHILE conditional expression evaluates to true. See the section called "The search for truth" near the beginning of this chapter.

General Forms:

```
LOOP {statement{s}} WHILE condexp DO {statement{s}} REPEAT
LOOP {statement{s}}WHILE condexp DO
    statement{s}
  .
  .
REPEAT
LOOP
    {statements}
```

```
WHILE condexp DO
      {statements}
        .
        .
REPEAT
```

MAT *arrayvar* = *exp*

-or-

MAT *arrayvar* = MAT *arrayvar*

Initializes all the locations of a dimensioned array variable to the specified value{s}. When assigning one matrix to another, the array on the right side of the equal sign must be the same size or smaller than the matrix on the left side. See also: DIM, MATREAD, and MATWRITE.

Example:

```
DIM CUSTOMER.ITEM(5)
MAT CUSTOMER.ITEM  = " "
```

MATCH *matchstring*

-or-

MATCHES *matchstring*

Pattern matching operator. The matchstring may be a composite of literals and/or match operators, appended to length specifications. During processing, the value must be the exact length of the length specifications parameter.

Matchstring Operators:

nA	Accept only "n" alphabetic characters
nN	Accept only "n" numeric characters
nX	Accept "n" wildcards (any character)
'literal'	Any literal string enclosed in single or double quotes.

The "n" parameter specifies the length of the match operator string. A length specification of zero (0) allows any length of the following match operator.

When combinations of matchstrings and literals are present, the entire matchstring must be enclosed in double quotes.

Examples of pattern matching:

Single Pattern Match:

```
        IF X MATCHES "3N'-'2N'-'4N" THEN
        PRINT "VALID SOCIAL SECURITY "
   END ELSE
        PRINT "INVALID SOCIAL SECURITY "
END
```

Multiple Pattern Matches:

```
IF X MATCHES "10N]1A9N" THEN...
```

Tests for ten numeric characters or one alphabetic character followed by nine numerics. Note the character separating the 2 pattern matchstrings is a value mark (]).

MATREAD *arrayvar* FROM {*filevar*}, *idexp* {LOCKED *statement*{*s*}} {THEN *statement*{*s*}} ELSE *statement*{*s*}

Reads the specified dimensioned array (item) from the optionally-specified file variable, or the default file variable if none is specified, and stores one attribute per element into the array previously defined with a DIM statement. See also: MATREADU, and the section on the THEN/ELSE construct and the section called "About Default File Variables" near the beginning of this section.

If more attributes are present in the item read than elements in the previously dimensioned array, then the extra attributes are appended to the last array element, with each attribute delimited by an attribute mark. If the number of attributes read is less than the array size, then the remaining array elements are assigned null values.

The ELSE condition is taken when the item is not on file. The THEN condition is taken when the item is read successfully.

As of release 2.2, the LOCKED clause is now supported in the syntax of this statement. This clause occurs before the THEN and/or ELSE clause{s} and specifies the statement{s} to execute if the group (or item in newer versions) is locked when the read is attempted. Earlier versions of generic Pick did not support this feature.

The LOCKED clause should only be used with READU, READVU, or MATREADU statements—*not* with READ, READV, or MATREAD statements.

MATREADU *arrayvar* FROM {*filevar*}, *idexp* {*LOCKED statement*{*s*}} {THEN statement{s}} ELSE statement{s}

Reads the specified dimensioned array (item) from the optionally specified file variable, or the default file variable if none is specified, and stores one attribute per element into the array previously defined with a DIM statement. The MATREADU statement is identical to the MATREAD statement, except that the *group* is "locked," preventing access to that group by any other process. Most other Pick implementations lock only the item during the read, and the group during an update. See also the section on the THEN/ELSE construct and the section called "About Default File Variables" near the beginning of this section.

If more attributes are present in the item read than elements in the previously dimensioned array, then the extra attributes are appended to the last array element, with each attribute delimited by an attribute mark. If the number of attributes read is less than the array size, then the remaining array elements are assigned null values. The ELSE condition is taken when the item is not on file. The THEN condition is taken when the item is read successfully.

As of release 2.2, the LOCKED clause is now supported in the syntax of this statement. This clause occurs before the THEN and/or ELSE clause{s} and specifies the statement{s} to execute if the group (or item in newer versions) is locked when the read is attempted. Earlier versions of generic Pick did not support this feature. The LOCKED clause should only be used with READU, READVU, or MATREADU statements—*not* with READ, READV, or MATREAD statements.

MATWRITE *arrayvar* on *{filevar,}idexp*

-or-

MATWRITEU *arrayvar* ON *{filevar,}idexp*

Writes dimensioned array (item) into the specified file variable. If the file variable parameter is omitted, the default file variable is used. See the section called "About Default File Variables" near the beginning of this section.

The MATWRITEU statement is identical to the MATWRITE statement, except the *group* remains locked. See also: RELEASE.

MOD (*dividend,divisor*)

Calculates the remainder (modulo) of the expression. Same as the REM function.

NEXT *variable*

Terminates a FOR..NEXT loop. See the FOR..NEXT statement.

General Form:

```
FOR variable = exp TO exp {STEP exp}
     statement{s}
     .
     .
NEXT variable
```

NOT (*logical.expression*)

Reverses the normal effect of a logical expression. Returns true if the (logical) expression evaluates to false. Returns false if the expression evaluates to true. See the section called "The search for truth" near the beginning of this chapter.

Example:

```
IF NOT(NUM(RESPONSE)) THEN PRINT "NOT NUMERIC"
```

NULL

Compiler directive to perform no operation, other than to provide an instruction where one is required but not intended to do anything. Typically used by confused programmers in a single line IF..THEN..ELSE construct as in the following example:

```
IF condexp THEN NULL ELSE statement{s}...
```

NUM (*exp*)

Evaluates to "true" (1) if the expression results in only numeric values. Evaluates to false (0) if the expression contains any nonnumeric characters. See the section called "The search for truth" near the beginning of this chapter.

OCONV (*exp,convexp*)

Converts the expression to external format, according to conversion code specified in convexp. See ACCESS Section for available conversions.

Examples:

```
PRINT OCONV (CHECK.AMOUNT,"MR2,$")
PRINT OCONV (CUST.ITEM(INVOICE.DATE),"D2/")
```

The ACCESS chapter contains information on the various conversion codes that are available to the OCONV function.

ON *indexexp* GOSUB *statement.label{,statement.label...}*

Transfers control to a local subroutine statement label according to the positional value of the index expression. The local subroutine must be terminated with a RETURN statement.

If the index expression evaluates to a number less than one, or to a number greater than the number of statement labels, then control passes to the next executable line in the program. As of release 3.1, Pick now supports alphanumeric statement labels. When using alphabetic labels, the label must be terminated with a colon (:).

Example:

```
ON RESPONSE GOSUB 8000,9000,9500
```

ON *indexexp* GOTO *statement.label {statement.label,...}*

Transfers control to a statement label according to the positional value of the index expression.

If the index expression evaluates to a number less than one, or to a number greater than the number of statement labels, then control passes to the next executable line in the program. As of release 3.1, Pick now supports alphanumeric statement labels. When using alphabetic labels, the label must be terminated with a colon (:).

Example:

```
ON RESPONSE GOTO 100,200,300,400,500
```

Open {"DICT,"} *file.exp* {TO *filevar*}{THEN *statement{s}*} ELSE *statement{s}*

Opens the specified filename expression and associates the file with the indicated file variable. If the "DICT" parameter is specified (or implied as an expression), then the dictionary level of the specified filename is opened and assigned to the file variable. If no file variable is specified, then the default file variable is opened and assigned. See also the section on the THEN/ELSE construct and the section called "About Default File Variables" near the beginning of this section.

OUT *variable*

Outputs a single ASCII character, using the decimal equivalent in the specified variable.

Compatibility: **Pick 2.2** and higher

PAGE {*expression*}

Terminates the current page of output, prints the optional FOOTING, positions to top of form, and prints the optional HEADING. The optional expression may be used to change the current value of the page number.

PRECISION *number-of-positions*

Defines number of decimal places to carry in results of mathematical expressions. As of release 2.2, the number-of-positions parameter must be in the range 0 to 6. The default precision is four (4). Some older Pick implementations only support precision in the range, 0 to 4.

PRINT ON *printfilenumber print.expression*

Directs printer output to one of 255 print reports in the range (0-254).

PRINT {*@(col{,row}):*}{*exp{,exp...}*} {*maskexp*}

Outputs literal or expression{s} to the current output device. If the "@" symbol is specified, the output is directed to the specified column and row coordinates. See the @function for more information on terminal and printer control functions (located at the beginning of PICK/BASIC statements and functions). If nothing follows the PRINT statement, a blank line is output.

The comma (,) between expressions specifies for the cursor to "tab right" 18 spaces prior to printing the next expression.

The colon (:) between expressions and parameters specifies that expressions are concatenated. A colon must appear between the @(col,row) parameter and the following expression.

The mask expression may be any legal mask expression. See the section on the Masking function. See also: CRT, PRINTER ON, and EXECUTE.

PRINTER CLOSE

Indicates that the current output is now complete, closes the spooler entry, and releases control to the spooler.

PRINTER OFF

Directs output from subsequent PRINT statements to the terminal. See also: CRT.

PRINTER ON

Directs output from subsequent PRINT statements to the system printer, via the spooler. See also: CRT.

PROCREAD *variable* {THEN *statement*{*s*}} ELSE *statement*{*s*}

Reads the calling PROC's primary input buffer and assigns its contents to the specified variable. When a successful read takes place, the variable is treated as a string of characters delimited by spaces. The FIELD function may be used to parse the variable. The INDEX function may be used to determine the number of entries (# of spaces + 1) in the (buffer) variable. The ELSE condition is taken when the program has not been executed from a PROC. Either a THEN or an ELSE construct must be present. See the section on the THEN/ELSE construct.

PROCWRITE *variable* {ELSE *statement*{*s*}}

Writes the specified string expression variable to the calling PROC's primary input buffer. In order for PROC to be able to deal with the information in the variable, each space in the variable defines a new parameter in the PROC's buffer. The ELSE statement{s} is (are) taken when the program was *not* run from a PROC.

PROMPT *exp*

Specifies the single character to display during subsequent INPUT statements that prompt for terminal input. The default prompt character is a question mark (?), which is used when the PROMPT statement is not used. A null prompt character may be defined with the statement, PROMPT "".

Examples:

```
PROMPT CHAR(0)
PROMPT ""
PROMPT ":"
```

PWR (*exp1,exp2*)

Raises value contained in exp1 to the power of the value of exp2. See also the ^ character in the section called "Reserved Characters."

READ *arrayvar* FROM {*filevar,*} *idexp* {LOCKED *statement*{*s*}} {THEN *statement*{*s*}} ELSE *statement*{*s*}

Reads item from the optionally-specified file variable and assigns each attribute to an array element in the dynamic array designated in arrayvar. See also: READU and the

THEN/ELSE construct.

If the file variable parameter is not specified, the default file variable is used. See the section called "About Default File Variables" near the beginning of this section.

The ELSE condition is taken when the item is not on file. The THEN condition is taken when the item is read successfully.

As of release 2.2, the LOCKED clause is now supported in the syntax of this statement. This clause occurs before the THEN and/or ELSE clause{s} and specifies the statement{s} to execute if the group (or item in newer versions) is locked when the read is attempted. Earlier versions of generic Pick did not support this feature.

The LOCKED clause should only be used with READU, READVU, or MATREADU statements—not with READ, READV, or MATREAD statements. As of release 3.1, the LOCKED clause will no longer lock the group when used with the READ statement. The READ and READV statements will now read a locked group.

READNEXT *id-variable* {*,posvar*}{FROM *selectvar*} {THEN *statement*{*s*}} ELSE *statement*{*s*}

Reads the next item-id from the active list and assigns it to the specified variable. The list must have been retrieved by a SELECT, SSELECT, GET-LIST, or QSELECT command executed immediately prior to starting execution of the PICK/BASIC program that contains the READNEXT statement, or by a preceding SELECT or EXECUTE statement within the program. See also: (PICK/BASIC) SELECT and the section on the THEN/ELSE construct.

The position variable (posvar) parameter indicates the position of the multivalue within an attribute, specified in an exploded sort, executed prior to the execution of the program. This variable allows multivalues to be retrieved in exploded sort sequence.

The ELSE condition is executed if no selection was performed or when there are no more items in the list.

READT *variable* {THEN *statement*{*s*}} ELSE *statement*{*s*}}

Reads a tape record, and assigns the value returned to the specified variable. The length of the tape record is specified by the most recently executed T-ATT command. See the section on the THEN/ELSE construct. As of release 2.2 this statement now works with streaming cartridge tape.

The ELSE condition is taken if the tape unit is not attached, or an end-of-file is encountered.

READU *arrayvar* FROM {*filevar,*}*idexp* {LOCKED *statement*{*s*} {THEN *statement*{*s*}} ELSE *statement*{*s*}

Reads item from the optionally-specified file variable and assigns each attribute to an array element in the dynamic array designated in arrayvar. The READU statement is identical to the READ statement, except that the *group* is "locked,"preventing access to that group by any other process. Most other Pick implementations lock only the *item* during the read, and the group during an update. See the section on the THEN/ELSE construct.

If the file variable parameter is not specified, the default file variable is used. See the section called "About Default File Variables" near the beginning of this section.

The ELSE condition is taken when the item is not on file. The THEN condition is taken when the item is read successfully. As of release 2.2, the LOCKED clause is now supported in the syntax of this statement. This clause occurs before the THEN and/or ELSE clause{s} and specifies the statement{s} to execute if the group (or item in newer versions) is locked when the read is attempted. Earlier versions of generic Pick did not support this feature.

The LOCKED clause should only be used with READU, READVU, or MATREADU statements—not with READ, READV, or MATREAD statements.

READV ***variable*** **FROM** ***{filevar,} idexp,attrexp*** **{LOCKED** ***statement{s}*****}** **{THEN** ***statements{s}*****}** **ELSE** ***statement{s}***

Reads an item from the optionally-specified file variable and assigns the value contained in the attribute number referenced in the attribute expression to the specified variable. See also: READVU, the section on the THEN/ELSE construct, and the section called "About Default File Variables" near the beginning of this section.

The ELSE condition is taken if the item is not on file. The THEN condition is taken when the item is read successfully.

As of release 2.2, the LOCKED clause is now supported in the syntax of this statement. This clause occurs before the THEN and/or ELSE clause{s} and specifies the statement{s} to execute if the group (or item in newer versions) is locked when the read is attempted. Earlier versions of generic Pick did not support this feature.

The LOCKED clause should only be used with READU, READVU, or MATREADU statements—not with READ, READV, or MATREAD statements. As of release 3.1, the LOCKED clause will no longer lock the group when used with the READ statement. The READ and READV statements will now read a locked group.

READVU ***variable*** **FROM** ***{filevar,} idexp,attrexp*** **{LOCKED** ***statement{s}*****}** **{THEN** ***statement{s}*****}ELSE** ***statement{s}***

Reads an item from the optionally-specified file variable and assigns the value contained in the attribute number referenced in the attribute expression to the specified variable. The READVU statement is identical to the READV statement, except that the *group* is "locked," preventing access to that group by any other process. Most other Pick implementations lock only the *item* during the read, and the group during an update. See also: READV and the section on the THEN/ELSE construct.

The ELSE condition is taken if the item is not on file. The THEN condition is taken when the item is read successfully.

As of release 2.2, the LOCKED clause is now supported in the syntax of this statement. This clause occurs before the THEN and/or ELSE clause{s} and specifies the statement{s} to execute if the group (or item in newer versions) is locked when the read is attempted. Earlier versions of generic Pick did not support this feature.

The LOCKED clause should only be used with READU, READVU, or MATREADU statements—not with READ, READV, or MATREAD statements.

RELEASE

-or-

RELEASE *idexp*

-or-

RELEASE *filevar,idexp*

Releases the *group* locked with a previous MATREADU, READU, or READVU statement, in the optionally-specified file variable. If the file variable and item-id expressions are both omitted, all groups currently locked by the current process are unlocked.

If the file variable parameter is not specified, the default file variable is used. See the section called "About Default File Variables" near the beginning of this section.

REM *text*

Defines user-specified remarks. Causes the entire source line to be ignored by the compiler.

The characters, * or !, may (and should) be substituted for the REM statement.

REM (*dividend, divisor*)

Calculates the remainder (modulo) of two numeric expressions. Same as the MOD function.

REPEAT

Terminates DO portion of LOOP..WHILE or LOOP..UNTIL statements. See the LOOP..WHILE or LOOP..UNTIL statements.

General Form:

```
LOOP {statement{s}} UNTIL condexp DO
     statement{s}
     .
     .
REPEAT
```

REPLACE (*arrayvar,attrexp;exp*)

-or-

REPLACE (*arrayvar,attrexp,valexp;exp*)

-or-

REPLACE (*arrayvar,attrexp,valexp,subvalexp,exp*)

Replaces the specified location within the dynamic array variable referenced by arrayvar with the value referenced in "exp" (expression). See also the INSERT function.

A "−1" may be specified as the attrexp, valexp, or subvalexp, which causes the exp to be replaced as the last element in the respective location. Alternate method, using dynamic array reference symbols:

strexp<arrayvar {,valexp{,subvalexp}}> = exp

Note: only the last form shown and the alternate method are acknowledged by the SMA standard.

RETURN

-or-

RETURN TO *statement.label*

Terminates an internal or external subroutine. Control resumes with the statement following the CALL or GOSUB command. The TO clause may only be used with an internal subroutine, and transfers control to the specified statement label. This is *not* recommended as it makes programs nearly impossible to figure out. As of release 3.1, Pick now supports alphanumeric statement labels. When using alphabetic labels, the label must be terminated with a colon (:).

REWIND {THEN *statement{s}*} ELSE *statement{s}*

Rewinds the magnetic tape on the attached unit. The ELSE condition is taken if the tape unit is not ready or attached with a T-ATT command. See the section on the THEN/ELSE construct. As of release 2.2, this statement now works with streaming cartridge tape.

RND (*numexp*)

Generates a random number between 0 and the value specified in the numeric expression, minus one. As of release 3.1, the RND function uses a new formula based on the minimal standards multiplicative linear congruent generator, also known as the Lehmer generator.

Example:

```
PAY.INCREASE.PERCENTAGE = RND(8) + 1
```

The RND function in this example generates a random number between 0 and 7. One is added to the result to make sure that everybody gets at least *some* sort of an increase, making the range between one and eight.

RQM {*number-of-seconds*}

-or-

RQM {*untiltime*}

Activates sleep function, placing process into an inactive mode until optional argument is satisfied. This statement terminates the current process' timeslice. Same as SLEEP statement.

The sleep parameter may either be an integer number of seconds, or the desired time, in 24-hour (military) format delimited by colons. If no argument is indicated, the process will sleep for one second.

SELECT

-or-

Select *var* {TO *selectvar*}

-or-

SELECT *filevar* {TO *selectvar*}

Creates a list of item-ids from the file specified in the file variable parameter, allowing sequential access to each item in the file. If the file variable parameter is not specified, the default file variable is used. See also: READNEXT and the section called "About Default File Variables" near the beginning of this section. When used with the TO clause, the item list is assigned to the specified select variable.

SEQ (*exp*)

Converts an ASCII character to its numeric equivalent. The inverse of CHAR.

SIN (*numexp*)

Calculates the sine of the angle specified in the numeric expression, and returns the result in degrees.

SLEEP {*number-of-seconds*}

-or-

SLEEP {*untiltime*}

Activates sleep function, placing process into an inactive mode until optional argument is satisfied. This statement terminates the current process' timeslice. Same as the RQM statement.

The sleep parameter may either be an integer number of seconds, or the desired time, in 24-hour (military) format (delimited by colons). If no argument is indicated, the process will sleep for one second.

Examples:

```
NAPTIME = 3600
SLEEP NAPTIME
UNTIL.WAKEUP.TIME = 8:00
SLEEP UNTIL.WAKEUP.TIME
```

SPACE (*numexp*)

Generates a string of spaces whose length is equal to the value of the numeric expression.

SQRT (*numexp*)

Calculates the positive square root of the number defined in the numeric expression.

STOP
-or-
STOP *errmsg#, "parameter"{, "parameter"..}*

Terminates program, but continues with PROC. The parameter{s} are passed to the error message handler and displayed with the message stored in the message number indicated by "errmsg#." See also: ABORT and ERRMSG.

Examples:

```
OPEN "INVOICES" TO INV.FILE ELSE STOP 201, "INVOICES"
READ CUST.ITEM FROM CUST.FILE, ID ELSE STOP 202,ID
```

STR *(exp,numexp)*

Generates a string of the variable expression repeated the number of times specified in numeric expression. See also: SYSTEM for retrieving the current device width for substituting as the numeric expression. For example:

```
PRINT STR("*",79)
```

Prints 79 "*" (asterisks) at the current cursor (or print head) position.

SUBROUTINE {*(argumentlist)*}
-or-
SUBROUTINE *subroutinename{(argumentlist)}*

Defines a program as an external subroutine. This statement must appear as the first line in an external subroutine, and all arguments defined in the optional argument list must be delimited by commas (,). See also: CALL. Some versions of Pick require that this statement appear as the first *executable* statement, meaning that the program could contain comment lines before the SUBROUTINE line.

All external subroutines should be cataloged prior to execution. Some versions of Pick do not require this as long as the CALLed program exists in the same file as the CALLing program.

SYSTEM *(exp)*

Interrogates the current value of pertinent system functions, as shown below: *The function differs between various Pick implementations.*

(0) Relates to last tape-handling error generated by the READT, WRITET, WEOF, or REWIND statements:

- 1 If not attached
- 2 Null variable
- 11 Record truncated

(1) Returns a 1 if the system printer is on, meaning that a PRINTER ON statement has

been issued or that the program was activated with a (P)option. Otherwise, a 0 is returned.

(2) Returns the page width as defined by the TERM command.

(3) Returns the page length as defined by the TERM command.

(4) Returns the number of lines remaining to print on the current page, based on the current terminal characteristics previously defined with the TERM command. See note below.

(5) Returns the current page number. SMA defines this as SYSTEM(6). See note below.

(6) Returns the current line counter. SMA defines this as SYSTEM(5). (Note: arguments 4,5,6 may only be used in conjunction with the HEADING and FOOTING statements within PICK/BASIC.)

(7) Returns the terminal type code, as defined by the TERM command.

(8) Returns the block size at which the tape was last attached. As of release 2.2, this function now works with streaming cartridge tape.

(9) Returns the current CPU millisecond count.

(10) Checks the current stack (STON) condition. Returns one (1) if the stack is on, or zero (0) if it is not on.

(11) Checks status of list function. Returns one (1) if a list is active or zero (0) if no list is active.

(12) Returns system time in milliseconds.

(13) Forces RQM (terminates timeslice) and returns a 1.

(14) Returns the number of bytes awaiting input in the input buffer.

(15) Returns verb option{s} in effect.

(16) Returns the number of levels of nested EXECUTE statements.

(17) Returns the ERRMSG item-ids from previous EXECUTE statement, separated by attribute marks.

(100) Returns release level, version, and version date on Pick XT and AT only.

TAN (*numexp*)

Calculates the tangent of the angle specified in degrees by numeric expression.

THEN/ELSE

In-line initiator. See the section at the end of PICK/BASIC on the THEN/ELSE construct.

TIME ( )

Returns the current system time in internal format. Internal time is represented as an integer number indicating the number of seconds past midnight. The parentheses following the function are required, and never contain any arguments. See also: DATE ( ).

TIMEDATE ( )

Returns the current system time and date in external format (hh:mm:ss dd mmm yyyy). The parentheses following the function are required, and never contain any arguments. See also: TIME ( ) and DATE ( ).

TRIM (*strexp*)

Removes all leading and trailing blanks from string expression, and leaves one blank wherever more than one blank was embedded within the string.

Example:

```
STRING = "   PICK   POCKET   GUIDE   "
STRING = TRIM(STRING)
```

After the TRIM, "STRING" would contain: "PICK POCKET GUIDE."

UNLOCK

-or-

UNLOCK *locknumber-exp*

Resets an execution lock, in the range 0 to 63. If no locknumber is specified, all locks set by the program are unlocked. See also: LOCK. Some implementations now support up to 128 locks.

UNTIL

In-line initiator in a FOR..NEXT statement. Multiline initiator in a LOOP statement. See also: FOR..NEXT and LOOP..WHILE.

WEOF {THEN *statement*{*s*}} ELSE *statement*{*s*}

Writes an end-of-file mark to tape. See the section on the THEN/ELSE construct. The ELSE condition is taken if the tape is not ready or attached. As of release 2.2, this statement now works with streaming cartridge tape.

WHILE

In-line initiator in a FOR..NEXT statement. Multiline initiator in a LOOP statement. See also: FOR..WHILE and LOOP..WHILE.

WRITE *arrayvar* ON {*filevar,*}*idexp*

Writes the item from the dynamic array specified in arrayvar into the specified file, using the item-id specified in the item-id expression. If the file variable parameter is not specified, the default file variable is used. See also: WRITEU and the section called "About Default File Variables" near the beginning of this section.

WRITET *exp* {THEN *statement*{*s*}} ELSE *statement*{*s*}

Writes the value of the expression to tape. The ELSE condition is taken if the tape is not ready or attached. See the section on the THEN/ELSE construct. See also: T-ATT in the TCL section. As of release 2.2, this statement now works with streaming cartridge tape.

WRITEU *arrayvar* ON {*filevar,*} *idexp*

Writes the item from the dynamic array specified in arrayvar into the specified file, using the item-id specified in the item-id expression. If the file variable parameter is not specified, the default file variable is used.

See also: WRITE and the section called "About Default File Variables" near the beginning of this section.

The WRITEU statement is identical to the WRITE statement, except that the *group* remains locked. See also: RELEASE.

WRITEV *exp* ON {*filevar,* }*idexp,attrexp*

Writes the value of the expression into the attribute designated in the attribute expression parameter, using the item-id specified in the item-id expression parameter. If the file variable parameter is omitted, the default file variable is used. This statement causes a READ to occur prior to the WRITEV, which accounts for the reason that this is inefficient. See also: WRITEVU and the section called "About Default File Variables" near the beginning of this section. Using a value of "−1" as the attrexp causes the string to be appended at the end of the item. Using 0 (zero) as the attrexp inserts the string at the front (top) of the item.

WRITEVU *exp* ON {*filevar,* }*idexp,attrexp*

Writes the value of the expression into the attribute designated in the attribute expression parameter, using the item-id specified in the item-id expression parameter. If the file variable parameter is omitted, the default file variable is used. This statement causes a READ to occur prior to the WRITEV, which accounts for the reason that this is inefficient. See also: WRITEV and the section called "About Default File Variables" near the beginning of this section. The WRITEVU statement is identical to the WRITEV statement, except that the *group* remains locked. See also the RELEASE statement.

XTD (*exp*)

Converts value in expression from hexadecimal to decimal. See also: DTX. As of release 3.1, this function now returns a 0 (zero) instead of a null value.

PICK/BASIC user exits

User exits are special functions that make direct references to assembler routines known as *modes*. They were added to the system to fulfill needs outside the standard boundaries of the PICK System prior to being replaced by extensions to the system. User exits have always been dangerous, and as long as they remain, will continue to be dangerous. EXTREME caution is advised in using them. *Caveat Emptor*.

The general form of user-exits:

```
... = OCONV (argument,"user.exit")
```

Example:

WHO = OCONV("","U50BB)

In other words, the user exits may be used in an assignment (on the right side of an equal sign) or after a PRINT or CRT statement.

Many of the functions performed by user exits can now be achieved by using the EXECUTE statement with the appropriate TCL command or PICK/BASIC statement.

U0079 Returns the same output as the "where" verb from TCL (PIB status and return stack information)

U014A Reads absolute sector

INPUT:
DA = drv.index<vm>blk.no<AM> mode {<vm> xlt1<vm> xlt2<AM>}
where:
drv.index = 1 for drive A, 2 for drive B, 3 for drive C, 4 for drive D
blk.no = logical block number
mode = 1 for convert ASCII data to hex data, 2 for transform and prefix character, 3 for transform and delete character, 4 for transform, prefix and drop MSB, 5 for transform, delete and drop MSB
xlt1/xlt2 = translation table as follows: hex {SVM hex}
where hex = 2 byte hexadecimal value

OUTPUT:
DA = status
Where:
status = '00' if successful, 'xx' (2 hex digits), otherwise fail

Compatibility: **Pick 3.1**

U014B Writes absolute sector.

INPUT:
DA = drv.index <vm>blk.no <AM>mode
where:
drv.index = 1 for drive A, 2 for drive B, 3 for drive C, 4 for drive D
blk.no = logical block number
mode = 1 for convert for hex data to ASCII data : DB = user.exit <AM>sector
where:
user.exit = 'U014B'
sector = hex 1024 image for binary 512 byte sector
OUTPUT UT:

DA = status
where:
status = '00' if successful, 'xx' (2 hex digits), otherwise fail.

Please note that the previous two user exits are included verbatim from the preliminary documentation from Pick Systems on release 3.1B. If they are unclear, please call Pick Systems for clarification.

Compatibility: **Pick 3.1**

U038E Soundex function

Example:

```
A 'DEMONS'
A = OCONV(A,'U0138')
A will contain the value D552.
```

Compatibility: **Pick 3.1**

U1072 Activates "SORT" from PICK/BASIC. Returns a sorted array. Each element to be sorted must be separated by attribute marks.

U10B9 Returns the international currency value of a domestic currency value. The BP file in the SYSPROG account contains a program called CURRENCY which demonstrates the use of this user exit.

Compatibility: **Pick 3.1**

U138E Converts American currency to foreign currency: '$' to '#', ',' to '.' and '.' to ','.

Compatibility: **Pick 3.1**

U138E;n Converts American currency to foreign currency and the '$' sign to the value specified in "n." Also converts ',' to '.' and '.' to ','.

Compatibility: **Pick 3.1**

U238E Converts foreign currency to American currency: '#' to '$', ',' to '.' and '.' to ','.

Compatibility: **Pick 3.1**

U238E;n Converts foreign currency to American currency and the money character to '$' from the value specified in "n": Also converts ',' to '.' and '.' to ','.

Compatibility: **Pick 3.1**

U2079 Returns the domestic currency value of an international currency value. The BP file in the SYSPROG account contains a program called CURRENCY which demonstrates the use of this user exit.

Compatibility: **Pick 3.1**

U2117 Returns information about the process running as a dynamic array variable. If the process is not logged on, attributes 1 and 2 are empty.

Example:

```
A = OCONV(0,'U2117')
A<1> = PCB in hex and PIB status
A<2> = Return stack separated by value marks
A<3> = 0 if the last process, 2 if current process, 1 if neither
```

Compatibility: **Pick 3.1**

U21A3 Opens a file with ICONV and reads the next attribute with OCONV. If the open is successful, the value 1 (one) is returned otherwise the value 0 (zero) is returned.

Example:

```
A = ICONV ('BP FDISK','U213A')
Y = OCONV ('','U213A'')
```

Compatibility: **Pick 3.1**

U4117 Returns the PCB in hex for the current line.

Compatibility: **Pick 3.1**

U5117 Returns the PCB in hex for line 0 (zero).

Compatibility: **Pick 3.1**

U3060 Returns 8 hexadecimal characters as a value from supplied string. Used by the PASSWORD program to encrypt passwords.

U3070 Returns the PCB for the current line.

Compatibility: **Pick 3.1**

U3079 Returns PCB-FID in hex in an ICONV function or the line (port) number in an OCONV function.

U307A Sleeps until specified 24-hour (military) time. See also: SLEEP or RQM. Suggestion: don't use this. This statement is documented so that you can replace this with a valid statement if it is encountered in your code.

U313C Returns the floppy drive and density if attached.

Example:

```
A = ICONV ('','U313C'')
```

Variable A will contain density and drive separated by an attribute mark. Drive values are either A or B. Density values are: 1 for 360K media, 2 for 1.2mb media, 3 for 720K media or 4 for 1.4mb media.

Compatibility: **Pick 3.1**

U407A Sleeps for specified number of seconds. See also: SLEEP or RQM.

U50BB Returns the same output as the "WHO" command VERB from TCL (port-number and current account name).

U60BB Returns the current account name.

Compatibility: **Pick 3.1**

U9116 Logon a specified port.

Example:

```
A = OCONV('6,SYSPROG','U9116')
```

Compatibility: **Pick 3.1**

UA116 Logoff a specified port.

```
A =OCONV (6,'UA116')
```

Compatibility: **Pick 3.1**

UF070 Returns the number of physical serial ports.

Compatibility: **Pick 2.2** and higher

UB0BA Peeks into memory.

Example:

```
A = ''
A = '0000';* this is the segment of memory
A = '09E6';* this is the offset into the segment
A = '00';* dummy
DATUM = OCONV(A,'UBOBA')
```

DATUM will contain the datum stored at memory location 0000:09E6.

Compatibility: **Pick 3.1**

UC0BA Pokes into memory.

Example:

```
A = ''
A = '0000';* this is the segment of memory
A = '09E6';* this is the offset into the segment
A = X'nn';* this is the data written to memory
DATUM = OCONV(A,'UCOBA')
```

DATUM is now the dummy variable. The memory location 0000:09E6 will now contain the data in A.

Warning: if you plan to modify a memory location then be sure you READ and display it. This location, as with most locations, must have the data OR'd or AND'd. This location contains Post/Wait, PS/2, Extended Memory, and SCT recognition bits.

Compatibility: **Pick 3.1**

PICK/BASIC: The THEN/ELSE construct

The THEN/ELSE construct and its implications on multiline statements. The following statements make use of the PICK/BASIC "THEN/ELSE" construct:

IF	OPEN	READV
LOCATE	READ	READVU
LOCK	READNEXT	REWIND
MATREAD	READT	WEOF
MATREADU	READU	WRITET

Some Pick implementations have added the THEN/ELSE construct to other statements, such as INPUT, WRITE, CLEARFILE, and DELETE. Consult your system manuals for more details.

Each of these statements are referred to as initiators of the THEN or ELSE clause that succeeds them.

The possible syntactic structures are:

1) *initiator* THEN *statements* ELSE *statements*
2) *initiator* THEN *statements*
3) *initiator* ELSE *statements*

When THEN and ELSE clauses are both present, the THEN clause may be considered to be the initiator of the ELSE clause. All other characteristics are identical, except that an ELSE clause may succeed a THEN clause. For simplicity's sake, this text will cover only the case of the THEN clause.

Within the THEN clause, the THEN token is the initiator, which requires a terminator. The clause may exist on one or more than one line. The nature of the terminator varies between these cases.

Single-line form

If the THEN clause is complete in one physical line, its terminator is a carriage return or an ELSE token.

initiator THEN *statement{s}* <cr>
-or-
initiator THEN *statement{s}* ELSE *statement{s}* <cr>
-or-
initiator ELSE *statement{s}* <cr>

The form for the single-line clause:

THEN *statement; statement;* ... ;<cr>

-or-
THEN *statement*; *statement*; ...;ELSE<cr>

The syntax of the ELSE clause is the same as that of the THEN clause, except that it may not be followed by another ELSE clause.

Multiline form

If the THEN clause spans more than one physical line, the THEN token must immediately be followed by an EOL (End-of-Line) character. This character may be either a <cr> or a ; (semicolon). In this case, the clause is terminated by END preceded by an EOL character.

```
initiator THEN<cr>
      statement{s}<cr>
      statement{s}<cr>
      statement{s}<cr>
END
```

There must be one or more statements between the THEN and its terminator. If there are several statements, they must be separated by EOL characters. If the THEN clause is the one-physical-line clause, the EOL character must be a semicolon. If the THEN clause spans more than one physical line, the EOL characters may be either (or both) <cr>'s or semicolons.

The form of the multiline clause:

THEN EOL *statement* EOL *statement* EOL EOL END EOL
-or-
THEN EOL *statement* EOL *statement* EOL EOL END ELSE EOL
statement EOL *statement* END EOL

In this case, each EOL character may be either a <cr> or a semicolon, which means that a multiline clause may be contained in either one or more than one physical line.

This case will normally appear as:

```
THEN<CR>
            statement<cr>
            statement<cr>
            statement<cr>
END<cr>
```

For program clarity, the statements are indented from the beginning of the initiator, and the THEN or END ELSE are outdented to the beginning of the initiator.

Multiple END statements

Multiline statements may have more than one END statement. The END statement then becomes the initiator for the ELSE condition as follows:

```
initiator THEN <cr>
     statement<cr>
     statement<cr>
     statement<cr>
END ELSE<cr>
     statement<cr>
     statement<cr>
     statement<cr>
END
```

Multiple END ELSE sequences may be used, provided that each ends with an END statement.

5
PROC

About compatibility with SMA standards

Everything in this section except for the (-n) functions of the "T" command is compatible with the SMA standard document 501, dated March 1987.

About logon PROCs

A logon PROC is one that starts automatically upon logging on to the system. This is how most systems whisk the user away into a menu when they log on. The way it works is that after the user has provided a valid account name and optionally the password, the MD of the account is checked to see if there is a PROC with the same name as the account. If such a PROC exists, it starts up automatically. Obviously, if no such PROC exists, control is transferred to TCL.

While logon PROCs are optional, they are useful for issuing several TCL commands, such as TERM-TYPE and SET-SYM.

PROC linkages

({DICT} *filename* {*itemname*})

-or-

({DICT} *filename* {*itemname*}) {label}

Transfers control to PROC in specified *filename*. If no *itemname* is specified, the default *itemname* is the value in the current position of the input buffer. Control is not returned to the calling PROC.

The *label* parameter indicates the statement label number where execution should begin.

[{DICT} {*filename*} {*itemname*}]

-or-

[{DICT} *filename* {*itemname*}] {*label*}

This example is like the former linkage, but control returns to the calling PROC upon completion. If no itemname is specified, the itemname defaults to the value in the current position of the input buffer.

Examples:

```
[PROCS EXAMPLE1]
```

Transfers control to 'EXAMPLE1' in the file called 'PROCS'. Control returns to the next line upon completion.

```
[PROCS EXAMPLE2] 25
```

Transfers control to 'EXAMPLE2' in the file called 'PROCS', then begins execution at statement label 25. Control returns to the next line upon completion.

```
[ ] 150
```

Transfers control to statement label 150 in the current PROC and begins execution.

```
(PROCS)
```

Transfers control to the PROCS file, using the item-id indicated in the input buffer.

PROC commands

+number

Adds value of decimal number to the current parameter of the presently active input buffer.

−number

Subtracts value of decimal number from the current parameter of the presently active input buffer.

A {*surroundchar*} {{(*parnum*} {,*charcount*{)}}

Moves data from the specified parameter number to the currently active output buffer. The "surroundchar" parameter specifies the character to place before and after the string, after it is moved. The "charcount" parameter specifies the number of characters to move.

Examples:

```
A"1
```

Moves contents of input buffer one to the currently active output buffer, surrounded by double quotes.

```
A(2,999)
```

Moves the second through 999th (or whenever it runs out of characters) to the currently active output buffer.

B

Decrements input pointer by one.

BO

Decrements output pointer by one.

C {text}

Comment; all data on line ignored by PROC processor.

D{{(}*parnum*} {*numbercharacters*{)}}{+}

Displays contents of the current parameter in the currently active input buffer. Default is currently active input buffer.

If the optional parameter number is specified, only the contents of the specified input buffer are displayed.

The D command, followed by a 0 (zero), displays the entire current input buffer. The + character suppresses the automatic linefeed at the end of the display.

F

Increments input pointer by one.

GO *statement label*

-or-

G *statement label*

-or-

GO A{*parnum*}

Transfers control to specified statement label. The first two forms transfer control *directly*, meaning that the statement label is explicitly stated. The latter form allows an *indirect* transfer according to the value of the label as extracted from a parameter in the input buffer.

Hstring{<}

Moves specified text string to currently active output buffer. The < character is the equivalent of a carriage return, and must follow each parameter when moving multiple parameters to the secondary output buffer (following the STON command).

IF {#} E {*operator* ERRMSG*number*} *command*

Tests for specified ERRMSG number. If true, performs specified PROC command.

Example:

```
IF E = 401 XNo items were selected...
```

IF {#} S *command*

Tests for active list. May be used after a SELECT, SSELECT, QSELECT, or GET-LIST command.

IF {#} A{*parnum*} {,n} {*operator*{*matchstr*}} *command*

Tests contents of buffer specified in "A{parnum}" expression with any logical or pattern matching operator, and performs the specified PROC command if successful. The optional "n" argument allows only the specified number of characters.

Logical Operators:

=	Equal to
#	Not equal to
<	Less than
>	Greater than
[	Less than or equal to
]	Greater than or equal to

The # character tests for the absence of the expression, when used left of the "A" command.

Pattern Matching Operators: (*Note:* the pattern matchstrings must be enclosed in parentheses):

(nA)	Accepts "n" alphabetic characters only.
(nN)	Accepts "n" numeric characters only.
(nX)	Accepts "n" of any characters.
('string')	Accepts literal string.

The "n" parameter in the pattern matchstring specifies the length of the match operator field. A length specification of zero (0) allows variable length input.

Examples:

```
IF A (3N'-'2N'-'4N) OInvalid SS#.
IF A = XXDone.
IF A = (0N) GO 10
IF A1 = QUIT X PROC Terminated Voluntarily
IF A1,1 = Q X PROC Terminated Voluntarily
IF # A1 GO 10
IF A1 = (0N) GO A1
```

IH\

Removes the current parameter from the currently active input buffer and replaces it with a null value. If the pointer is in the middle of a parameter, the parameter is truncated, starting at the current position.

IH\

Inserts a new null parameter in front of the current parameter in the currently active input buffer. If the pointer is in the middle of a parameter, the parameter is truncated starting at the current position and a new null parameter is added after the truncation.

IH *string*

Inputs data string into active input buffer.

IP {*promptcharacter*}

Inputs data from terminal into active input buffer. The default prompt character is a colon (:).

IS {*promptcharacter*}

Inputs data into secondary input buffer. The default prompt character is a colon (:).

IT

Inputs data from tape label into primary input buffer.

As of release 2.2, two responses are now available to the PROC "IT" (Input from Tape) command. They are C to continue or O to override character.

O {*text*} {+}

Outputs literal text to terminal at next available line on screen. Thc + character suppresses the automatic linefeed/carriage return after output.

P

Processes command currently in output buffer.

PH

Processes command currently in output buffer, and suppresses ("hushes") all terminal output from PROC command.

PP

Prints output buffers prior to processing.

PW

Prints output buffer prior to processing, prompts with a question mark, and waits for user response before execution.

Valid Responses:

G or <cr> Go. Proceed with process.
S Skip. Proceeds with next command in PROC.
X (or N) Cancel. Returns control to TCL.

PX

Processes command in output buffer, stops execution of PROC upon completion.

Combining options:

Several of the above "processing" options may be combined, as shown in the following examples.

PHX

Process, hush output, terminate.

PWH

Print, wait, process, and hush.

PQ

Required on first line of every PROC.

RI {*startparameter*}

Resets both input buffers to null.

Use of "startparameter" resets to null all parameters following specified parameter and the entire secondary input buffer.

RO

Resets both output buffers to null.

S{*parnum*}

"Sets" the input pointer to specified parameter number; activates specified parameter number as currently active input buffer.

SP

Selects the primary input buffer, and positions the pointer to the beginning of the input buffer.

SS

Selects the secondary input buffer, and positions the pointer to the beginning of the secondary input buffer.

STOFF

-or-

ST OFF

Selects primary output buffer and directs subsequent output to primary output buffer.

STON

-or-

ST ON

Selects secondary output buffer and directs subsequent output to secondary output buffer.

T {*function,function,...*} {+}

Directs output to terminal and controls special terminal display functions:

Functions of the T Command:

+	Suppresses carriage return after output
B	Rings terminal bell
C	Clears terminal screen
(column,row)	Outputs value at column and row coordinates
In	Outputs ASCII value of the integer character indicated by "n"
Xx	Outputs HEX/ASCII value of the hexadecimal character indicated by "x"
"text"	Outputs literal text.

Compatibility: **Pick SMA**

Special @ control functions:

(−1) Clears the screen and positions the cursor to home position (0,0)
(−2) Positions the cursor to the home position (0,0)
(−3) Clears to the end of screen from the current cursor position
(−4) Clears to the end of the line from the current cursor position

Compatibility of above: **Pick SMA**

The following are compatible only with generic Pick and the AT/XT releases:

(−5) Enables the blink function
(−6) Disables the blink function
(−7) Enables the protect function
(−8) Disables the protect function
(−9) Moves the cursor position back one position
(−10) Moves the cursor up one line

The following additional control functions have been added to the T command on the Pick XT and AT releases:

(−11) Activates screen protect
(−12) Deactivates screen protect
(−13) Activates reverse video
(−14) Deactivates reverse video
(−15) Activates underlining
(−16) Deactivates underlining
(−17) Beginning of the input buffer

The following control functions may only be used on Port 0 (zero), equipped with a color graphics display on the Pick XT or AT:

Background Color Controls:

(−33) White
(−34) Brown
(−35) Magenta
(−36) Red
(−37) Cyan
(−38) Green
(−39) Blue
(−40) Black

Foreground Color Controls (Full Intensity):

(−41) White
(−42) Brown
(−43) Magenta
(−44) Red
(−45) Cyan
(−46) Green
(−47) Blue
(−48) Black

Foreground Color Controls (Half Intensity):

(−57) White
(−58) Brown
(−59) Magenta
(−60) Red
(−61) Cyan
(−62) Green
(−63) Blue
(−64) Black

Additional Control Functions:

(−89) Activates monochrome display unit in 80 by 25 black and white mode
(−93) Activates color graphics monitor in 80 by 25 color mode
(−94) Activates color graphics monitor in 80 by 25 black and white mode

U*entrypoint modeid*

Transfers control to user assembly code subroutine. Must be 4-digit hexadecimal number. Note: the following "infact" user modes have unofficially been part of the Pick system for many years and because they are not "official", no support is usually provided for them. Note also that if you are not extremely careful in using these, you can easily crash your machine and possibly do harm to your data. *We assume no liability for errors and/or omissions, and have recorded these for posterity's sake. Caveat Emptor.*

PROC User Exits

U01A6

Used for cursor control. Now made obsolete by the "T" command.

Format:

```
U01A6
control code{,control code ...}
(continuation of PROC)
```

Control codes:

(col,row)	Positions cursor at specified column and row
B	Rings bell
C	Clears screen
In	Outputs integer value of "n"
Xx	Outputs hexadecimal character "x"
"text"	Outputs literal text

U01AD

Retrieves a value from an attribute of an item in a file.

Format:

```
U01AD
filename itemname amcexp output-code
error-return line
(continuation of PROC)
```

Output-codes:

A	Outputs to alternate output buffer
P	Outputs to primary input buffer
S	Outputs to current output buffer
T	Outputs to terminal
V	Verifies that file exists, no output
VA	Verifies non-null attribute

Note: this function allows for indirect references to values from the input and output buffers by using the following special symbols:

% Current input buffer value
# Current output buffer value

Example of direct reference:

```
PQ
U01AD
CONTROL-FILE CO.NAME 1 S
XCan't find CO.NAME or CONTROL-FILE
```

This example reads attribute 1 of the item called "CO.NAME" in the file called "CONTROL-FILE" and places it in the current output buffer.

Example of indirect reference:

```
PQ
U01AD
%2 %3 %4 P
XSomething went wrong...
DO
```

This example reads the attribute number as defined in the fourth location of the input buffer, using the item-id from the third location and the filename from the second location.

U11AD

Retrieves multiple values from an attribute of an item in a file. See also: U01AD.

U01B8

Retrieves and optionally formats a value from a file or a text string.

U01BC

"n"-way branch.

U11BC

Pads value in secondary input buffer with zeros (0's).

Format:

```
U11BC
number-of-zeros
(continuation of PROC)
```

U218D

Disables break key.

U21A2

Functions exactly like the "RO" command, resetting the Primary (and Secondary) output buffers.

U21AD

Retrieves multiple values from an attribute of an item in a file, without advancing the multivalue counter. See also: U01AD.

U21BC

Deletes all entries, or last entry, from output buffer.

Format:

```
U21BC
condition-flag
```

When condition flag returns a zero (0), all entries are deleted. When one (1) is returned, just the last entry is deleted.

U307A

Functions exactly like the (TCL) command, "SLEEP untiltime", instructing the process to sleep until the specified military time.

U318D

Enables break key.

U31AD

Returns current portnumber.

Format:

```
U31AD
output-code
(continuation of PROC)
```

See also: U01AD for explanation of output codes.

U31BC

Subroutine call.

U407A

Functions exactly like the (TCL) command, "SLEEP numberseconds," instructing the process to sleep for the specified number of seconds.

U41AD

Replaces string in the primary input buffer.

Format:

```
U41AD
string
(continuation of PROC)
```

U41BC

Subroutine recall.

U50BB

Functions exactly like the (TCL) command, "WHO", returning the current portnumber and account name.

U51BC

Subroutine return.

U61BC

Functions exactly like the "PH" command, disabling terminal output from the process.

P91BC

Transfers to another PROC, without affecting current input buffer(s).

Format:

```
Hprocname
P91BC
```

Note: this user-exit *must* follow the letter "P" (to Process).

UA1BC

Moves entries from the current pointer position of the input buffer to the end of the input buffer.

UE070

Returns the current reel number to the active input buffer. (Added in release 2.2).

UDO7O

Returns "WHO" output to active input buffer.

X {*text*}

Terminates PROC and outputs text on terminal. Also used to designate the end of an internal and external PROC subroutines.

6
Spooler

About spooler options

Most spooler commands allow options. Sometimes these options have numeric arguments. In many cases, valid combinations of options are available, but need to be made clear to the options interpreter. Generally, it's a good idea to separate options with blanks when options contain numbers, as in the following example:

```
SP-ASSIGN HS F1 3
```

This example assigns for hold file output, to formqueue 1, with 3 copies. Notice that spooler options do not have to be enclosed in parentheses like options with other TCL commands. There is, however, an important rule to keep in mind: *if numeric options are within parentheses, parameters outside of the parentheses will be ignored!*

Spooler commands

:STARTSPOOLER {(*option*{s})}

Initializes spooler and returns to normal operation.

Options:

- n Starts spooler process on specified portnumber. (Used primarily by developers to test the spooler code.)
- C Clears all but permanent file control blocks (hold files). Does *not* return space to overflow table.
- D Used in conjunction with the "n" option above to enable the debugger on the line.
- I Initializes and DESTROYS all spooler queue entries. Does *not* return space to overflow table.
- L Links workspace for inactive lines.

LISTABS {*options*}

Outputs current spooler assignment parameters for every port on the system. See also: SP-ASSIGN for interpretation of the displayed status codes.

LISTPEQS {*options*}

Outputs list of spooled entries.

Options:

'acctname'	Displays spooler entries created by specified account name.
n	Integer number, in the range (0-600), indicating the spooler entry to display.
n-n	Specifies beginning and ending spooler entries to display.
A	Outputs the status of all reports created from current account.
C	Outputs count of spooled entries and total storage (frames) used.
E	Outputs print file absolute location.
F	Outputs status of jobs queued for output in queue order (0-125).
H	Outputs hold files only.
L	Outputs active and deleted reports.
P	Directs output to system printer, via the spooler.

Status codes:

A	Available
C	Closed
G	Align
H	Hold file
I	Immediate
L	Locked
N	No close
O	Currently being output
P	Printer
R	Requested
S	Spooled
T	Tape
X	Aborted

LISTPTR {*options*}

Outputs the printer control block status for all printers.

Options:

n{-n}	Specifies beginning and ending printer numbers.
N	Activates NOPAGE function on output to terminal.
P	Directs output to system printer, via the spooler.

SP-ASSIGN {*options*}

Sets spooler output assignment for current process.

Note: an SP-ASSIGN command with NO options resets the assignment back to the default state. This *must* be done prior to using the SP-EDIT command on hold files when attempting to de-spool.

Options:

- n Integer number in the range (1-125) indicating the number of copies (Default = one).
- ? Outputs resulting setting, or current setting when entered alone.
- C Activates *choke* function. Choke means that the spooler will require no more than 20 frames to print the job, and will *recycle* the 20 frames. Must be used with an I option, and may not be used with the H option.
- Fn Directs output to formqueue "n", where "n" is an integer number in the range (0-125).
- H Directs output to hold file {s}.
- I Instant print. Begins output (assuming device is ready) as soon as the first frame of output is completed.
- M Suppresses "Entry n" message.
- O Indicates to leave file open upon completion of process, which allows placing multiple print jobs in one physical spooler entry. See also: SP-OPEN and SP-CLOSE. To close the entry, use the SP-ASSIGN command without options.
- Rn Initiates the print file "n", where "n" is an integer number in the range (0-125), for use with BASIC "PRINT ON" statements.
- S Suppresses printing on the system printer. Normally used with H option.
- T Attaches tape unit as output device.

Note: the "n", "Fn", "Rn", and "Qn" options *must* be separated by a blank from any other options present in the command line.

Examples of the SP-ASSIGN command:

```
SP-ASSIGN HS?
SP-ASSIGN 13 F2?
```

SP-CLOSE

Closes the currently open spooler entry. See also: SP-OPEN. Entries are automatically closed if a LOGTO, OFF, or SP-ASSIGN (without an R option) is issued.

SP-EDIT {*options*}

Accesses spooler entries for processing or deletion. When options are omitted, allows access to all entries generated from current account.

Options:

- 'acctname' Accesses entries generated from the specified account.
- n{-n} Integer number, in the range (0-600), of spooler entry, or beginning and ending hold spooler entries.
- D Delete {s} hold file{s}.

F{b{-e}}	Integer number, in the range (0-125), specifying the beginning and ending form queue{s} to access.
H	Suppresses tape label when directing output to tape.
L	Activates "look" function, and displays first 500 bytes of spooler entries.
MD	Manager (also called "magic") priority. Delete{s} spooler entries.
MS	Manager priority. Spool{s} spooler entries.
N	Activates NOPAGE function when spooling to terminal.
O	When used with the L option, allows looking at spooler entries already being output.
P	Directs hold file to currently assigned printer.
R	Changes output parameter settings to currently assigned parameter{s}.
T{W}	Directs output to tape. W indicates to wait for tape to be readied, if not yet already.
U	Accesses all spooled entries generated from current process.
V	Converts hold file to data file, without trimming blanks and blank lines.

Examples:

```
SP-EDIT MSP
SP-EDIT MSP1-5
SP-EDIT MD1-10
SP-EDIT MUD
```

SP-KILL {*options*}

Stops output of currently active spooler entry on specified printer.

Options:

n{-n}	Integer number, in the range (0-19) indicating which printer to stop.
A	Stops spooler entry or entries created from current account.
B	All spooler entries.
Dn{-n}	Deletes printer{s}. The beginning and ending printer number{s} must be in the range (0-19). Note: the maximum number of printers will vary between various PICK-class systems.
F{b{-e}	Returns spooler entries to available hold file status. The beginning and ending parameter{s} must be in the range (0-600).
N	Suppresses abort message on output when directed to a printer.
O	Unlinks spooler entry already being output.

Examples:

```
SP-KILL 1
SP-KILL OF7
```

SP-OPEN

Specifies that spooler is to leave the spooler entry open after completion of the process. See also: SP-CLOSE and SP-ASSIGN O.

SP-STATUS {*options*}

Displays status of all spooler-controlled devices.

Options:

n{-n} Integer number indicating the beginning and ending printer number{s} to display.
B Outputs status of all printers.
P Directs output to system printer, via the spooler.

SP-TAPEOUT {*options*}

Retrieves reports previously spooled to magnetic tape, and outputs to current device assignment.

Options:

A Converts EBCDIC format to ASCII format.
L Allows output of tapes created with each line being treated as a tape record.
U Converts all lowercase characters to uppercase.

STARTPTR *printer#, formqueue#, #ejectpages, printer specification,* {A} {(S{X*linecount*} {(D)}

Activates and initializes parallel or serial printer.

The printer specification is composed of two parameters; the type (P or S), and the address or location of the device.

The letter A may follow the printer specification. When used, it allows for forms alignment on the newly started printer.

Printer types:

P Parallel. This requires special hardware. Consult your vendor to find out if more than one parallel printer is supported.
S Serial. Can go in any serial I/O port.

Examples of printer specifications:

P0 Parallel printer 0.
S12 Serial printer on port 12.

Options:

D Enables debugger on line. (Used primarily by developers to test spooler code.)
S Suppresses first form feed on serial printer.
Xn Specifies the number of lines per page for serial printers.

Examples:

```
STARTPTR 0,0,0,P0
STARTPTR 1,1,0,S12
```

STOPPTR *{options}*

Stops the specified printer at the end of the current print job. The default printer is printer number zero (0).

Options:

n Integer number of printer to stop, in the range (0-19).
B Stops all printers.

7
Pick PC-AT

This section is specifically for users of the Pick System on the PC-AT, PC-XT, or compatibles. The documentation included in this section is current through release 3.1.

Release 3.1 features and enhancements summary

Miscellaneous enhancements

- Intel 286/386/486 extended memory supported with improved performance up to 16 megabytes
- Intel 486 implementations support added
- New menu-driven installation procedure
- Ability to select/override serial drivers
- System upgrade option added
- Serial I/O problems with extra ports at boot-up addressed
- Monitor debugger problems addressed
- Parallel printer problems addressed
- UPGRADER account added to allow administrative system upgrades
- PICK-SETUP account added to allow administrative system initialization
- Pick User Reference Manual updated
- R83 ASSEMBLER account and manual updated
- Archive 409 60/150MB external tape supported for PS/2
- Digiboard 4-port card supported for PS/2
- POWER-OFF now handles users/spooled items correctly
- REBOOT procedure now updates SYSTEM-CONFIG,ACC file to indicate controlled system shutdown and waits one minute after flushing buffers before continuing with procedure to allow time for disk caching controllers to flush
- Dictionary of ACC file now contains location items for 33 users
- All incorrectly sized files in SYSPROG were resized
- ERRMSG file has been updated for all new verbs, PROCs, and programs
- MSG command now checks parameter ranges and unlocks message (ABS) frame when aborted

- Num Lock key enabled as default
- Resident ABS buffers expanded to 32K
- ABS buffers 900 through 1023 reserved by and for Pick Systems
- ABS buffers 710 through 770 reserved for VIA Systems
- Monitor and Virtual embedded messages updated to be user-friendly
- Hard disk scan added to write and verify sectors with patterns X'00'/X'FF'/X'AA'/X'55'/X'CC' to find bad sectors more efficiently

3.1 PICK/BASIC enhancements

- Alphanumeric statement labels now supported in PICK/BASIC
- International currency format conversion user-exit added to PICK/BASIC
- SOUNDEX user-exit added to PICK/BASIC
- BLIST program/command added to format PICK/BASIC programs
- CATALOG command no longer requires the source code to be present
- DTX and XTD functions now return 0 (zero) instead of null, EQUATE statements now allow negative numbers
- LOCKED clause no longer locks a group when used with the READ statement; Pick System notes that the LOCKED clause should only be used with READU, READVU, or MATREADU statements
- READ and READV statements will now read a locked group
- RND function has been updated to use the "minimal standards multiplicative congruent generator", (aka Lehmer generator)
- User exit '00B9', added for SOUNDEX
- User exit '10B9', added for converting international currency format to US currency format
- User exit '20B9' added for converting USA currency format to international currency format
- User exit '014A' added to read absolute sectors
- User exit '014B' added to write absolute sectors

3.1 ACCESS enhancements

- S option added to suppress number of items counted message
- H option changed to suppress only header and not the item count
- Item translations now truncate at 512 characters

3.1 Spooler enhancements

- Parallel printer drivers now use error status bits for more reliability
- S option added to STARTPTR command to suppress top of page
- :STARTSPOOLER no longer aborts with numeric parameters

3.1 Tape enhancements

- :SET DMA command added to redefine default SCT DMA channel
- ACCOUNT-SAVE command now allows account name to be specified on command line;
- RESTORE-ACCOUNTS command/program now restores all accounts on save media

- SAVE verb now defaults to LABEL EOF LABEL DATA format. Some tape units will not restore saved data in EOF LABEL EOF DATA format.
- SCT driver modified to setup/enable DMA to prevent DMA problems
- SCT drivers updated to wait longer for handshaking delays
- SCT drivers will not disable IRQ 5; tape IRQ is enabled if a SCT is identified and remains on while the system is in use
- M option added to SET-SCT command to use the maximum number of memory buffers for improved tape reliability and streaming
- SET-SCT command now verifies parameters used with command
- T-ATT command now verifies parameters used with command
- End of reel restore problem corrected to continue with next reel
- T-LOAD no longer overrides D-pointers
- V option added to T-LOAD for verifying T-DUMP media
- T-VERIFY command added to verify integrity of FILE-SAVE or ACCOUNT-SAVE media

3.1 TCL enhancements

- :FILES command now handles spooled items properly
- BREAK-KEY-ON and BREAK-KEY-OFF verbs added
- BUFFERS program/command added to display system virtual buffer usage
- CL verb added for compatibility with Advanced Pick, same as COPY-LIST
- CHECK-ACCOUNT and CHECK-FILES commands added to perform "dummy" saves
- COLDSTART modified to verify system integrity and to ensure that system was properly shutdown prior to proceeding with normal COLDSTART procedure
- COMPARE command now allows A option to compare entire attribute
- CONFIG program/command added to display current hardware configuration
- CREATE-BFILE verb added to create PICK/BASIC files and change pointer to "DC"
- DELETE-ACCOUNT PROC now accepts account name with command
- DIR command added to display DOS directories from Pick
- DISK-USAGE program/command added to display current disk usage
- DISKCOPY command added to duplicate diskettes
- DISKCOMP command added to verify diskettes
- DL verb added for compatibility with Advanced Pick, same as DELETE-LIST
- EL verb added for compatibility with Advanced Pick, same as EDIT-LIST
- EXPORT program/command added to provide Pick to DOS file transfers
- FILE-SAVE command now displays accounts that will be saved, those that will not be saved, and a user-specified start or delay time
- FIND program/command modified to not write Q-pointer in file, now creates a list in POINTER-FILE using the item-id FILENAME-FIND, and if the file being searched is a dictionary, the item-id is D-FILENAME-FIND
- FORMAT verb now supports DOS format and verification
- FORMAT verb now supports V option to only verify diskette
- FORMAT verb now supports F option to only format diskette
- GETBUF subroutine provided in SYSPROG's file for inputting formatted data

- HALT-SYSTEM command added to unconditionally shutdown system, without waiting for users or printers
- IMPORT program/command added to provide DOS to Pick file transfers
- International date format in multiple languages supported
- INIT-ABS program/command added to initialize a range of ABS frames to 'NEP'
- INPUT program/command added that calls subroutine "GETBUF"
- LIST-PORTS program/command modified to properly display multiple pages
- LISTF program/command added as an alternate to LISTFILES, which shows all dictionary and data sections with indentation
- LL verb added for compatibility with Advanced Pick, same as LIST-LISTS
- PRIME program/command added to return the next higher prime number from input provided
- SET-DATE-FORMAT program displays dates in five languages: English, French, German, Italian, and Spanish
- SET-SHUTDOWN-DELAY program/command added to allow a user-specified interval prior to shutdown—for users with caching hard-disk controllers to allow enough time to flush
- SL verb added for compatibility with Advanced Pick, same as SAVE-LIST
- SIEVE program (in SYSPROG's BP file) modified to compute prime numbers correctly
- TO verb added for compatibility with Advanced Pick, same as LOGTO
- UPDATE-ACCOUNTS program/command added to assist in upgrade of prior R83 releases to current release

2.0 Printer support

As of release 2.0, Pick now supports up to three parallel printers.

2.2 Changes to hard disk and diskette handling

In release 2.2, there was a major enhancement to the handling of disk and off-line media. By enhancing the use of buffers and ROM BIOS calls, performance of diskette handling was dramatically improved.

As of release 2.2, all disk sectoring formats are now supported and the 17-sector track restriction has been removed.

The FORMAT command now supports 5¼ and 3½ inch diskettes. Pick now flushes as least one write-required frame to disk every ten seconds.

2.2 Changes to streaming cartridge tape handling

As of release 2.2, Pick no longer writes an empty 512-byte block between each block of data like in earlier releases, which provides the ability to read SCT's created by other systems to be read in Pick. At the same time, it eliminates backward compatibility with earlier versions. A new option is provided for restore. It is the "O" (for Old format) option when being supplied to the prompt for file restore device.

Pick Systems advises users to *not* write EOF marks at the beginning of SCT's because this can lead to problems where tapes are unreadable. The FILE-SAVE and ACCOUNT-SAVE PROCs have been modified not to write EOF marks anymore.

Blocks of data are now written to tape from 512-byte buffers. The number of buffers set aside for the tape buffer is determined by the SET-SCT command.

Finally, the system is now able to recognizc unlabeled tapes. Formerly, if the tape was not labeled, the first 512-byte block of data was lost. Now, if the system senses that there is no label, it automatically positions at the beginning of the first block where it can be treated as data.

2.2 Changes to terminal assignment

Prior to release 2.0, the terminal characteristics for each port were maintained in an item called TERMTYPE in the SYSPROG BP file. In 2.0, the terminal characteristics were moved to attribute 2 of the port location/definition item in the DICT of the ACC file. The terminal characteristics are read in from a program called TERM-TYPE, which should be placed into each accounts logon PROC. You may use the editor to maintain individual port characteristics. For example, to change the terminal characteristics for line 0, you would enter:

```
>ED DICT ACC 00<cr>
TOP
.L2<cr>
001 Memory Mapped Monitor
002  79,24,1,0,2,8,80,60,1
EOI 002
.R<cr>
(enter your new characteristics, followed by a <cr>)
.FI<cr>
'00' FILED.
```

2.2 Extensions to PICK/BASIC

See also: EXECUTE and the @ function in the PICK/BASIC section.

Four user exits have been added to provide PEEK and POKE memory read/write capabilities and IN and OUT port I/O capabilities. See the program called IO.TESTS in the BP file of the SYSPROG account for examples of how they are used. SYSTEM functions 12 through 17 have been added. See the PICK/BASIC section for detailed explanation.

2.2 Extensions to PROC

1. See the "T" command in the section on PROC.
2. Two responses are now available to the PROC "IT" (Input from Tape) command.

They are **C** to continue or **O** to override character.

3. A new user exit has been added:
UE070 Returns the current reel number to the active input buffer.

2.2 Changes to the system debugger

The END and OFF commands have been changed.

2.2 Changes to the END command

Formerly, if the system debugger (!) was entered from the PICK/BASIC debugger (*), an END would return control to the PICK/BASIC debugger. Now, it returns directly to TCL.

2.2 Changes to the OFF command

Formerly, if the system debugger (!) was entered from the PICK/BASIC debugger (*), an OFF would return control to the PICK/BASIC debugger. Now, it logs off.

DOS considerations

About partitions

If you intend to provide a partition for DOS, it *must* be set up prior to loading Pick. When Pick loads, it takes up the **largest** unused partition. Pick needs a minimum of two and half megabytes in the partition.

The COPYPICK command

A DOS program called COPYPICK is available from your dealer or Pick Systems. This program allows moving Pick items into a DOS partition and must be executed from DOS.

Under DOS, the COPYPICK command has the following format:

```
C>COPYPICK<cr>
```

The program then prompts for options:

- D Diagnostics. When supplied as the first option, summary diagnostics are provided. When in the second option position, for example, after the I option, more detailed diagnostics are provided.
- I Includes the (Pick) item-id as a line within the DOS file.
- N Numeric item-ids. Prompts for beginning and ending range numbers, and items are moved in ascending sequential order.

After answering the options prompt, the system prompts with:

```
PICK Account name:
PICK File (DICT FILE or FILE or FILE,DATA):
DOS File:
Pick Item or * for all:
```

After the copy, a count of the total number of records and attributes is displayed.

See your DOS documentation for restrictions on filenames.

2.2 The FDISK command

The DOS FDISK command is also relevant. The FDISK command has also been added to the Pick system in release 2.2 and has similar operational characteristics to its DOS counterpart.

2.2 Graphics support

A new (unofficial and unsupported) user-exit is now provided with Pick for pixel-addressable graphics. It is illustrated in the program called MMVIDEO, which can be found in the BP file of the SYSPROG account.

2.2 Booting the Pick system

There are two methods to reboot Pick on the XT/AT:

1. Using the REBOOT verb discussed later in this section
2. By pressing the CTRL, ALT, and DEL keys simultaneously on port 0 (zero)

During the initial loading process, a series of percent signs (%) are displayed. In the three second gap while these appear on the monitor, and before the options prompt appears, several valid options are possible:

- A Allows changing the number of ABS frames.
- F Indicates that system will recognize Streaming Cartridge Tape (SCT). (Release 2.2)
- S Toggles overlapped SCT and disk I/O processing. Increases system performance when using tape and disk simultaneously, which defaults to not enabled (Release 2.2)
- W Toggles the ROM BIOS multitasking capability, which defaults to off on two-user systems and to on for systems with three or more users (Release 2.2).

Rebooting automatically takes place from the hard disk, unless the Pick PC system diskette #1 is present in the diskette drive, in which case, the following displays on the screen:

```
OPTIONS: K) ill, A)BS only, F) ile & ABS, Q)uick file & ABS
```

- K Deletes the Pick partition.
- A Used to restore the Pick monitor and ABS section only. (This is typically referred to as an "ABS load".) After loading, control transfers to the COLDSTART procedure, which reloads everything except the data files.
- F Used to reinitialize the hard disk partition in which Pick is resident, followed by a restore of the monitor, ABS section, and file area. (This is typically referred to as a "full restore".) See also: FILES.
- Q Exactly like the F option, except that the disk is *not* initialized.

2.2 File restore options

Formerly, the following options appeared for the file restore device:

H High density floppy
S Standard density floppy.
Q Quarter-inch SCT.

The prompt for file restore device now includes a new option and a change to an old option:

O Old SCT. Used when the SCT was created on a pre-2.2 release.
Q Quarter-inch SCT. Used when the SCT was created on a 2.2 or higher release.

When prompted to change diskettes, two responses are valid:

C Continue, after correct diskette has been inserted.
Q To quit for any reason.

Shutting down the system

See the POWER-OFF command later in this section.

2.2 Changes to logon

A change has been made to the way the logon process is handled. After three unsuccessful logon attempts, the port is rendered *inactive*, preventing further attempts. To *reactivate* the port, press any key (other than the <cr>) followed by two <cr>'s.

2.2 ABS frame usage

The following chart shows which of the ABS frames are available for use in the Pick AT version. As of release 2.2, Pick Systems provides 704 ABS frames. Pick Systems advises assembler programmers to use frames above 550.

The * indicates that this frame or group of frames is checked during the VERIFY-SYSTEM command.

ABS frame(s)	*Status*
001 – 109	Reserved by Pick Systems
110	available
111 – 116	Reserved by Pick Systems
117	available
118	Reserved by Pick Systems
119	available
120 – 129	Reserved by Pick Systems
130	available
131 – 184	Reserved by Pick Systems
185	available
186 – 207	Reserved by Pick Systems
208	MAINLINK
209 – 220	Reserved by Pick Systems

221	available
222–223	JET
224–226	Reserved by Pick Systems
227	available
228–280	Reserved by Pick Systems
281	available
282–284	Reserved by Pick Systems
285	available
286–311	Reserved by Pick Systems
312–313	COMPU-SHEET
314–324	Reserved by Pick Systems
325–337	available
338–339	Reserved by Pick Systems
340–380	JET
381–383	Reserved by Pick Systems
384–396	available
397–398	Reserved by Pick Systems
399	ACCU-CURSOR
400–403	Reserved by Pick Systems
404	available
405	Reserved by Pick Systems
406	available
407	Reserved by Pick Systems
408–417	ACCU-PLOT
418–419	Reserved by Pick Systems
420–421	COMPU-SHEET
422	Reserved by Pick Systems
423–428	COMPU-SHEET
429	Reserved by Pick Systems
430–459	ACCU-PLOT
460–467	COMPU-SHEET
468–469	Reserved by Pick Systems
470–485	MAINLINK
486–511	COMPU-SHEET
512–550	JET
551–703	available
710–770	Reserved for VIA Systems
900–1023	Reserved by and for Pick Systems

Pick-AT/XT TCL commands

:FILES

Initiates a full restore as an alternative to the "options" prompt. The proper media type must be indicated with the SET-FLOPPY or SET-SCT prior to using this command.

Compatibility: **Release 2.2** and higher

:SET-DMA DMA-channel

Redefines the SCT DMA channel from its default values.

ADDENDA

Activates PROC to display information about Operating System enhancements made by Pick Systems. This command is no longer provided as of release 3.1.

ADDENDUM *number*

Activates PROC to display information about a specific feature related to Operating System enhancements made by Pick Systems. Use this after the ADDENDA command. This command is no longer provided as of release 3.1.

BEEP

Activates PICK/BASIC program to continuously beep on a CRT until someone reaches over and slams their fist down on any of the keys.

BLIST *filename itemlist** {(*options*)}

Utility to format and list PICK/BASIC source code.

Options:

P Directs output to system printer, via the spooler.
U Updates source item(s). See the PROC called BLIST in the MD of your account. Attribute two contains a number that is used to control the number of spaces to indent from the left margin. The default setting is two.

Compatibility: **Pick 3.1**

BREAK-KEY-OFF

Disables BREAK key. Prevents user from entering the PICK/BASIC or System Debuggers.

Compatibility: **Pick 3.1**

BREAK-KEY-ON

Enables BREAK key. Allows user to enter the PICK/BASIC or System Debugger.

Compatibility: **Pick 3.1**

BUFFERS

Displays current system virtual buffer usage.

CAT {*filename*}

Activates PROC to display information about the compile date/time for a PICK/BASIC program file.

CHECK-ACCOUNT

Prompts for account name, then performs "dummy" save of account.

CHECK-FILE

Prompts for account name and filename, then performs "dummy" save of file.

CL *listname*

Synonym for COPY-LIST command. Provided for compatibility with Advanced Pick.

Compatibility: **Pick 3.1**

CLOCK

Activates program to demonstrate operation of real-time clock.

COLOR {*foreground*} {*,background*} {*options*}

Sets foreground and/or background colors on the color graphics monitor. The options allow special visual attributes to be activated or deactivated, and may only be used from port 0 (zero).

Valid Color Choices:

BLACK, BLUE, BROWN, CYAN, GREEN, MAGENTA, RED, WHITE

Valid options for visual attributes:

/B or /BLINK	Activate blinking
/F or /FULL	Full intensity foreground
/H or /HALF	Half intensity foreground
/NB or /NOBLINK	Deactivate blinking
/NR	Deactivate reverse video
/NOREVERSE	Deactivate reverse video
/R or /REVERSE	Activate reverse video

CONFIG

Displays system configuration. Added in release 3.1.

COPYDOS DOS.*path* {(*options*)}
TO: (*filename* {*itemname*} { }

Copies data, in Pick storage format, from a DOS partition into the Pick partition.

Addressing the DOS.path:

drive: \ *filename*

-or-

drive: \ *directory* \ *filename*

-or-

drive: *directory* \ *directory* \ *filename*

The pattern continues. Effectively there could be many directories.

Options:

D Displays diagnostic information during translation.
F Flags characters. System prompts for further information.
L Creates list-type (indirect) item. (Release 2.2)
M Creates multiple (Pick) items.
O Overwrites (duplicate) Pick item{s}.
P Strips most significant bit off characters as they are converted, except for flagged and/or translated characters (Release 2.2).
R Indicates DOS data is in a random file.
S Indicates DOS data is in a sequential file.
T Translates characters. System prompts for further information.
X Creates hexadecimal image of DOS file.

When file type (S or R) is omitted, the default is S.

Note: when this is executed without the T and F options, DOS end-of-line characters (carriage returns or X'OD') are automatically converted to attribute marks (X'FE'). Line feeds (X'0A' and nulls X'00') are deleted.

CREATE-BFILE *filename* modulo{,separation} modulo{,separation
(modulo{,separation} = *dictionary*; modulo{,separation = *data section*)

-or-

CREATE-BFILE DICT *filename modulo*{,*sep*}

-or-

CREATE-BFILE DATA *filename*{,*filename*} *mod*{,*sep*}

Similar to the CREATE-FILE command, but used for creating files for use with PICK/BASIC. After creating, the file D-pointer is changed to a "DC". The *modulo* should be a prime number and maybe up to 32,267, provided that the separation is one (1).

Modulo is the number of groups to allocate for primary file space. Separation is the number of frames per group. The default separation is one.

Compatibility: **Pick 3.1**

CS

Clears the terminal screen.

DCD {*portnumber*}

Displays the current status of the DCD (Data Carrier Detect) on a specified port, or for the current port if one is not specifically requested. DCD is used to sense changes in the signal being transmitted over the wire to the terminal; when it drops, the terminal is automatically logged off. Note: special cabling is required prior to enabling this feature on a line (Release 2.2)

DCD-OFF {*portnumber*}

Disables the monitoring of Data Carrier Detect on the specified portnumber. If the portnumber is omitted, the current port is affected. This command may not be issued on or against line 0 (zero). The default setting is off.

DCD-ON {*portnumber*}

Enables the monitoring of Data Carrier Detect on the specified *portnumber*. If the *portnumber* is omitted, the current port is affected, and may not be issued on or against line 0 (zero). The default setting is off.

DEFINE-TERMINAL

Allows the addition or modification of term types for using different types of terminals on the system. All information needed for the process is requested from the menu presented upon issuing the command. See also: TEST-CURSOR.

As of release 2.2, the following additional terminal characteristics have been added to DEFINE-TERMINAL. Each of these codes are preceded by an "at sign" (@) when used in PICK/BASIC or PROC.

Code	*Description*
(−11)	Activate screen protect
(−12)	Deactivate screen protect
(−13)	Activate reverse video
(−14)	Deactivate reverse video
(−15)	Activate underlining
(−16)	Deactivate underlining
(−17)	Activate slave printer
(−18)	Deactivate slave printer
(−19)	Move cursor right
(−20)	Move cursor down
(−21)	Activate graphic character set
(−22)	Deactivate graphic character set

Code	*Description*
(−23)	Keyboard lock
(−24)	Keyboard unlock
(−25)	Control character enable
(−26)	Control character disable
(−27)	Write status line
(−28)	Clear status line
(−29)	Initialize terminal mode
(−30)	Download function keys
(−31)	Nonembedded stand-out on
(−32)	Nonembedded stand-out off
(−99)	Returns a 1 if the terminal uses embedded attributes or 0 (zero) if it does not. Returns null if not defined through DEFINE-TERMINAL.
(−100)	Half-intensity (except on memory mapped monitor)
(−101)	Full-intensity (except on memory mapped monitor)

DIR {\ DOS.*path*{\ *subdirectory...*}} {(*options*)}

Displays file information from DOS floppy diskette.

Options:

P Directs output to system printer, via the spooler.
N Suppresses wait at end of page. (Opposite of NOPAGE).
W Displays in wide format, five files per line.

Compatibility: **Pick 3.1**

DISK-USAGE

Activates PICK/BASIC program to display disk usage statistical information.

Compatibility: **Pick 3.1**

DISKCOMP {(P)}

Compares two floppy diskettes.

Compatibility: **Pick 3.1**

DISKCOPY {(*options*)}

Copies a floppy diskette.

Options:

C Compares duplicate with original.
F Formats diskette before copying.
R Repeats duplication. User prompted for number of copies.

Compatibility: **Pick 3.1**

DL *listname*

Synonym for DELETE-LIST command. Provided for compatibility with Advanced Pick.

Compatibility: **Pick 3.1**

EL *listname*

Synonym for DELETE-LIST command. Provided for compatibility with Advanced Pick.

Compatibility: **Pick 3.1**

EPSON

Activates PICK/BASIC program to change characteristics for the EPSON printer.

EXPORT {*filename*} {*itemlist*} {(*options*)}
TO: DOS.*file*

Moves one or more items from a Pick file to a DOS diskette. Must be executed from the Pick partition.

Options:

- A Appends segment mark at the end of Pick item(s). When used with the T option, Pick items are separated and DOS files are terminated with specified character.
- C Concatenates (combines) Pick selected item(s) into one DOS file. Unless the A option is used, Pick files are not separated by any delimiter.
- D Displays diagnostic information during transfer. May be combined with the P option.
- I Includes (Pick) item-id(s) with the DOS file. Each item-id is preceded by a line-feed character.
- N Sorts Pick item-ids numerically.
- O Overwrites duplicate DOS file.
- P Directs output to system printer, via the spooler.
- S Creates DOS file using same name as the Pick item-id.
- T Translates (replaces) specific characters during export. User is prompted for further information.

Compatibility: **Pick 3.1**

FC

Displays the current status of "flow control" or DSR (Data Set Ready) and X-ON/X-OFF protocol on a specified port, or for the current port if one is not specifically requested. When the DSR signal is off or the X-OFF protocol is invoked, the output to the port is suspended.

Compatibility: **Pick AT/XT 2.2** and higher

FC-OFF {*portnumber*}

Disables the flow control on the specified *portnumber*. If the *portnumber* is omitted, the current port is affected. May not be issued on or against line 0 (zero). The default setting is on. See also: FC-ON, MODEM-ON, and MODEM-OFF.

Compatibility: **Pick AT/XT 2.2** and higher

FC-ON {*portnumber*}

Enables the flow control on the specified *portnumber*. If the *portnumber* is omitted, the current port is affected. May not be issued on or against line 0 (zero). The default setting is on. See also: FC-OFF, MODEM-ON, and MODEM-OFF.

Compatibility: **Pick AT/XT 2.2** and higher

FDISK

Activates menu to allow any of the following functions:

- Change partition pointer, which affects the boot process next time it is used
- Delete the Pick partition
- Display partition information
- Create a PICK partition
- Select next fixed disk drive (Release 2.2)
- Undo changes to partition data, leaving them the way they were prior to invoking FDISK (Release 2.2)

This command may only be issued from the SYSPROG account while on port 0 (zero). See also the REBOOT command.

FILECOMP

Activates PICK/BASIC program to compare and analyze the contents of two files.

FIND

Activates PICK/BASIC program to search a file for the existence of one or more strings of characters in any attribute. As of release 3.1, the item-id of the item that this process writes to the POINTER-FILE is: filename-FIND. For example:

```
PROCLIB-FIND
```

Compatibility: **Pick AT/XT**

FKEYS

Activates PICK/BASIC program used for maintaining function key definition items. Pick Systems advises reviewing the program in the SYSPROG BP file prior to using it.

FORMAT *{option}*

Formats floppy diskette for use only with the Pick System. This command may only be issued from the SYSPROG account. As of release 2.2, the FORMAT command now supports 5 1/4 and 3 1/2 inch diskettes.

Options (All added in Release 3.1):

D Formats for use the DOS.
F Formats diskette only.
V Verifies diskette only.

HALT-SYSTEM

Immediately halts system without waiting for users or printers.

Compatibility: **Pick 3.1**

IMPORT DOS.*path* {*(options)*}
TO: *(filename {itemname}*

Moves data from a DOS diskette or DOS hard partition into a file in the Pick partition. The DOS.path must include the drive-id and the DOS directory, subdirectory (or subdirectories), and filename.

Example:

```
>IMPORT A: \AUTOEXEC.BAT<cr>
TO: (TEMP<cr>
```

Options:

D Displays diagnostic information during transfer.
F Flags characters. User prompted for further input.
L Creates list-class (indirect) item.
M Creates multiple items. User prompted for further input.
O Overwrites item if duplicate item-id exists.
P Parity strip. Characters converted to values 0-127. Flagged or translated characters are not stripped.
R DOS data is in random file mode.
S DOS data is in sequential file mode (default).
T Translates characters. User prompted for further input.
X Creates hexadecimal image of DOS file.

Notes:

- If neither the R nor S option is specified, the S option is assumed.
- If neither the F nor T option is specified, IMPORT will automatically translate the DOS characters X'OD' (carriage return) to X'FE' attribute mark). Also, X'0A' (linefeed) and X'00' (null) characters are deleted.

- If no PICK filename is provided at the "TO:(" prompt, the DOS filename is used as the Pick itemname.
- If the DOS file is larger than 25,000 bytes and the M option is not used, the process will break the DOS file into multiple items and append a sequential number to the end of each item-id. If the L option is used, a "list-class" item is created and this breaking up process does not take place.

Compatibility: **Pick 3.1**

INIT-ABS

Activates PICK/BASIC program for initializing ABS frames. User is prompted for range of frames.

Compatibility: **Pick 3.1**

LIST-LISTS

Displays saved-lists from POINTER-FILE. See also: LL.

Compatibility: **Pick 3.1**

LIST-PORTS {(Z)}

Displays the baud rate, parity bits, stop bits, and word length for every connected port on the system. See also: SET-PORT. (Release 2.2)

Option:

Z Displays the status for all configured ports, connected or not.

LISTF

Displays dictionary and data files from current account in hierarchical format.

LL

Displays saved-lists from POINTER-FILE. See also the LIST-LISTS command.

Compatibility: **Pick 3.1**

MODEM-OFF

Disables the flow control on the current port. May not be issued on or against line 0 (zero). The default setting is on. See also: FC, FC-ON, FC-OFF, and MODEM-ON (Release 2.2).

MODEM-ON

Enables the flow control on the current port. May not be issued on or against line 0 (zero). The default setting is on. See also: FC, FC-ON, FC-OFF, and MODEM-OFF (Release 2.2)

MONO {*/options*}

Sets options for the monochrome display unit. The options allow special visual attributes to be activated or deactivated. May only be used from port 0 (zero).

Valid options for visual attributes:

/B or / BLINK	Activate blinking
/F or /FULL	Full intensity foreground
/H or / HALF	Half intensity foreground
/NB or /NOBLINK	Deactivate blinking
/NR	Deactivate reverse video
/NU	Deactivate underlining
/NOREVERSE	Deactivate reverse video
/NOUNDERLINE	Deactivate underlining
/R or /REVERSE	Activate reverse video
/U	Activate underlining
/UNDERLINE	Activate underlining

OKIDATA

Activates a menu to allow the changing of printer characteristics for the Okidata parallel printer.

PICK-SETUP

Activates process to establish administrative guidelines for system, including selection of ABS frames, date format, monitor keyboard, system time and date, shutdown delay, restoration and update of accounts, creation of accounts, and assigning passwords. See also: SET-DATE-FORMAT, SET-KBRD, SET-SHUTDOWN-DELAY, SET-DATE, SET-TIME, RESTORE-ACCOUNTS, UPDATE-ACCOUNTS, CREATE-ACCOUNT and PASSWORD.

Compatibility: **Pick 3.1**

POWER-OFF

Brings the system to an "orderly shutdown" by flushing memory to disk, disabling all users, and parking the disk drive heads prior to halting the system. May only be executed from port 0 (zero) when all other users are logged off. As of release 2.2, this command will not work if any lines other than zero are active, which includes spooler-controlled lines (printers). As of release 3.1, this command now handles users and spooled items correctly.

PRIME

Enter number: number<cr>

Activates program to provide next higher prime number from number provided.

Compatibility: **Pick 3.1**

REBOOT

Causes the system to reinitialize, rather than using the CTRL-ALT-DEL keys. May only be issued from port 0 (zero). Disables all users and flushes memory prior to rebooting. See also: FDISK and POWER-OFF. As of release 2.2, this command will not work if any lines other than zero are active, which includes spooler-controlled lines (printers). As of release 3.1, this procedure now updates the SYSTEM-CONFIG,ACC file to indicate a controlled system shutdown. It also waits one minute after flushing buffers before continuing with procedure, to allow time for disk caching controllers to flush.

RESTORE-ACCOUNTS

Activates PROC to restore multiple accounts from a FILE-SAVE tape or diskette(s). See also: ACCOUNT-RESTORE (Release 2.2).

SET-BAUD {*portnumber,*} *baud rate*

Allows changing the baud rate for lines 1 and 2 on the XT, and for 1 through 10 on the AT. The default baud rate for each line is 9600. When the line (port) number is not specified, the current line is affected. See also: SET-PORT command.

The valid baud rate choices are:

110,150,300,600,1200,2400,4800,9600 (and 19200 on release 2.2 and higher)

SET-DATE *mm/dd/yy*{*yy*} {(U)}

Sets the system date to specified setting. See also: SET-DATE-EUR and SET-DATE-STD.

Note: this command is now a PROC that executes the verb called SET.DATE.

Option:

U Updates the hardware real-time clock, as well as the system (software clock).

SET-DATE-EUR

Toggles the standard date format to European format: *dd/mm/yy*. See also: SET-DATE-FORMAT.

SET-DATE-FORMAT {*country.code*} {(*options*)}

Changes format of domestic date/time format from items in the DATE-FORMAT file.

Supported Country Codes:

US American
GR German
IT Italian
SP Spanish
UK English/United Kingdom

Options:

S Sets system date format using SYSTEM-CONFIG DATE-FORMAT item.

U Updates SYSTEM-CONFIG DATE-FORMAT item using specified *country code*.

Compatibility: **Pick 3.1**

SET-DATE-STD

Toggles the European date format to North American format: *mm/dd/yy*. See also: SET-DATE-FORMAT.

SET-FLOPPY {*(density,drive)*}

Used after the T-ATT command to designate the density to read/write diskettes and which floppy drive to use, when more than one is present. Drive choices are typically A or B. See also: FORMAT. Don't forget to rewind the diskette with the T-REW command prior to attempting any read or write operation. Usually, this doesn't take too long.

The defaults are: drive A, High density.

As of release 2.2, 3 1/2 inch floppies are supported.

Density choices:

S Standard density (360Kb for 5 1/4 inch, 720Kb for 3 1/2 inch)

H High density (1.2Mb for 5 1/4 inch, 1.44Mb for 3 1/2 inch)

SET-FUNC *filename itemname*

Specifies name of item to use in assigning function keys for use only by port 0 (zero). Each function key may be assigned one character. See the file called FUNCKEYS on the SYSPROG account. The default upon booting is that the function keys are undefined. See the item called SET-KBRD.DOC in the DOC file in the SYSPROG account for more information on defining function keys.

SET-KBRD *filename itemname*

Specifies name of item to use in assigning the type of keyboard for use only by port 0 (zero). The items available in the KEYBOARDS file on the SYSPROG account include: BRITISH (ENGLISH), DVORAK, FRENCH, FRENCH 2, GERMAN, ITALIAN, SPANISH, SPANISH 2, and USA (the default). See the item called KBRD.DOC, in the DOC file on the SYSPROG account. It contains a detailed explanation for constructing keyboard definition items. As of release 2.2, Pick Systems now provides support for 101/102 keyboards.

SET-KEYS {*keyboard.name*}

Allows user to modify monitor keyboard information stored in the KEYBOARDS file.

SET-LPTR

-or-

SET-LPTR *number*

-or-

SET-LPTR {*number*},{*delay*},{*burst*},{*slice*}}

Used to display or change performance parameters on parallel printers. To obtain an optimum blend of printer and system performance, experiment with different settings. When no parameters are provided, the current settings are displayed. A printer number may be specified to display its current settings. Like the TERM command, existing parameters may be left intact by providing two successive commas where the parameter would normally appear.

The *number* parameter indicates the printer number in the range 0 to 3.

The *delay* parameter indicates the number of times to attempt to send a character to the printer. The higher the value, the slower the system performance, but faster printer performance. The default is 300, and the value must be in the range 1 to 4095.

The *burst* parameter indicates the number of characters to transmit to the printer in one packet. Relates to size of printer (RAM) buffer. The default is 200, and must be in the range 1 to 255. Pick System suggests that 15 provides good performance.

The *slice* parameter indicates the number of timeslices that the printer waits prior to receiving its next timeslice. The default is 1, and it must be in the range 1 to 15. Pick Systems advises using a number equal to or greater than the number of users on the system.

SET-PORT {*portnumber*{,*baud*,*parity*,*stopbits*,*wordlength*}}

Activates the program to display or change baud rate, parity bits, stopbits, and wordlength for a port. When no *portnumber* is specified, the existing settings are displayed.

The valid *baud* rates (as of release 2.2) are:

110,150,300,600,1200,2400,4800,9600, and 19200. The default baud rate is 9600.

To leave an existing parameter intact, use two successive commas (like the TERM command).

Parity may be **N** for none, **O** for odd, or **E** for even. *Stopbits* may be either **1** or **2**. *Wordlength* may be either **7** or **8**. See also: LIST-PORT.

SET-SCT (*blocksize*)

(Pick XT version.) Used after the T-ATT command to designate that the Streaming Cartridge Tape should be used for any subsequent "tape" operations. If the *blocksize* is omitted, it will default to 16384. The *blocksize* must be between 2048 and 16384, and a multiple of 512.

SET-SCT {*buffers*} {({*blocksize*} {*options*}}

(Pick AT version.) Used after the T-ATT command to designate that the Streaming Cartridge Tape should be used for any subsequent "tape" operations.

The *buffers* parameter indicates the number of 512-byte buffers to assign for the tape buffer. The default (and minimum) is 128. The maximum is a function of how much memory is present on your system. Up to half of the memory may be allocated. For example, if your system has 640Kb of main memory, the maximum number of buffers is 640. If the blocksize is omitted, it defaults to 16384. The blocksize must be between 512 and 32500, and be a multiple of 512.

Options:

M Assigns number of buffers using the total of real memory minus 256K or 768 buffers, or 384K on a 640K system. Pick Systems strongly encourages the use of this option to increase tape streaming and decrease the number of stop/starts, which decrease tape reliability. This option was added in release 3.1.

R Indicates that the tape is in "old" format, meaning that it was created on a version prior to 2.2.

SET-SHUTDOWN-DELAY *{delay}* {(*options*)}

Displays or alters the delay number of seconds prior to shutdown. For users with disk caching hard-disk controllers. Allows time for disk to flush. Delay may be a positive number between 1 and 65536. All by itself, the command displays the current setting. The default setting is 512.

Options:

S Sets monitor shutdown delay using SHUTDOWN-DELAY item in SYSTEM-CONFIG file.

U Updates SHUTDOWN-DELAY item in SYSTEM-CONFIG file with specified value.

Compatibility: **Pick 3.1**

SET-TIME *hh:mm(:ss)* {(U)}

Sets the system time to specified setting. Note: This command is now a PROC that executes the verb called SET.TIME.

Option:

U Updates the hardware real-time clock, as well as the system (software clock).

SETUP.SIO

This program was provided with release 2.0 to alter the parity, stopbits, and wordlength for a port. As of release 2.2, it has been renamed SET-PORT.

SL *listname*

Synonym for SAVE-LIST command. Provided for compatibility with Advanced Pick.

Compatibility: **Pick 3.1**

T-ERASE

Performs a re-tension and erases a Streaming Cartridge Tape.

T-RETEN

Re-tensions Streaming Cartridge Tape by moving all the way to the end of the tape, then rewinding. Recommended prior to using tape for any purpose. Automatically performed during FILE-SAVE and ACCOUNT-SAVE.

T-STATUS

Indicates the type and drive number of the currently attached off-line storage device.

T-VERIFY {(*options*)}

-or-

T-VERIFY *acctname* {(*options*)}

Verifies integrity of FILE-SAVE or ACCOUNT-SAVE media. In default mode, when no options are provided, only the account names are displayed, and the media is compared with the file system. All errors found are displayed.

Items are displayed in file hierarchy format as follows:

Account>Dictionary Level>Data Level>Item-ID {Errors}

Options:

- A Verifies and displays all accounts on media, until an "end-of-save" occurs. This option *must* be used if no account name is provided.
- D Suppresses duplicate item-id's in group.
- E Displays errors only.
- F Sequentially displays only files found on media, in hierarchy format. When used with I option, items are also displayed.
- G Suppresses group hash testing on all items. Ignores errors if items are in the wrong group.
- I Displays items from media in file hierarchy format. Items display continuously in place, unless this option is combined with the F option, which displays each item on a separate line.
- L Logs errors to user-specified log file. Attribute 1 of items written in log file will contain the error message from the ERRMSG file. Attribute 2 will be the element that caused the error, in hierarchical format.
- N Activates the NOPAGE function on output to the terminal.
- P Directs output to system printer, via the spooler.
- Q Queries user on each error found. User has option to continue, quit, or skip file system comparisons for the current file.
- T Verifies contents of media only, without comparing to file system. When this option is used, the F, I, and Q options must also be used.

TA {*portnumber*}

Displays status of type-ahead buffer on specified portnumber, or current port if omitted. See also: TA-OFF and TA-ON (Release 2.2).

TA-OFF {*portnumber*}

Disables type-ahead buffer on specified portnumber, or current port if omitted. See also: TA and TA-ON (Release 2.2).

TA-ON {*portnumber*}

Enables type-ahead buffer on specified portnumber, or current port if omitted. See also: TA and TA-OFF (Release 2.2).

TERM-TYPE

Activates PICK/BASIC program to automatically set the terminal characteristics for the current line. The item read in to set the characteristics is found in the DICT of the ACC file. The item-id is the 2-digit portnumber. The editor is used to maintain individual port characteristics. For example, to change the terminal characteristics for line 0, you could enter:

```
ED DICT ACC 00<cr>
TOP
.L2<cr>
001 Memory Mapped Monitor
002  79,24,1,0,2,8,80,60,1
```

TEST-CURSOR

Activates program to test the various terminal capabilities such as clear screen, clear to end of line, "X,Y" addressing, reverse video, etc. See also: DEFINE-TERMINAL (Release 2.2).

TO *acctname*{*,password*}

Synonym for LOGTO command.

Compatibility: **Pick 3.1**

UPDATE-ACCOUNTS *acctname* {*acctname...*}

Activates process to update MD verb definitions to new release for one or more accounts. Any conflicts found will be logged in the CLASHES file, with a new data section being added for each account. For example, if the account called DUMMY was run through this process, the clashes would be stored in CLASHES,DUMMY. To see the existing data sections, use: LISTFILES DUMMY.

Compatibility: **Pick 3.1**

WHICH

Provides current release level.

XCS {*portnumber*}

Displays status of Extended Character Set for specified portnumber or current port if omitted. When XCS is enabled, the high-order bit is not stripped from input, which allows characters in the (decimal) range 128 to 239 to be used. See also: XCS-OFF and XCS-ON (Release 2.2).

XCS-OFF {*portnumber*}

Disables extended character set on specified portnumber or current port if omitted. See also: XCS and XCS-ON (Release 2.2)

XCS-ON {*portnumber*}

Enables extended character set on specified portnumber or current port if omitted. See also: XCS and XCS-OFF (Release 2.2).

8
RUNOFF

About compatibility with SMA standards

Most of RUNOFF is compatible with the SMA standard. The exceptions to the SMA standard are noted and occur only in the options available with the HEADING and FOOTING commands. Only one command in generic Pick, the .NOPAGING command, is not part of the SMA standard.

Format of RUNOFF command

RUNOFF {DICT} *filename itemlist** {(*options*)}

Activates output function of RUNOFF text processor.

Options:

n Any integer number. Specifies the number of times to overstrike a character or characters designated as boldface.
C Suppresses .CHAIN and .READ output.
I Outputs next item name.
J Suppresses highlighting function.
N Activates NOPAGE function on output to terminal.
P Directs output to system printer, via the spooler.
S Suppresses boldface and underline function.
U Outputs all characters in uppercase.

Special control characters

@ Print next character in boldface
@^ Begin boldface
@\ End boldface

&	Underline next character
&^	Begin underline
&\	End underline
^	Print next character in uppercase
^^	Begin uppercase
\	Print next character in lowercase
\\	End uppercase
_	Treat following character as a literal
<	Begin following text at next tabstop
>	End following text at next tabstop

RUNOFF commands

Many RUNOFF commands have an acceptable abbreviated form. The abbreviated form follows all of the full commands that recognize the abbreviated form.

.* {*text*}

Comment line. All text or commands on line are ignored by RUNOFF processor.

.BEGIN PAGE

-or-

.BP

Terminates current page, prints optional FOOTING, ejects a page, increments page counter, and prints optional HEADING.

BOX *leftmargin,rightmargin*

-or-

.BOX OFF

Encloses following text in a "box" of vertical bars on the output page. The BOX command, followed by the OFF parameter, disables the BOX function.

.BREAK

-or-

.B

Outputs partially filled line before processing next line.

.CAPITALIZE SENTENCES

-or-

.CS

Activates automatic capitalization of sentences following a period (.), exclamation point (!), question mark (?), colon (:), or a semicolon (;) that is followed by one or more spaces.

.CENTER

-or-

.C

Centers following line between current left and right margins.

.CHAIN {DICT} {*filename*} *itemname*

Transfers control to specified *itemname*. If filename is not specified, the current filename is used. Control does not return to the source item. See also: READ.

.CHAPTER *text*

Ejects page, increments page and chapter counters, and outputs the literal, "CHAPTER", followed by the optional text centered between the current margins. The chapter, page number, and text are accumulated for the table of contents.

.CONTENTS

Outputs the current table of contents, as defined by previous .CHAPTER and .SECTION commands.

.CRT

Directs output to terminal.

.EC

End case. Disables any previous .UPPERCASE or .LOWERCASE commands.

.FILL

-or-

.F

Activates line fill function. Words from the source item are printed one at a time on the output line until no more words can fit on the line, and then a new line is begun. In other words, individual lines in the source item are combined to form continuous paragraphs of the proper width. See also: STANDARD.

.FOOTING {{*text*} {*'options'*}...}

Defines following line as text to output at the bottom of each page. If the line following the .FOOTING command is null, then the footing is suppressed.

Options:

- C Centers line on page according to current page width as set by the TERM command.
- D Outputs current system date.
- F Outputs filename.
- Fn Outputs filename left-justified in "n" spaces (Not part of SMA standard).
- I Outputs item-id.
- In Outputs item-id left-justified in "n" spaces. (Not part of SMA standard).
- L Performs carriage return/linefeed.
- P Outputs current page number, right-justified in a field of four spaces.
- Pn Outputs current page number, left-justified in "n" spaces. (Not part of SMA standard.)
- PN Outputs current page number, left-justified. (Not part of SMA standard.)
- T Outputs current system time and date.

.HEADING {{*text*} {*'options'*}...}

Defines following line as text to output at the top of each page. If the line following the .HEADING command is null, then the heading is suppressed.
See also: .FOOTING.

.HILITE {*character*}

-or-

.HILITE OFF

Prints the optionally-specified character along the right margin. If the character is omitted, or the word "OFF" appears after the command, then the HILITE function is disabled.

Any character, other than a period (.), may be specified as the highlight character.

.INDENT {-} *numberspaces*

-or-

.I {-} *numberspaces*

Indents the following line the specified number of spaces. Left margin is *not* reset.

The *numberspaces* may contain a negative number to cause "outdenting." If the *numberspaces* argument is omitted, one (1) is assumed.

.INDENT MARGIN {-} *numberspaces*

-or-

.IM {-} *numberspaces*

Increments the left margin by the specified number of spaces. The *numberspaces* may contain a negative number to move the left margin farther to the left.

.INDEX *text*

Inserts text with current page number into index. Text must be enclosed in double quotes if it contains embedded blanks. See also: .PRINT INDEX.

.INPUT

Prompts for input from terminal screen. The entered text is then output as though it had been stored in the document.

.JUSTIFY

-or-

.J

Activates fill mode and justifies lines to the right margin by placing extra spaces between words on the line. See also: STANDARD and FILL.

.LEFT MARGIN *marginsetting*

Sets left margin tabstop to specified column number. Left margin is automatically set to zero (0) in the STANDARD command.

.LINE LENGTH *numbercharacters*

Specifies the maximum number of characters per output line. This number, plus the left margin setting, (minus one), denotes the right margin position. Line length is automatically set to seventy (70) in the .STANDARD command.

.LOWERCASE

-or-

.LC

Outputs all text in lowercase. See also: .EC.

.LPTR

Directs output to system printer, via the spooler.

.NOCAPITALIZE SENTENCES

-or-

.NCS

Deactivates automatic capitalization of sentences function.

.NOFILL

-or-

.NF

Disables line fill and justification functions. Outputs text line for line exactly as stored. See also: .FILL and .JUSTIFY.

.NOJUSTIFY

-or-

.NJ

Disables justification function. Line fill function remains in effect and lines are output with a "ragged" margin. See also: .JUSTIFY.

.NOPAGING

-or-

.N

Activates NOPAGE function on output to terminal. (Not part of SMA standard.)

.NOPARAGRAPH

Disables paragraph function. See also: .PARAGRAPH.

.PAGE NUMBER *pagenumber*

Sets current page number to specified number. If *pagenumber* is omitted, one (1) is assumed.

.PAPER LENGTH *paperlength*

Specifies the maximum number of print lines per output page.

.PARAGRAPH {-} *numberspaces*

-or-

.P {-} *numberspaces*

Specifies number of spaces for paragraph indentation. Any line beginning with a blank is indented the specified number of spaces. The *numberspaces* may contain a negative number to cause the paragraph to "outdent".

.PFILE *printfile#*

Directs subsequent output to specified *printfile number*, just like the PRINT ON statement in BASIC. Typically used to provide a separate spooler entry for containing the table of contents created with the .CONTENTS command.

.PRINT
text

Displays following line of text on terminal. Typically used to provide a prompt message for use with a subsequent INPUT command.

.PRINT INDEX

Outputs index created with previous .INDEX commands. This command may *not* be used with the .SAVE INDEX command. See also: .INDEX command.

.READ {DICT} {*filename*} *itemname*

Transfers control to specified RUNOFF item for output and returns control upon completion. If the *filename* is omitted, the current *filename* is used. See also: .CHAIN and the I option with the RUNOFF command.

.READNEXT

Extracts top entry of list created by an external {S}SELECT statement prior to output and inserts next value into text of item. See also: {S}SELECT in ACCESS.

.SAVE INDEX *filename*

Saves entries defined in previous .INDEX commands in specified filename, using the item-id of the current RUNOFF item. The *filename* of the index *must* be different than the RUNOFF text filename to avoid destroying data.

.SECTION *section-number text*

Specifies section level number to increment by one and stores the resulting section number and optional text in the table of contents. See also: .CONTENTS.

.SET TABS *tabstop{tabstop...}*

Specifies tabstop locations at specified column position{s}. Tabstops must be in ascending sequence, and zero (0) is not valid. Up to 30 tabstops may be set. See also: C (column) in the EDITOR section.

Any word following the "less-than" symbol (<) will begin at the next tabstop. Any word following the "greater-than" symbol (>) will end at the next tabstop. Note: tabs are only in effect while in .NOFILL mode.

.SKIP {*numberlines*}
-or-
.SK {*numberlines*}

Outputs specified number of blank lines on page, taking into account any previously specified .SPACING commands. If *numberlines* is omitted, then one (1) is assumed.

.SPACE *numberlines*
-or-
.SP *numberlines*

Outputs specified number of blank lines on page, regardless of any previously specified .SPACING commands. If *numberlines* is omitted, then one (1) is assumed.

.SPACING *numberlines*

Specifies interline spacing to the specified number of lines (e.g., .SPACING 2 sets double spacing). See also: .SK and .SP.

.STANDARD

Specifies for RUNOFF to use the following default parameters:

.CAPITALIZE SENTENCES
.CRT
.FILL
.FOOTING (null)
.HEADING (null)
.JUSTIFY
.LEFT MARGIN 0
.LINE LENGTH 70
.PARAGRAPH 5
.UPPERCASE

The SMA standard for .STANDARD is:

.CAPITALIZE SENTENCES
.FILL
.JUSTIFY
.FOOTING (null)
.HEADING (null)
.LEFT MARGIN 0
.LINE LENGTH 70
.PARAGRAPH 5
.END CASE

.TEST PAGE *numberlines*

-or-

.TP *numberlines*

Counts the number of lines remaining to output on the current page. If the *numberlines* parameter is less than the count returned, then the following text is output on the current page, otherwise, a page is ejected and the text is output on the new page. This command prevents blocks of text from being split across a page boundary.

.UPPERCASE

-or-

.UC

Outputs text in uppercase characters, unless specifically altered by the lowercase special control character, (\ ). See also: .EC.

9
System debugger

The system debugger is used for assembly code debugging. It has the capability of accessing and changing data directly on the disk. A thorough familiarization with this section is recommended prior to using the debugger, as it can be *very* destructive.

Symbol file definitions

PSYM Permanent symbol table.
OSYM Object symbol table.
TSYM Temporary symbol table.

Note: These definitions are the standard tables for classic Pick. These files are not always provided with each version of Pick and may actually go by different names. Usually, there is a PSYM file provided with the Assembler account, which may have to be purchased or obtained separately.

The SET-SYM command

SET-S *filename* {T}

Sets symbol file pointer for use by system debugger. Filename is typically PSYM.

Option:

T Sets secondary file pointer to TSYM file.

Term conventions and definitions

To address any disk location, usually three pieces of information are required: The *Data Format* Specification, the *Data Reference* Specification and the *Data Window* Specification. This information may seem a little confusing at first. Several examples of how to put these pieces together are provided after the descriptions of the specifications.

DFS: The Data Format Specification

The DFS specifies the output display format mode of operation to use. It precedes the address of the data to access. The DFS, once set, will remain in the designated mode until explicitly changed. All of the following are invalid with the use of the A or the L commands, and will generate error messages.

Options:

- C Character format.
- I Integer format. Automatically generated by any reference to a symbol of the type: H, T, D, or F. A window specification of greater than six bytes will default to one byte.
- X Hexadecimal format.

DRS: The Data Reference Specification

The DRS specifies either a direct or an indirect disk address.

Address Specifications:

Represented by the character preceding the address, as follows:

.address Indicates the address is a hexadecimal number.
,address Indicates the address is a decimal number.

The formats shown in this section use the default hexadecimal representations.

Direct Reference:

!fidaddr.dataaddr
-or-
!dataaddr
where fidaddr (frame id address) is the logical frame, and dataaddr (data address) is the address of the unlinked data frame.

Both of these parameters may be preceded by a period (.), indicating that the address is a hexadecimal value, or a comma (,), which indicates that the address is a decimal value.

!/fidaddr.dataaddr

Same as above, but the frame is assumed to be in linked format.

Indirect References:

Implicit:

!R*regaddr*

where register number address is the reference to data pointed to by a register number in the range 0–15.

!/symbolname

where symbolname is the name of the symbol, as defined in either the PSYM or TSYM files. This command will display the register number, displacement, format type, and window of the symbol.

Note: the symbol table must be set prior to using the indirect reference to a symbol name.

Explicit:

!*symbolname

References the data pointed to by the symbolic name of the register or storage register.

!Rregaddr.dataaddr

Applies the displacement, (dataaddr), to the location pointed to by Rfidaddr in order to obtain a storage register, with which the data may be addressed.

!*fidaddr.dataaddr
-or-
!*dataaddr

This command is like the previous data address commands, but treats the specified location as a storage register. The displacement, dataaddr, is applied to the frame address to find the address of the storage register.

!symbolname**
-or-
!fidaddr.dataaddr**
-or-
!dataaddr**

References the storage at which the storage register points, with one condition: If the first byte of the medial storage register is a X'82', then the element is interpreted as a BASIC indirect string element and the storage register is taken from two bytes beyond this location. If any of the data fields are invalid as storage registers, then the message ERR! will appear. Some machines will croak.

DWS: The Data Window Specification

The DWS indicates the number of bytes to display and has the general form:

;window

Designates window as a tally for display, or a half-tally for the trace and y-trace, which represents the number of bytes to display. The maximum is limited to the size of the frame being requested.

Offset Specifications:

Explicit:

;offset, window

Designates offset and window, where offset is a positive or negative tally indicating the offset from the DFS, and window is a positive number. This form works for traces, except in the case that the location is an indirect reference from a storage register whose location is specified by the form !fidaddr.dataaddr.

Implicit:

;C*offset*

-or-

;C*offset.window*

Where offset and window are functionally the same as above, and the C (code) designates the number of fields. If the window specification is not included, then the implicit window derived from the field type is used, otherwise the specified window is used.

The possible designators for the C parameter are as follows:

B	Field width = 1 bit
C	Field width = 1 byte
D	Field width = 4 bytes
F	Field width = 6 bytes
H	Field width = 1 byte
R	Field width = 8 bytes
S	Field width = 6 bytes
T	Field width = 2 bytes

;C

Where the C parameter is as above, but in this form, an offset of zero is used, along with the implied window and DFS.

The general form for bit (B) display:

;B*offset.window*

Specifies bit display, starting at bit zero, the offset from the addressing base, for a width of window bits. Bits and bit fields may be traced with either trace. The displacement specified by a symbolically addressed bit is in bits. Therefore, the form *fidaddr.dataaddr* will treat the dataaddr as a bit count in the direct-reference form.

Examples of the DFS, DRS, and DWS

```
!C4888,12;4<cr>
```

This reads : in character format, frame 4888, displaced (or offset) in 12 bytes, retrieving a window of 4 bytes.

```
!X.FEC.C;.A<cr>
```

This example reads : in hexadecimal format, frame FEC, displaced in C bytes, retrieving a window of A bytes.

```
!C.FEC,12;4
```

This example shows that different combinations of decimal and hexadecimal parameters can be specified.

Display prompts and special functions

After a valid address has been specified, the debugger accesses the requested location and displays its current contents. The cursor is positioned to the right of an "=" sign, indicating that the debugger is ready to either accept any of the following special functions or change the contents of the window.

The following commands are expected in response to the equal (=) character that appears as the result of a legal debugger command.

..=<cr>

(Carriage Return). Returns control to the command processor. Leaves window unchanged.

..=<lf>

(Linefeed). Displays the next window of data, on the same line.

..=<control>N

Displays the address of the next window and the next window on the next line.

..=<control>P

Displays the address of the previous window and the previous window on the next line.

..='*string*

Replaces the characters specified in string at the beginning of the displayed window for the length of string, which may not exceed forty bytes. The string must terminate with a <cr>, <lf>, <control>N, or <control>P. This command is used to change data displayed in character format (see DRS).

..=*decimal number*

Places the value of the decimal number in the displayed window, filling from the right, if the window is 1,2,4, or 6 bytes in length, and does not cross a frame boundary. The string must terminate with a <cr>, <lf>, <control>N, or <control>P.

..=.*hexadecimal string*

Places the value of the hexadecimal string in the displayed window, filling from the left. The string must contain an even number of hexadecimal characters, and may not exceed 38 hexadecimal characters. The string must terminate with a <cr>, <lf>, <con-

trol>N, or <control>P. This command is used to change data displayed in hexadecimal format (see DRS).

..=*binary string*

Binary String. The binary string is a sequence of 1's and 0's less than 40 characters in length. Places the value of binary string in the displayed window, starting with the first bit in the window. The string must terminate with a <cr>, <lf>, <control>N, or <control>P.

..=0

(Zero). Clears the window to null, if the type is not bit display. The string must terminate with a <cr>, <lf>, <control>N, or <control>P. Only functional on binary string.

..=A

Redisplays the address of the last window, along with the window.

..=C

-or-

..=C*window*

-or-

..=C*offset.window*

Changes the display type, window, and offset if specified, and redisplays either the original field with the new type and/or window specification, or the resultant field if the offset is changed. The string must terminate with a <cr>, <lf>, <control>N, or <control>P.

System debugger commands

!A{DRS}

Displays the current instruction location of the virtual code address. The DFS is meaningless to this command and will generate the error message, ILLGL SYM (illegal symbol).

!ADDD *decnum decnum*

Adds two decimal numbers and displays result in decimal.

!ADDX *hexnum hexnum*

Adds two hexadecimal numbers and displays result in hexadecimal.

!B{DRS}{.0}

Sets a breakpoint at specified data reference location, causing a break each time the address is encountered.

The optional zero (0) indicates that every entry point in the frame is to be treated as a breakpoint, in which case, the dataaddr parameter is omitted from the DRS.

The DRS may contain a maximum of two numeric parameters, hence no window specification is expected.

A plus (+) character is displayed for each breakpoint successfully entered into the table, until the table is full. The maximum number of breakpoints is four.

!C{DRS}

Activates character display format. See section on DFS-Data Format Specifications.

!D

Displays table containing current breakpoints, traces, data breakpoints (y-trace tables), and frame replacement specifications.

!DB

Toggles the debugger availability flag. Must be executed from SYSPROG.

!DIVD *decnum decnum*

Divides two decimal numbers and displays result in decimal.

!DIVX *hexnum hexnum*

Divides two hexadecimal numbers and displays result in hexadecimal.

!DTX *decnum*

Converts decimal value to hexadecimal equivalent and displays result.

!DTX{*radix*} *decnum*

Converts decimal value to a specified radix (base) and displays result. Default radix = 16.

!E{*numberlines*}

Specifies number of instructions to execute prior to returning to debugger command level.

The numberlines parameter must be in the range, (0−250). The E command, followed by a <cr>, disables previous iteration counter setting.

!END

-or-

!end

Terminates debugger process and returns control to TCL.

A change was made to this command in release 2.2. Formerly, if the system debugger was entered from the PICK/BASIC debugger, an END would return control to the PICK/BASIC debugger. Now, it returns directly to TCL.

!*Foldfidaddr.newfidaddr*

Frame replacement function. Replaces entries in oldfidaddr as entries in newfidaddr. Both parameters may be either decimal or hexadecimal numbers. See section on Address Specifications under DRS - Data Reference Specifications.

!G{DRS}

Go function. Transfers control to address specified in the DRS, with the exception of not allowing window specifications. The G command, followed by a <cr>, continues execution, if possible, from the current virtual address location.

!H

Toggles the ECHO flag.

!I{DRS}

Activates Integer display format. See section on DFS-Data Format Specifications. The I command, followed by a <cr>, will display subsequent output in Integer format.

!K{DRS}

Kills breakpoint previously specified with the B command. See B command for limitations of breakpoint addresses. The K command, followed by a <cr>, kills all current breakpoints in the table. A minus (−) character is displayed for each breakpoint entry successfully removed from the table.

!L{DRS}

Displays the link fields of the frame implied in the DRS. A DFS may not be used with this command and will generate an error message.

!M

Toggles modal trace function on or off. The modal trace function, when on, enters the debugger each time a frame boundary is crossed.

!ME {*line#*}

Assigns all PCB and symbolic reference data specifications to the specified line number. The ME command, followed by a <cr>, resets the pointer to the current virtual process' PCB.

! MULD *decnum decnum*

Multiplies two decimal numbers and displays result in decimal.

!MULX *hexnum hexnum*

Multiplies two hexadecimal numbers and displays result in hexadecimal.

!N {*tally reference counter*}

Prints the instruction address and other characteristics for the number of times specified in the tally reference counter prior to return to the debugger command level, unless a real error is encountered, in which case entry to the command level is automatic.

The N command, followed by a <cr>, cancels this function, such that all breaks will re-enter the debugger command level.

!OFF

Terminates process, logs process off of system, and returns control to logon message.

A change was made to this command in release 2.2. Formerly, if the system debugger was entered from the PICK/BASIC debugger, an OFF would return control to the PICK/BASIC debugger. Now, it logs off.

!P

Toggles the LISTFLG function, either enabling or disabling output display.

!R (*regaddr*)

Indicates indirect reference to specified register number address. See the section on DFS-Data Format Specifications.

!SUBD *decnum decnum*

Subtracts two decimal numbers and displays result in decimal.

!SUBX *hexnum hexnum*

Subtracts two hexadecimal numbers and displays result in hexadecimal.

!T {DRS}

Sets a trace table entry, indicating to the debugger to display the specified data element, along with its address, on each break. If the DRS is omitted, the T command toggles the trace function on or off. The system will display the appropriate condition.

A plus (+) character is displayed for each trace table entry successfully entered into the table, until the table is full. The maximum number of trace table entries is four.

!TIME

Displays the current system time and date.

!U {DRS}

Removes trace table entries previously specified with the T command. A minus (−) character is displayed for each trace table entry successfully removed from the table.

The U command, followed by a <cr>, clears all commands previously specified with the T command.

!X {DRS}

Activates Hexadecimal display format. See section on DFS-Data Format Specifications.

The X command, followed by a <cr>, displays subsequent output in Hexadecimal format.

!XTD *hexnum*

Converts hexadecimal number to its decimal equivalent and displays result.

!XTD {*radix*} *hexnum*

Converts radix (base) to its decimal equivalent and displays result. Default radix = 16.

!Y {DRS}

Sets a y-trace table entry indicating to display the specified data element, along with its address, each time the data element changes. If the DRS is omitted, the Y command toggles the function on or off.

The current value of the data, stored in aligned words, is kept with the address data, so that the table element size will change with varying sizes of data.

A plus (+) character is displayed for each entry successfully entered into the table, until the y-trace table is full. The maximum number of entries is four.

This slows down execution speed drastically.

!Z {DRS}

Cancels data break commands set by previous Y command.

The Z command, when followed by a <cr>, cancels all data breaks set by previous Y command.

A minus (−) character is displayed for each entry successfully removed from the y-trace table.

* * * *

10

PICK/BASIC debugger

The PICK/BASIC debugger is used for tracing execution locations and variables in PICK/BASIC programs.

About compatibility with SMA standards

There are no SMA standards at present for the PICK/BASIC debugger.

Symbol definitions

The symbol definitions are automatically defined during the compile process, and concatenated to the object code pointer in the dictionary level of the program file.

Entering the debugger

There are several ways to enter the debugger. Some of them are voluntary. Among the voluntary methods are:

- Pressing the "break" key while a PICK/BASIC program is executing
- Running the program with a D option

For example:

```
RUN BP ENTER.CUSTOMER (D)<cr>
```

or, if the program is cataloged, providing a D option after the program name at TCL:

```
ENTER.CUSTOMER (D)<cr>
```

- Placing a "DEBUG" statement in the source code of the program at the point where you want to enter the debugger

The other means of entering the debugger is, of course, involuntarily, which occurs during a "fatal" error condition, like trying to write to a diskette that is still in its jacket or referencing a file that hasn't been opened. Refer to the PICK/BASIC Error Message chapter for clues to the causes and cures of most of the fatal error conditions. The debugger is usually gracious enough to give you an error message number and a vague clue of why the program died.

Prompt character

The prompt character, asterisk (*), appears in the leftmost column of the terminal display screen, indicating that the debugger is ready to accept any legal command.

Operators

Perform a logical comparison function and are used in conjunction with the "B" command for setting breakpoint conditions.

=	Equal to
>	Greater than
<	Less than
>=	Greater than or equal to
<=	Less than or equal to
#	Not equal to

Referencing Variables

*/variable

-or-

*/variable(*n*)

-or-

*/variable(*n*,*n*)

-or-

/

Displays current value of specified string or array variable and allows operator to change current value.

If the literal, "*", is entered, then the values of all variables defined in the program are displayed.

*/*variable*{(*dimension1*{,*dimension2*})}

Displays current value of array element defined in specified variable. The variable name, followed by a <cr>, displays all elements in the array, when more than one is defined, until the last element is displayed or the break key is pressed.

Zone output specification

***[{*leftmargin, rightmargin*}]**

-or-

***[**

Sets left and right margins for output zone limits of debugger display. The [command, followed by a <cr>, removes zone limits.

PICK/BASIC debugger commands

***?**

-or-

***$**

Displays current program name, execution linenumber, and object code verification status.

B*variable operator variable

-or-

B*variable operator "literal"

-or-

B$*operator linenumber

Sets a breakpoint in the trace table, indicating that control shall pass to the debugger when the test condition defined in the command expression is met. The dollar sign ($) character specifies program line numbers for execution/breaks.

A plus (+) character is displayed for each breakpoint successfully entered into the table until the table is full. The maximum number of breakpoints is four.

Note: the spaces between the arguments in the above syntax are simply there for readability—they are not allowed when composing breakpoints, as shown in the following examples:

Examples:

```
*BAMOUNT.DUE>0
```

enters the debugger when "AMOUNT.DUE" is greater than 0.

```
*B$=117
```

enters debugger before executing line 117.

***D**

Displays the contents of the Break and Trace tables.

***DE**
-or-
DEBUG

Transfers control to the system debugger. See also: System Debugger.

***E{*numberlines*}**

Specifies the number of instructions to execute prior to returning to debugger command level.

The E command, followed by a <cr>, disables previous iteration counter setting.

***END**

Terminates program execution and returns control to TCL.

***G{*linenumber*}**

"Go to" function. Transfers control to a specific program (source) line number. The G command, followed by a <cr>, resumes program execution from the current program line number.

Note: if the program was compiled without EOL (End-Of-Line) characters, then the only number allowable for the "GOTO" is one (1).

***K{*breakpoint-number*}**

Kills a breakpoint previously set with the B command, and removes the entry from the breakpoint table.

The K command, followed by a <cr>, removes all breakpoint entries from the table.

***L{*startingline-numberlines*}**
-or-
***L{*numberlines*}**
-or-
***L{*}**
-or-
***L**

Displays source code program lines, beginning from specified starting line number, or from current position, if no starting line number is specified. If the message "NO SOURCE" displays, use the Z command. The L command, followed by an * (asterisk), displays the entire program. The L command, followed by a <cr>, displays the current program source code line.

*LP

Toggles the line printer bit, either directing debugger output to the terminal screen or the spooler.

*N{*numbertimes*}

Instructs the debugger to ignore breakpoints for the next number of times encountered. The N command, followed by a <cr>, resets the bypass, and breakpoints are processed at each occurrence.

*OFF

Terminates program execution, logs process off system, and returns control to the logon message.

*P

Toggles the LISTFLG function, either enabling or disabling output display.

*PC

Closes the currently open spooler file entry, releasing control to the spooler.

*R

Removes the top return stack address of the local subroutine from the stack, causing the program to return from current subroutine as though a RETURN statement was encountered.

*S

Displays the contents of the subroutine stack.

*T{*variable*}

Sets a trace table entry, indicating to the debugger to display the specified data element, along with the contents of the break and trace tables, on each break. A plus (+) character is displayed for each trace table entry successfully entered into the table, until the table is full. The maximum number of trace table entries is six. The T command, followed by a <cr>, toggles the trace function on or off.

*U{*trace table entry*}

Removes trace table entries previously specified with the T command. A minus (−) character is displayed for each trace table entry successfully removed from the table. The U command, followed by a <cr>, clears all trace table entries previously specified with the T command.

*V

Verifies PICK/BASIC object code. No longer serves any useful function.

*Z {DICT} *filename itemname*

-or-

*Z<cr>

FILE/PROG NAME?*filename itemname*

Tells the debugger where to find the source code to use with the object code being executed, and is required before using the L command. The Z command, followed by a <cr>, prompts for the filename and itemname.

11
System error messages

Many error messages that still remain in the ERRMSG file are no longer used, or are too obscure to document. They are still included in the unlikely case that they will ever be needed.

Error messages have their own unique "language", and are handled by a special program contained in the operating system used to format their output according to the various instructions contained in the message, much the same as in PROC.

Error message functions

The following chart illustrates the various instructions available to the error message processor and explains what they mean:

Instruction	*Description*
A	Outputs argument at current screen coordinate
A(n)	Outputs argument, left-justified, in a field of "n" blanks
D	Outputs system date at current screen coordinate
E	Outputs error message item-id, enclosed in brackets
Hstring{+}	Outputs literal string at current screen coordinate The optional + sign is used to hold the cursor position, typically for input
L	Issues a linefeed
L(n)	Issues "n" linefeeds
R(n)	Outputs the next argument, right-justified, in a field of "n" blanks
S(n)	Positions the cursor to column (position) "n" on the current row (line)
T	Outputs system time at current screen coordinate
X	Ignores the next argument in the argument list

Testing error messages

The PRINT-ERR verb can be used to test error messages. It has the general format:

PRINT-ERR *filename item-id*

The filename is usually ERRMSG.

The sequence of error messages

There are several important error messages to know about. The first is an item called "LOGON," that resides in the SYSTEM file. It is used to display the *logon* message, that is, the message that displays on a terminal when the terminal is logged off.

When you log on, the next error message that is activated is an item also called "LOGON," which resides in the ERRMSG file.

After that, error messages "335" is displayed. That's the one that welcomes you to the system and optionally tells you the time, date, and release number.

When you log off, error message "336" is displayed.

The standard Pick system error messages

1 **PASSWORDS CAN ONLY BE CHANGED ON SYSPROG**

2 **Uneven number of delimiters ('" \).**

There must be an even number of single quotes ('), double quotes (") and/or backslashes (\ ) in any TCL command.

3 **Verb?**

Unrecognizable command issued at TCL. Most often cause is the fact that the verb is not defined in the current accounts' Master Dictionary.

5 **The word "item" is illegal.**

Means that the item referred to as "item" has an "X" in attribute one in the dictionary, defining it as "protected" attribute.

7 **A value must follow the HEADING, FOOTING, tag or GRAND-TOTAL connective.**

Each of these modifiers must be followed by a text string enclosed in double quotes.

8 **A window specification string must follow the window connective.**

9 **System D-pointer missing.**

10 **Filename missing.**

The specified filename either has an incorrect file definition item, or points to a file that cannot be located.

11 **Frame locked at location x 'location'.**

Displayed when using the LOCK-FRAME command to permanently corelock a particular frame.

13 **Data level descriptor (filename in dictionary) is missing.**

Means that the D-pointer to the data section of a file has been changed or deleted from the dictionary.

15 **The filename is preceded by an illegal connective.**

Indicates that a connective (such as AND, BY, or BREAK-ON) preceded the filename. Connectives are followed by attribute names, not filenames.

17 **WITHIN is valid only in COUNT, LIST, SUM, or STAT statements.**

18 **The last word may not be a connective.**

Typically caused by ending an ACCESS sentence with a connective, such as AND.

19 **A value without an attribute name is illegal.**

Typical cause is a value enclosed in double quotes in an ACCESS sentence without a WITH clause or enclosing itemnames with double instead of single quotes.

20 **Error in the USING syntax.**

21 **Meaningless item-id in statement.**

22 **TO before item-id valid only in a CHANGE statement.**

24 **The word "item" cannot be identified.**

The specified Attribute-Defining-Item either is improperly formatted, or does not exist as entered.

25 **WITH may not immediately precede a value.**

Means that the Attribute-Defining-Item is missing between WITH and value. Form of selection criteria is: WITH attributename {operator} "value".

26 **Attribute values may not both precede and follow an attribute name.**

Form of selection criteria is:
WITH *attributename* {*operator*} "*value*."

27 **The word WITH is missing**

29 **At least one item-id must be specified for a WITHIN-type statement.**

30 **Error in M/DICT definition of the verb.**

Invalid verb definition. Check verb definition (in MD) for nonhexadecimal characters in attribute two, and compare the verb definition with the same item in SYSPROG's MD or the NEWAC file.

53 **Item list required for WITHIN.**

71 **An illegal connective modifies the word 'word'.**

An Attribute-Defining-Item has been preceded by an illegal connective, such as an "AND" connective.

72 **The value "value" is meaningless.**

Returned upon unsuccessful execution of the user-exit Un1AD, where "n" is the entry point.

79 **The number of separate AND clause sets cannot exceed 9.**

There is a maximum of 9 AND clauses in an ACCESS sentence.

80 **A system error has occurred in model: modename, which may be due to sort-key(s) preceding selection criteria.**

This is normally caused by using an "AND" connective without a "WITH" connective.

82 **Your system privilege level is not sufficient for this statement.**

An operation was attempted that is prohibited by definition of the system privilege level. Check account name in SYSTEM file. Attribute 8 may either be: SYS0 (lowest priority), SYS1, or SYS2 (highest priority).

91 **End tape check - n file(s).**

92 **End of recorded data - n file(s).**

Displayed at the end of a T-EOD command.

93 **Attach the tape unit.**

A tape operation command must be preceded by a T-ATT (tape attach) command. After attachment, it need not be reattached unless a different blocksize is required.

94 **End of file.**

Displayed when an EOF (End of File) mark is encountered during a T-FWD (tape forward) or T-BCK (tape backward) command.

95 **Tape attached to line 'n'.**

Tape must be detached from specified line number with the T-DET command prior to any operations.

96 **BOT**

Beginning-of-tape. Displayed when T-BCK (tape back) command was issued on the first file on the tape.

97 **End of tape.**

Displayed when any tape moving command reaches the end of tape.

98 **Parity error!**

Means big trouble. Hopefully, this does not display during a full restore. It normally means that the tape has media problems and is unreadable. Parity errors are a good reason to check your FILE-SAVE tape immediately after it is created, using a "dummy" restore. A dummy restore is done using the SEL-RESTORE command. When asked for the account name, use a word that is *not* a valid account name (like Rumpelstiltskin) and a filename that is also *not* valid (like Skywalker, in case there is a Rumpelstiltskin account you were not aware of).

100 'item' is not 'whatever'.

118 The form 'with attribute and attribute' is undefined.

158 An illegal connective of the form "value" modifies "value".

163 Attribute for SORT, BREAK-ON, or TOTAL connective is missing.

164 Total or control break connective not succeeded by attribute definition.

Means that a TOTAL or BREAK-ON modifier was not followed by a valid attribute name.

166 The A-correlative attribute name 'item' is illegal.

167 Missing terminal quote ("/') in A-correlative: 'item'.

Look at the specified attribute name in attribute 8 for the A correlative.

Make sure that there is an even number of quotes.

168 Illegal A-correlative.: 'n'.

Indicates that the A correlative has an unrecognizable syntax. Could be a million or so different reasons. Look at the Correlative section of the ACCESS chapter for syntax on the A correlative.

169 Missing left paren in A-correlative: "n".

Look at the specified attribute name in attribute 8 for the A correlative. Make sure that each set of parentheses is "opened" and "closed".

170 Missing right paren in A-correlative: "n".

See error message 169.

173 Missing semicolon in A-correlative.

192 Erroneous object string.

193 Basic object code cannot be copied to an item.

194 Don't copy to the same item in the same file.

This error occurs when the following syntax is used in a COPY process:

```
COPY old-filename *
TO:new-filename
```

Simply put, COPY copies the "first" item in "old-filename" to an ITEM called "new-filename", and then tries to do the same for the "next" item in "old-filename".

To correct this, precede "new-filename" with a left-parenthesis, as follows:

```
COPY old-filename *
TO:(new-filename
```

196 'item' is too large to be an item.

197 This get-list or save-list specification is incorrect.

198 The list pointed to by pointer item 'item' is defective.

199 Insufficient workspace for item 'item'.

Typically displayed when a very large PICK/BASIC is executed. The best way to correct is to break up the program into smaller, more manageable subroutines.

200 'POINTER-FILE' IS NOT A POINTER TYPE (DCODE = 'DC') FILE.

201 'filename' is not a filename.

Indicates that a filename specified in a TCL command does not exist, or is improperly defined in the Master Dictionary of the current account.

202 'item-id' not on file.

Normally appears in conjunction with a GET-LIST command followed by an ACCESS command. Typically indicates that an item has been deleted from the file since the list was saved.

302 Item name?

Indicates the itemname or itemlist specification is missing from the TCL-II command.

204 File definition 'filename' is missing.

File (D−) pointer missing from M/DICT.

205 No statements to be assembled.

An assembly process was attempted on an item that either does not exist, or has no lines to assemble.

208 Error in item-id list.

210 File 'filename' is access protected.

An operation was attempted on a file that has access code locks present. See System Administrator for gaining access to file. Literally means that the access and update codes do not match the user logon corresponding entry in the SYSTEM file. Ensure that the correct account is being used.

211 Mode 'modename' no assembled code can be found.

Displayed upon attempting to MLOAD or MVERIFY an assembler object frame that contains no object code.

212 Mode 'modename' has no frame statement.

The first line of an assembler program must contain a FRAME statement, otherwise it is incapable of being verified or loading into the ABS area.

213 Mode 'modename' location counter error at line "n".

Output from MLOAD verb. Indicates that continuity of object code location counter in assembled assembly code is corrupted or has an illegal value. Reassemble mode or restore good item from FILE-SAVE tape.

214 Mode 'modename' overflows frame frame# at line symbol line#.

215 Mode 'modename' hex error at line no. line#.

Output from MLOAD verb. Indicates that there is illegal object code in item. Reassemble or restore good item from FILE-SAVE tape.

216 Mode 'modename' loaded; frame = fid; size = size; cksum = check-sum.

Displayed after successful loading of an assembler (object) frame into the ABS area.

217 Mode 'modename' verified; frame = frame; size = size; cksum = checksum.

Displayed upon execution of the MVERIFY command, used to compare the contents of the frame in the ABS area with the actual code.

218 Mode 'modename' frame = frame has "n" mismatches.

Displayed when an MVERIFY operation (the verb used in VERIFY-SYSTEM) has found that the object code in the file item does not exactly match the code loaded in the corresponding frame in the ABS area. This error may be corrected by reloading the mode, or all ABS frames.

219 Illegal command: command.

Displayed when the RUNOFF process interprets an illegal command.

220 'itemname' exited.

Used by Editor.

221 'itemname' filed.

Used by Editor.

222 'itemname' deleted.

Used by Editor.

223 'itemname' exists on file.

224 'item' is a pointer item. It may not be loaded into a nonpointer file.

225 TSYM must be dict & data mod/sep 1,137,1.

The TSYM (Temporary symbol table) file must be created with both a dictionary and a data section.

226 Tape format error.

See error message 98. This is even more insidious than parity errors, because this kind of problem does *not* get detected during a T-CHK. It literally means that the tape is not "logically" constructed properly.
These types of errors can usually be detected by running a fake or dummy restore after a FILE-SAVE.

234 Item size exceeds 32,000 bytes.

Source unknown. Normally, an abort will occur if an item exceeds the 32K limit. The editor has its own message for this problem. Let us know if you find what causes this.

235 Attempt to write into update protected file!

239 'filename' is not a pointer type (dcode= 'dc') file.

240 a "SELECT" or "SSELECT" must be used preceding a 'save-list' statement!

Displayed when a SAVE-LIST command is not preceded by a GET-LIST, SELECT, SSELECT, OR QSELECT command.

241 Successful compile!! n frames used.

Displayed when a PICK/BASIC program miraculously survives the compile process. Note: this message has absolutely nothing to do with the program running successfully.

242 'itemname' decataloged.

Displayed when removing the object code for a PICK/BASIC program with the DECATALOG command.

243 list saved - n frames used.

Displayed after saving a list with the SAVE-LIST command.

244 'item' cataloged!

Displayed when using the CATALOG command on a PICK/BASIC program.

245 'item' list deleted.

246 'item' is no longer a list or no longer on file.

247 'item' is basic object code.

Usually displayed when an operation such as EDIT is performed on the DICT (dictionary) level of a program file, where the object pointers are stored. Not generally a good idea; that's why it is prevented. If you really want to play around with the object code, use the system debugger and the DUMP command.

260 Invalid batch lock command: command.

265 PROC stack overflow.

267 PROC transfer to 'procname' cannot be completed.

Displayed when a PROC attempts to link another PROC that it cannot find.

268 The destination of the PROC "GO" statement: GO n, cannot be found.

This error normally means that there is a statement in the PROC telling the PROC to "GOTO" a specific statement label, which cannot be found.

269 Input to proc buffer cannot exceed 298 characters.

270 Format error in the proc statement: PROC statement.

Displayed when an illegal statement is encountered in a PROC. Another possible cause is when a PROC gets updated (edited) while it is being run. Never, ever, change PROCs while they are running!

272 A value exists for the attribute referenced by the element: element.

273 Error in column-number/field-width or format specification at: location.

274 Unrecognizable batch-string element: element.

275 Y or F sub-element error at batch-string element: element.

276 D-2 update without d-1 being specified, at batch-string element: element.

277 J element missing at batch-string element: element.

278 Error in processing secondary batch-string element: element.

279 Incorrect scaling factor in f* batch-string element: element.

280 File-definition batch element error at: element.

281 D1 must have Y11 storage correlative error at: location.

282 Invalid parameter for SELECT list.

289

	TERMINAL	**PRINTER**
PAGE WIDTH:	**termwidth**	**printerwidth**
PAGE DEPTH:	**termdepth**	**printerdepth**
LINE SKIP:	**lineskip**	
LF DELAY:	**lfdelay**	
FF DELAY:	**ffdelay**	
BACKSPACE:	**backspace**	
TERM TYPE:	**termtype**	

See the TERM and the SET-TERM commands in the TCL section.

290 The range of the parameter "parameter" is not acceptable.

This is used by two processes: First, the TERM and SET-TERM commands, to indicate arguments that are too high. Second, this is used by the LIST-LABEL and SORT-LABEL commands when the total width of output for the labels exceeds the device width to which the output is being directed. Simply fix the TERM characteristics and try again.

293 **Total number of contiguous frames: n.**

Displayed in the POVF command.

298 **Format error in specifications.**

316 **Numeric parameter missing.**

331 **The account file is missing.**

Indicates that ACC (Accounting History File) has been deleted, improperly defined in the SYSPROG account or SYSTEM file, or the Q-pointer to it in the current account MD is missing or improperly constructed. This error sometimes occurs when logging on to a system while a restore is in progress. If a restore is *not* in progress, the problem can be corrected by performing a SEL-RESTORE of the ACC file from a FILE-SAVE, or by correcting the Q-pointer.

335 **The PICK System for the IBM PC-AT Ver 2.n.**

See "The Sequence of Error Messages" at the beginning of this section.

336 **Logged off at time on date.**

See "The Sequence of Error Messages" at the beginning of this section.

337 **User is not logged on.**

This displays when sending a message to a user who is not currently logged on.

338 **Account file statistics were not updated due to either insufficient workspace to contain the account file item, or system dictionary changed while you were logged on.**

Indicates that the ACC item is too large for available workspace. As a procedural recommendation, periodically clear the DATA section of the ACC file, but *not* while anyone is logged on. Additionally, if accounting statistics are not required, change attribute 9 in the SYSTEM file from "U" (Update ACC) to "L", and avoid altering the SYSTEM file while users are logged on.

340 **Connect time = n mins.; cpu = n units; lptr pages = n.**

341 **PC-AT System verified.**

342 *****PC-AT RELEASE 1.0-SYSTEM DOES NOT VERIFY!***.**

390 **'frame' LOADED.**

391 **'frame' VERIFIED.**

398 **The file D-pointer requires a V(ertical) correlative for this statement.**

The file D-pointer must contain a V code in attribute 8 to process ACCESS sentences containing the WITHIN connective.

399 **The maximum of 20 levels for a WITHIN-type statement has been exceeded.**

401 **No items present.**

Possibly the second-most popular error message ever displayed, right after error message 3 (Verb?). This error means that the attempted selection criteria did not allow any items to be selected for processing. Also happens on empty files.

403 **End of list.**

404 **n items selected.**

Displayed after the successful completion of a SELECT, SSELECT, GET-LIST, or QSELECT.

405 **n items listed.**

Displayed at the end of most ACCESS reports unless otherwise suppressed or indicated.

406 **item count = n, byte count = n, avg. bytes/item = n, avg. items/group = n, std. deviation = n, avg. bytes/group = n.**

This is the summary line of HASH-TEST and ISTAT.

407 **n items counted.**

408 **One item counted.**

410 **A synonym (q-type) file cannot be specified in this statement.**

This error means that an attempt was made to issue a DELETE-FILE or CLEAR-FILE command on a file designated as a Q-pointer. Fortunately, this is not allowed.

411 **'DICT' or 'DATA' must be specified in a CLEAR-FILE statement.**

This error means that a CLEAR-FILE command did not indicate which level, either DICT or DATA to clear.

412 **Insufficient disk space available for the file.**

This error occurs when there is not a large enough block of contiguous disk space to fulfill the modulo request in the CREATE-FILE command. If the overflow table is heavily fragmented, consider doing a full restore to get all available overflow back into one contiguous block. Another alternative is buying another disk drive.

413 **The filename already exists in the master dictionary.**

This means that there is an item in the MD of the current account with the same item-id as the one requested in the CREATE-FILE command that just croaked.

414 **Illegal or missing modifier used in defining the file area(s).**

This indicates an error in the syntax of the CREATE-FILE command when creating a new file. See the CREATE-FILE command in the TCL section.

415 'item' exists on file.

Displayed by the COPY process, when the O (overwrite) option is *not* in effect, indicating that a duplicate item-id existed on the destination file, preventing the copy from taking place.

416 Range error in modulo or separation parameter.

This typically displays when one or both of the modulos are omitted from the CREATE-FILE command. See the CREATE-FILE command in the TCL section.

417 File 'filename' created; base = base, modulo = modulo, separ = sep (1).

Displayed upon the successful completion of the CREATE-FILE command.

418 File definition item 'filename' not copied

Displayed by the COPY process when a D-pointer is encountered. These are *never* copied.

419 The specified file cannot be cleared or deleted!

This displays when someone foolishly tries to clear the SYSTEM file or their MD.

420 Dictionary file deletion cannot be done without deletion of data-section(s) first.

This means that an attempt was made to delete the dictionary level of a file without first deleting the DATA level.

421 Statistics of item : total = n, average = n, count = n.

Displayed by the STAT command.

422 Byte statistics for: item total = n, average = n, items = n, cksum = n, bits = n.

Displayed by the CHECK-SUM command.

423 Total of attribute = n

Displayed by the SUM command.

425 INVALID FRAME-ID REQUEST

This means that a frame-id less than 0 or greater than maxfid was requested. You are lucky you did not get a referencing illegal frame abort.

426 Data file already exists!

This displays when attempting to create a new DATA level on an existing dictionary using a name that already exists in the dictionary.

427 There is no data section for this file.

428 'item' object pointer not found.

Results when an attempt is made to DECATALOG a PICK/BASIC program that is not compiled, or has no source item in the data section.

429 **'item' program object verifies.**

430 **'item' program object does not verify.**

432 **'item' item-name used in a program-file dictionary, compile aborted.**

This error means that there is an item in the DICT (dictionary) of the program file that is *not* an object code pointer item, but has the same name as the source program attempting to be compiled. For example, this problem would occur if you tried to compile a program called "BP" in the "BP" file. If it worked, it would hammer the pointer to the DATA section.

521 **Too many characters in word to block.**

Indicates that one of the words to block print would exceed the device width to which output is being directed.

522 **BLOCK-CONVERT file missing or improperly defined.**

This either means that the BLOCK-CONVERT file has been deleted or that the Q-pointer from the current account is invalid.

523 **Block output would exceed page width.**

524 **The letter 'character' is missing from the block-convert file.**

Displayed by the BLOCK-PRINT command when a requested character is missing from the BLOCK-CONVERT file.

525 **Input character 'character' is improperly formatted in BLOCK-CONVERT file.**

530 **Already logged on**

This displays when attempting to log on a line that is already on.

531 **Process roadblocked.**

This occurs when trying to log off a line that has been marked "roadblocked" by the monitor, due to disk accesses by the process.

532 **Illegal user id.**

This displays when trying to log a port on to an account that does not exist in the SYSTEM file.

533 **Logon successful.**

Indicates that the LOGON verb worked.

534 **Logoff successful.**

Indicates that the LOGOFF verb worked.

535 **Illegal line number.**

This displays when trying to log on a port that is outside the actual available number of ports.

536 **ALREADY LOGGED OFF.**

This displays when logging off a line that is already logged off.

550 **A required numeric parameter is missing or invalid.**

552 **Item 'item' has invalid format.**

604 **'label' is an undefined label reference.**

630 **'stop' in effect. Use 'resume'!**

631 **Spooler is waiting for printer cable to be attached!**

632 **Spooler is waiting because the printer is off-line!**

633 **Spooler is waiting for the tape to be detached!**

634 **Spooler is waiting for the printer to be detached!**

637 **The spooler needs the next reel of tape to continue!**

638 **The spooler is writing a file on tape.**

640 **The spooler is printing a file on the printer.**

641 **Hold file # n added.**

644 **An open file for line # n is being processed.**

645 **A closed file for line # n is being processed.**

646 **The current job has been aborted.**

651 **The spooler is not active.**

652 **Too many pages!**

653 **No file being output or file originated on another line!**

654 **Illegal output string length!**

655 **Not attached!**

656 **End of spool queue.**

657 **Not a hold file.**

658 **Illegal number! Use Sp-status.**

659 **Line printer ready.**

660 **Insufficient privileges; or device is attached to a spooler!**

700 **Run-time f-correlative abort.**

701 **Invalid function correlative definition: definition.**

705 **Illegal conversion code : 'conversion'.**

This indicates that there is an invalid conversion code. Be careful that there are no embedded spaces in the conversion line.

706 **The translate conversion-code : code is illegal.**

708 **'value' cannot be converted.**

780 **Item 'item' not on file.**

781 **'item' added.**

782 **'item' updated.**

783 **'item' deleted.**

802 **n items dumped.**

Displayed at the end of a T-DUMP or S-DUMP.

803 **n item(s) loaded.**

Displayed at the end of a T-LOAD.

805 **n items copied.**

806 **n items updated.**

808 **SYSTEM PRIORITIES**
INTERACTIVE PRIORITY **priority**
BATCH PRIORITY **priority**
SUPER HIGH PROCESS n
TIME SLICE (MS) timeslice

911 **Unable to run binary save — other users still logged on!**

950 **Linkfield error-group at n - Frame n Links: n...**

951 **Illegal forward link. Group at n Frame n Links n...**

952 **Illegal backward link. Group at n Frame n Links n...**

953 **Should link back to: Group at n Frame n Links n...**

954 **New error items created in TSYM.**

990 **Error in ABS-DUMP frame limits specifications.**

992 **n item(s) have been restored.**

993 **Account name must be specified.**

999 **Core PIBs Lines On PCBO Wsstart Wssize Sysbase/mod/sep Maxfid Ovf.**

1004 **'item' not on file.**

1011 **TRULY BIZARRE ERROR IN THE SELECTION PROCESSOR. TRY TO GENERATE A REPRODUCIBLE CASE. CALL YOUR SYSTEM SOFTWARE SUPPORT GROUP.**

Yes, this is a real message.

1050 **THAT IS AN OBSOLETE BASIC VERB (RUN OR CATALOG). PLEASE OBTAIN THE CURRENT DEFINITION.**

1051 THAT IS A PROGRAM CATALOGED UNDER PRE-R80 PROTOCOLS. PLEASE RECATALOG THE PROGRAM.

1059 No tape defined!

1060 Illegal tape op!

1065 Not detached!

1080 Tape device code is illegal.

1081 Tape device code is undefined.

1082 Tape device is assigned to 1/4-inch Streaming Cartridge Tape.

1083 Tape device is assigned to low density (320K) floppy using drive 'drive'.

1084 Tape device is assigned to std. density (360K) floppy using drive 'drive'.

1085 Tape device is assigned to high density (1.2M) floppy using drive 'n'.

1090 ASSIGNMENT SUCCESSFUL.

1091 Invalid floppy drive parameter.

1092 Invalid floppy media type parameter.

1093 Requested floppy drive is not installed.

1094 Requested floppy drive not supported by PICK.

1095 Cannot set high density media in standard density drive.

1099 Hold entry #.

1100 Start code locked.

1101 Null printer number.

1102 Printer number too big.

1103 No form number.

1104 Illegal character.

1105 Printer must be stopped.

1106 Form number too big—exceeds 125.

1107 TOO MANY PAGES IN THE PAGE SKIP—EXCEEDS 9.

1108 Negative number.

1109 Too many print files.

1110 Illegal printer type—not P or S.

1111 Illegal line number or parallel printer number.

1112 Illegal parallel printer number.

1113 Illegal serial printer number.

1114 The device or line which you specified is being used as another printer on the system.

1115 Allocation attempted on uninitialized PRINTER.

1116 There is no job enqueued for output on the forms you specified. Therefore, alignment is not possible.

1117 Your align was just aborted by someone. Please start the align process over.

1118 The printer control block has been initialized. Hopefully, the correct paper is in the printer, and the correct lpi is set.

1119 You are attempting to start printer a on line n, which is not stopped.

1121 You are improperly logged on.

1122 Your output specification is no output. Reassign your line if you wish to output a holdfile.

This occurs during an SP-EDIT of a hold file, choosing the Y response to the question, "SPOOL? ". The error occurs because the current output assignment for the process is assigned to hold output. Cancel the hold assignment with another SP-ASSIGN, followed by *no* options, and then SP-EDIT again.

1123 Line # n is already logged on.

This error occurs when attempting to start a serial printer on a port that is already in use by a terminal.

1126 PRINTER # n CONTROL BLOCK HAMMERED. CLEARED TO NULL.

This displays when using the SP-KILL Dn, where "n" is the number of a printer to delete from the printer queue.

1129 n Form q elements unlinked.

1130 Printer list elements Stak Lk Ln Curpos Begfid Cp Fo Frms Date Time Acct.

Used by LISTPEQS command.

1131 Printer list elements. # Stak Lk Ln Status Cp Fo Frms Date Time Acct.

Used by the LISTPEQS command.

1132 n queue elements.

1133 n frames in use.

1134 Printer assignments Printer Output queues Page Dev or Status Type Number skip line #

Used by the LISTPTR command.

1140 **Your open files were closed.**
Displayed when using the SP-CLOSE command.

1141 **Line Status Cop Form**
 # ies #

1143 **Align terminated; printer stopped.**

1144 **The tape is not available for use just now.**

1145 **Illegal specification number specification.**

1147 **Not attached.**

1148 **Tapeout terminated because of assign T or null assignment.**

1149 **Fatal spooler abort!!**

1150 **There is something wrong with the syntax of your verb's options.**

1151 **Entry # n**

1160 **Your output specification is no output. Reassign your line if you wish to output a holdfile.**

1161 **End of requested print files.**

1162 **End of print file control block.**

1169 **Illegal printer number—must be between 0 and 7 inclusive.**

1170 **Printer # n set to stop.**

1171 **and is inactive.**

1172 **but is still active.**

1173 **Printer # control block set to null.**

1174 **is unallocated.**

1175 **Parallel printer # n has been deleted.**

1176 **Serial printer # n has been deleted, and its process sent to Logon.**

1177 **Printer # n is inactive.**

1178 **The job being output on printer # n is not your print file.**

1179 **Job aborted on printer # n.**

1180 **Print file # n was not unlinked because it is being output.**

1181 **Print file # n was not unlinked because it is unused.**

1182 **Print file # n was not unlinked because it is not spooled.**

1183 **Printer file # n was not created on the account onto which you are now logged.**

1184 Print file # n was unlinked and is available as a hold file.

1200 The spooler is inactive.

1201 The spooler is active.

1202 Needs to start printers.

1203 Needs to log disk errors.

1204 The SPOOLER is in an unambiguous state.

See error message 1011.

1209 The control block for printer # n is in an ambiguous state. Delete the printer from the spooler system.

1210 Printer # n # is.

1211 unallocated.

1212 serial.

1213 parallel.

1214 ,inactive.

1215 ,active.

1216 ,stopped.

1217 ,and on line.

1218 ,and off line.

1219 The printer cable is off.

1220 There is no controller for this printer.

1221 The printer is defined as parallel printer # n.

1222 The printer is running on line n.

1229 Print file being output is element n.

1230 Open file for line #n.

1231 Closed file for line #n.

1232 Generated on account.

1233 , which is n frames long.

1234 and the output is choked.

1235 .

1239 Erroneously, the printer has not output queues assigned to it.

1240 Assigned output queues:

1241 ,

1242 ,

1243 The number of inter-job pages to eject is n.

1250 This system does not have parallel printers.

12

PICK/BASIC error messages

The standard PICK/BASIC error messages

Some of the messages contained in this chapter are no longer described in the Pick documentation. They are left here for compatibility with previous versions of the system and for historical significance. Many are also good for a laugh.

About SMA standards

There are no published standards for PICK/BASIC error messages.

B0 **Program "programname" compiled. n frames used.**
Displayed when a PICK/BASIC program miraculously survives the compile process.

B10 **Variable has not been assigned a value; zero used!**
Displayed when executing a BASIC program that references a variable that has not previously been referenced. Also occurs when writing dimensioned arrays that have not been "set" to null with a MAT assignment.

B11 **Tape record truncated to tape record length!**
This occurs in programs that write tape records when a tape record exceeds the number of bytes at which the tape was attached.

B12 **File has not been opened.**
Indicates that a read or write operation was attempted on a file that has not previously been opened with an OPEN statement.

B13 **Null conversion code is illegal; no conversion done!**
This means that the conversion code expression in an ICONV or OCONV statement evaluated to null and that it did not do exactly what was expected.

B14 **Bad stack descriptor.**

Indicates that the number of arguments passed with a CALL statement differ than the number of arguments in the SUBROUTINE statement in the external subroutine. Also occurs when a filevariable is used as an operand.

B15 **Illegal opcode: "opcode".**

Try recompiling the program.

B16 **Nonnumeric data when numeric required; zero used!**

Typically occurs when a mathematical function is attempted on a string variable. Probably the second-most popular error message, in terms of appearance.

B17 **Array subscript out-of-range.**

This fatal error occurs when referencing a subscript less than zero or greater than the number of subscripts (attributes) declared in the DIM or DIMENSION statement that established storage space for the dimensioned array.

B18 **Attribute number less than −1 is illegal.**

Occurs when the attribute expression of the READV or WRITEV statement evaluates to a negative number.

B19 **Illegal pattern.**

Indicates a meaningless pattern in a MATCH or MATCHES statement.

B20 **COL1 or COL2 used prior to executing a FIELD stmt; zero used!**

This means that a reference was made to either the COL1( ) or COL2( ) functions prior to issuing a FIELD statement.

B21 **Line line matread: number of attributes exceeds vector size.**

This error occurs when the number of attributes returned in a MATREAD is greater than the number of attributes established in the DIM statement. All "extra" attributes are stuffed into the "last" defined vector, delimited by attribute marks, so at least the item will survive a MATWRITE operation. Just do not try to refer to ANYTHING in the last vector location. Over dimensioning is O.K.

B22 **Called program is not a subroutine.**

The statement, SUBROUTINE followed by the program name, must be on line one of each external subroutine.

B24 **Divide by zero illegal; zero used!**

This indicates that a number was attempted to be divided by zero. Check the divisor to make sure that it has been assigned a value.

B25 **Program 'programname' has not been cataloged.**

This message displays when a CALL statement is issued, referring to an external BASIC program subroutine which has not been cataloged.

B26 **UNLOCK attempted before LOCK.**

This indicates that an attempt was made to UNLOCK one of the 48 system execution locks prior to its having been locked.

B27 **RETURN executed with no GOSUB.**

This typically occurs when an internal subroutine is executed without having been transferred to with a GOSUB statement, causing the RETURN statement to force this error.

B28 **Not enough workspace.**

This typically occurs when running a large BASIC program that may be dealing with one or more large data items. Program size is limited to 32,000 bytes. The solution is to break the program into smaller subroutines until this limitation is removed from the Pick System.

B29 **Calling program must be cataloged.**

CATALOG all mainline programs and external subroutines.

B30 **Array size mismatch.**

This occurs when a mainline program and an external subroutine both refer to the same dimensioned array, but each declares a different number of attributes. Also occurs in a "MAT copy " (MAT A = MAT B) when the number of vectors are different.

B31 **Stack overflow.**

This occurs when a program calls too many nested subroutines.

B32 **Page heading exceeds maximum of 1400 characters.**

A HEADING statement in BASIC cannot exceed 1400 characters.

B33 **Precision declared in subprogram 'programname' is different from that declared in the mainline program.**

This indicates that there is a PRECISION statement in an external subroutine that specifies a different number of decimal places than that of the PRECISION statement in the mainline program.

B34 **File variable used where string expression expected.**

This indicates that some reference was made to a variable that has been declared as a file variable in an OPEN statement.

B41 **Lock number is greater than 47.**

This means that the expression evaluated in the LOCK statement contained a number greater than 47. BASIC divides the number by 48 and the remainder is used as the lock number. In release 2.2 and higher, the number of locks has been increased to 64.

B100 **Compilation aborted; no object code produced.**

This is displayed when a compile fails for any reason. As a general rule of thumb, ignore all but the FIRST message that displays when a compile fails. Find and fix the program indicated with the first message and then recompile.

B101 Missing "END", "NEXT", "WHILE", "UNTIL", "REPEAT" or "ELSE"; COMPILATION ABORTED, NO OBJECT CODE PRODUCED.

Not always what it appears. This can be accurate, in that there may be a missing NEXT clause in a FOR..NEXT sequence. Find and fix the problem indicated with the FIRST message and then recompile.

B102 Bad statement.

This compile-time error indicates that there is something syntactically wrong with the line displayed immediately above this message. Look for misspelled statements and/or unclosed quotes or parentheses.

B103 Label 'label' is missing.

Displayed when a GOTO statement refers to a statement label that *cannot* be located in the program. Make sure that the statement label is the *first* executable parameter on the line. If it follows an asterisk, for example, it will never be seen by the compiler. This also occurs when a reference to a dimensioned array is made without indicating a subscript (vector).

B104 Label 'label' is doubly defined.

Indicates that there are two occurrences of the same statement label.

B105 'variable' has not been dimensioned.

This displays when a nondimensioned variable is treated as a dimensioned variable.

B106 'variable' has been dimensioned and used without subscripts.

This is displayed when a reference is made to a dimensioned array without being followed by a subscript (attribute) specification.

B107 "ELSE" CLAUSE MISSING.

B108 LINE line "NEXT" STATEMENT MISSING.

B109 Variable missing in "NEXT" statement.

This occurs when the NEXT statement is not followed by the variable declared in the FOR statement.

B110 END statement missing.

This often occurs when the END statements do not balance in a program, meaning that there may be a missing END statement somewhere in series of IF...THEN clauses.

B111 "UNTIL" OR "WHILE" MISSING IN "LOOP" STATEMENT.

This means that no UNTIL or WHILE conditional expression is specified in the LOOP construct.

B112 REPEAT missing in LOOP statement.

This means that the REPEAT statement cannot be located for the initiating LOOP statement.

B113 Terminator missing.

This displays when a line containing quoted literals is missing one or more of the quote marks, or when "garbage" follows a legal statement. Also occurs at the end of a popular Arnold Schwarzenegger film.

B114 Maximum number of variables exceeded.

PICK/BASIC allows for about 3,200 variables in a program. This is normally enough for most people. If not, try moving some of the variables to an external subroutine.

B115 label 'label' is used before the equate stmt.

This occurs when a reference is made to a constant prior to its being declared with the EQU or EQUATE statement.

B116 label 'label' is used before the COMMON stmt.

All variables must be declared in the COM or COMMON statement prior to being used in a program. This can be avoided, as can other problems, by *not* using the COMMON statement.

B117 label 'label' is missing a subscript list.

This displays when a reference is made to a dimensioned array variable without indicating a subscript (attribute) specification.

B118 label 'label' is the object of an EQUATE statement and is missing.

Indicates that the variable after the TO portion of an EQU statement has not been declared, or is used elsewhere in the program.

B119 Warning-precision value out of range-ignored.

Indicates that a precision of greater than 6 was specified, in releases 2.2 and higher. Releases 2.1 and lower supported a maximum precision of 4.

B120 Warning-multiple precision statements-ignored!

This nonfatal error message indicates that more than one PRECISION statement is specified in the program. All but the first are ignored.

B121 Label 'label' is a constant and cannot be written into.

This occurs when an attempt is made to change the value of a constant declared in an EQU or EQUATE statement.

B122 Label 'label' is improper type.

Indicates an invalid expression follows the TO in an EQU or EQUATE statement.

B124 Label 'label' has literal subscripts out of range.

Indicates a reference to a subscript (attribute) greater than the number of subscripts declared for the array in the DIM or DIMENSION statement; alternately, may indicate a subscript less than one.

B125 LABEL 'label' HAS A JUMP GREATER THAN 32K BYTES.

B126 OBJECT CODE EXCEEDS 65K.

You are on your own.

B127 OBJECT CODE AND SYMBOL TABLE EXCEED 64K.

Try compiling with the "S" option, which suppresses symbol table generation.

B128 LABEL 'label' EQUATED ARRAY SUBSCRIPT OUT OF RANGE.

Similar to error message B124. This means that an EQU or EQUATE statement makes a reference to a subscript (attribute) location greater than the number of subscripts defined for this array in its DIM or DIMENSION statement.

B130 LINE line THERE IS AN UNRATIONALIZABLE EQUATE.

B154 FOR STATEMENT WITH NO NEXT STATEMENT.

Each FOR.. statement *must* be terminated with a NEXT. If it is, then look at the statements between the FOR and the NEXT to see if there is an extra END statement that would logically cause the compile to think that the end of the program had been reached.

B199 FORMAT ERROR IN SOURCE FILE DEFINITION.

Displayed when a compile is attempted. This means that the D-pointer to the dictionary of the program file does *not* have a "DC" in attribute 1. It may be corrected with the editor.

B209 File is update protected.

Indicates that an update (write operation) was attempted on an update-restricted file.

B210 File is access protected.

Indicates that a read operation was attempted on a read-restricted file.

B222 'CSYM' is not a filename or needs a data level.

This displays when the pointer to the CSYM file is missing or improperly defined in the MD of the current account.

13
ASCII

ASCII	*Decimal*	*Hex*	*Keyboard*
NUL	0	00	
SOH	1	01	<ctl>A
STX	2	02	<ctl>B
ETX	3	03	<ctl>C
EOT	4	04	<ctl>D
ENQ	5	05	<ctl>E
ACK	6	06	<ctl>F
BEL	7	07	<ctl>G
BS	8	08	<ctl>H
HT	9	09	<ctl>I
LF	10	0A	<ctl>J
VT	11	0B	<ctl>K
FF	12	0C	<ctl>L
CR	13	0D	<ctl>M
S0	14	0E	<ctl>N
SI	15	0F	<ctl>O
DLE	16	10	<ctl>P
DC1	17	11	<ctl> Q (X-ON)
DC2	18	12	<ctl>R
DC3	19	13	<ctl> S (X-OFF)
DC4	20	14	<ctl>T
NAK	21	15	<ctl>U
SYN	22	16	<ctl>V
ETB	23	17	<ctl>W

ASCII	*Decimal*	*Hex*	*Keyboard*
CAN	24	18	<ctl>X
EM	25	19	<ctl>Y
SUB	26	1A	<ctl>Z
ESC	27	1B	ESCAPE
FS	28	1C	
GS	29	1D	
RS	30	1E	
US	31	1F	
(blank)	32	20	
!	33	21	
“	34	22	
#	35	23	
$	36	24	
%	37	25	
&	38	26	
′	39	27	
(	40	28	
)	41	29	
*	42	2A	
+	43	2B	
,	44	2C	
−	45	2D	
.	46	2E	
=	47	2F	
0	48	30	
1	49	31	
2	50	32	
3	51	33	
4	52	34	
5	53	35	
6	54	36	
7	55	37	
8	56	38	
9	57	39	
:	58	3A	
;	59	3B	

ASCII	*Decimal*	*Hex*	*Keyboard*
<	60	3C	
=	61	3D	
>	62	3E	
?	63	3F	
@	64	40	
A	65	41	
B	66	42	
C	67	43	
D	68	44	
E	69	45	
F	70	46	
G	71	47	
H	72	48	
I	73	49	
J	74	4A	
K	75	4B	
L	76	4C	
M	77	4D	
N	78	4E	
O	79	4F	
P	80	50	
Q	81	51	
R	82	52	
S	83	53	
T	84	54	
U	85	55	
V	86	56	
W	87	57	
X	88	58	
Y	89	59	
Z	90	5A	
[	91	5B	
\	92	5C	
]	93	5D	
^	94	5E	
-	95	SF	

ASCII	*Decimal*	*Hex*	*Keyboard*
'	96	60	
a	97	61	
b	98	62	
c	99	63	
d	100	64	
e	101	65	
f	102	66	
g	103	67	
h	104	68	
i	105	69	
j	106	6A	
k	107	6B	
l	108	6C	
m	109	6D	
n	110	6E	
o	111	6F	
p	112	70	
q	113	71	
r	114	72	
s	115	73	
t	116	74	
u	117	75	
v	118	76	
w	119	77	
x	120	78	
y	121	79	
z	122	7A	
{	123	7B	
|	124	7C	
}	125	7D	
~	126	7E	
DEL	127	7F	
(Following are high-order ASCII characters)			
	128	80	
	129	81	
	130	82	

ASCII	Decimal	Hex	Keyboard
	131	83	
	132	84	
	133	85	
	134	86	
	135	87	
	136	88	
	137	89	
	138	8A	
	139	8B	
	140	8C	
	141	8D	
	142	8E	
	143	8F	
	144	90	
	145	91	
	146	92	
	147	93	
	148	94	
	149	95	
	150	96	
	151	97	
	152	98	
	153	99	
	154	9A	
	155	9B	
	156	9C	
	157	9D	
	158	9E	
	159	9F	
	160	A0	
	161	A1	
	162	A2	
	163	A3	
	164	A4	
	165	A5	
	166	A6	

ASCII	*Decimal*	*Hex*	*Keyboard*
	167	A7	
	168	A8	
	169	A9	
	170	AA	
	171	AB	
	172	AC	
	173	AD	
	174	AE	
	175	AF	
	176	B0	
	177	B1	
	178	B2	
	179	B3	
	180	B4	
	181	B5	
	182	B6	
	183	B7	
	184	B8	
	185	B9	
	186	BA	
	187	BB	
	188	BC	
	189	BD	
	190	BE	
	191	BF	
@	192	C0	
A	193	C1	
B	194	C2	
C	195	C3	
D	196	C4	
E	197	C5	
F	198	C6	
G	199	C7	
H	200	C8	
I	201	C9	

ASCII	*Decimal*	*Hex*	*Keyboard*
J	202	CA	
K	203	CB	
L	204	CC	
M	205	CD	
N	206	CE	
0	207	CF	
P	208	D0	
Q	209	D1	
R	210	D2	
S	211	D3	
T	212	D4	
U	213	D5	
V	214	D6	
W	215	D7	
X	216	D8	
Y	217	D9	
Z	218	DA	
[	219	DB	
\	220	DC	
]	221	DD	
^	222	DE	
_	223	DF	
'	224	E0	
a	225	E1	
b	226	E2	
c	227	E3	
d	228	E4	
e	229	E5	
f	230	E6	
g	231	E7	
h	232	E8	
i	233	E9	
j	234	EA	
k	235	EB	
l	236	EC	

ASCII	*Decimal*	*Hex*	*Keyboard*
m	237	ED	
n	238	EE	
o	239	EF	
p	240	F0	
q	241	F1	
r	242	F2	
s	243	F3	
t	244	F4	
u	245	F5	
v	246	F6	
w	247	F7	
x	248	F8	
y	249	F9	
z	250	FA	
[	251	FB	START BUFFER
\	252	FC	SUBVALUE MARK
]	253	FD	VALUE MARK
^	254	FE	ATTRIBUTE MARK
-	255	FF	SEGMENT MARK

Glossary

The Pick system is unique in many respects, not the least of which is its own set of terminology. In writing this guide, it was necessary to create some new terms in order to reduce the amount of redundant redefining of functions and parameters.

The following term conventions and definitions are used consistently throughout the PICK Pocket Guide.

<cr> Abbreviation for carriage return. On some keyboards, the key for a <cr> may be called NEWLINE, LINEFEED, RETURN, or ENTER.

ABS frame A frame containing the object code for the operating system. Name derived from "**Ab**solute location".

ABS section The virtual memory storage area between frames 0 and 704, which contains the object code for the operating system and all the frames set aside for user and application system assembler code.

account A collection of logically related files associated with one user or one function on a PICK system.

acctname Acronym for "**account name**", as it appears in SYSTEM file.

ACC file A file found in the SYSTEM file which is used to maintain temporary and, optionally, permanent usage statistics. These statistics include the time and date the user logged on to a particular account, the portnumber used, the total number of minutes and hours used, the total number of pages sent to a printer, and the number of CPU units used during the session. In the dictionary of the ACC file, an item is stored for each port to indicate the port's physical location in attribute 1 and the terminal characteristics in attribute 2. This information is used by the **LISTU** command and, on Pick PC-AT implementations, the **TERM-TYPE** command. The item-id for this item is the portnumber. Use the standard editor to update or add these items.

ACCESS The nonprocedural data retrieval language of PICK. It is used to produce reports using English-like sentences. It is sometimes referred to as ENGLISH or RECALL.

AMC Acronym for **A**ttribute **M**ark **C**ount, or the relative position of an attribute within an item. Used by ACCESS to locate the attribute for retrieval.

argumentlist A list of expressions, each separated by a comma, used to designate information shared between programs using the CALL and SUBROUTINE statements from PICK/BASIC.

arrayvar Acronym for dynamic "**array var**iable". A variable defined for the storage of data elements in a meaningful pattern, as used in PICK/BASIC.

attrexp Acronym for "**attr**ibute mark count **exp**ression"; a PICK/BASIC expression which yields a number to be used as an attribute mark count (AMC) reference.

attribute Synonym for *field* in the PICK world. A specific piece of data which, along with other attributes, constitutes an item or record. The following example illustrates an item with six attributes:

```
001 JES & Associates, Inc.
002 P.O. Box 19274
003 Irvine
004 CA
005 92714
006 714-553-8200
```

attribute mark The reserved character used to separate attributes in an item. For example:

```
Hexadecimal Value-FE
Decimal Value-254
ASCII Value-
<control> {<shift>} ^
```

attrname Acronym for "**attr**ibute **name**". A data element referred to by its name via an Attribute-Defining-Item in the dictionary of the file.

base fid The first "**f**rame-**id**" in the block of (primary) space used to define a file.

baud rate The speed at which data is transmitted to or from a device. For example, CRTs are typically set to a baud rate of 9600 baud, indicating that they are to receive 9600 bits (960 bytes) per second.

bit Acronym for **B**inary D**i**gi**t**. The means by which data is stored on a computer. Each bit represents either a "1" or a "0" with an electrical charge.

byte Eight bits. One character of storage. For example, the character, "A", requires one byte of storage, and is represented in the binary form, "01000001".

buffer A (disk) ABS or data frame while it is in main memory.

BLOCK-CONVERT file The file which contains definitions for "big" letters produced with the BLOCK-PRINT command. It also contains the descriptions of the opcodes produced by a BASIC command in conjunction with the A option.

BP file The file in the SYSPROG account which contains PICK/BASIC source code provided with the Pick System.

col,row Acronym for "**col**umn and **row**", the "X,Y" coordinates for positioning the cursor on the terminal screen in PICK/BASIC. The column indicates how many positions to move horizontally across the screen. The row indicates how many lines to move vertically down the screen.

condexp Acronym for "**cond**itional **exp**ression"; a PICK/BASIC expression which evaluates to a zero (false) or a numeric nonzero (true).

conversion Define an action to be taken on a specified attribute or the results of a correlative during the postprocessing phase of an ACCESS process, which is just before the data is printed and/or displayed. For historical significance, the technical standard committee of the Pick Spectrum Association (formerly SMA) has dubbed a conversion as *reversible-mapping*, meaning that it can either work on an internal-to-external basis or an external-to-internal basis.

convexp Acronym for "**conv**ersion **exp**ression", a PICK/BASIC expression which evaluates to any legal conversion (or correlative), as defined in the section on ACCESS. Note: The "A" and "F" correlatives may *not* be used in the conversion expression.

correlative Define an action to be taken on a specified attribute or set of attributes during the preprocessing phase of an ACCESS process, which is before data is selected and/or sorted. For historical significance, the technical standard committee of the Pick Spectrum Association (formerly SMA) has dubbed a correlative as "non-reversible-mapping", meaning that it cannot be reversed from its output to its input. For example, this would be the case of a formula that added several numbers together to produce a result.

CRT Acronym for **C**athode **R**ay **T**ube. Refers to a terminal with a video screen. Also called VDT or Visual Display Terminal.

CURSOR file (Pick PC-AT only) The file that contains user-definable terminal drivers. See the DEFINE-TERMINAL command in the TCL section.

decnum Acronym for "**dec**imal **num**ber", as used in the ADDD, DIVD, MULD, and SUBD commands documented in the TCL section.

del Acronym for **del**imiter. (As used in the Editor section). Any nonnumeric character used in a multipart editor command to provide a logical separator between parameters. The character chosen as the delimiter must *not* appear in the string of characters being affected by the command.

delimiter May be either:

1) A character used to provide for separation of parameters within a command or function, as in the Editor commands and some correlatives.
2) A special character used to separate data elements in an item or string. Special characters are from X'FC'-'FE'. See chapter 13, ASCII for definitions.

dictionary The level of the file hierarchy which contains the items that define the data in the related data section for use with the ACCESS. The dictionary also contains an item (or multiple items) that provide the physical disk location for the data file (or files).

exp Abbreviation for "**exp**ression"; a variable, literal, constant, string, function, expression enclosed in parentheses, or a combination of variables and/or literals separated by operators used in a PICK/BASIC program.

ERRMSG file The file that contains the parameterized error messages for the system. See the ERRMSG section for an explanation of how the error message handler works.

fid Acronym for "**f**rame **id**". The integer or hexadecimal reference to any particular frame of data on the disk.

file A collection of logically related items.

filename The specific name of a file to access. May also be a Q-pointer to any file on the account or system. Valid filename references may be any of the following four formats:

1) *filename*. This means the DATA section of the specified file on any file-handling command.

   For example:

   LIST CUSTOMER-FILE

2) *DICT filename*. This refers to the DICT (dictionary) level of the specified file.

   For example:

   List DICT CUSTOMER-FILE

3) *dictfilename,datafilename*. This format is used with files having been created with more than one data section. See the CREATE-FILE command in the TCL section.

   For example:

   LIST STAFF, EXECUTIVES

4) *DATA filename*. This unique form is used *only* in the CREATE-FILE, DELETE-FILE, and/or the CLEAR-FILE commands.

   For example:

   CLEAR-FILE DATA CUSTOMER-FILE

filevar Acronym for "**file var**iable expression"; the filename variable assigned as the object of an OPEN statement in a PICK/BASIC program.

frame The basic storage area of the system. Historically, each frame is 512 bytes in length and is capable of storing 500 bytes of data, with the first 12 bytes reserved for linkage fields. Note: some PICK systems now have data frame sizes other than 512 bytes; consult your vendor if you do not know the size of the frames on your system. All of the software implementations of PICK have ABS frames greater than 512; typically they are either 2K (2048 bytes) or, in some cases, 4K (4096 bytes).

GFE Acronym for **G**roup **F**ormat **E**rror. A condition indicating errors in the virtual storage (data) frames of a file. Before the introduction of PICK tools for correcting GFEs, this acronym was sometimes taken to mean "Gone For Ever."

group The name given to a statistically grouped series of items stored in a PICK file. Can logically represent many frames in a linked format. The number of groups in a file is indicated by the modulo of the file.

hashing The process of passing an item-id through a mathematical algorithm to determine the primary frame of the group in which the item belongs. This represents the standard data access method used in the PICK system, sometimes referred to as a "hashed open bucket" access method.

hexnum Acronym for "**hex**adecimal **num**ber", as used in the ADDX, DIVX, MULX, and SUBX commands documented in the TCL section.

idexp Acronym for "item-**id exp**ression"; a PICK/BASIC expression which evaluates to an item-id.

indexexp Acronym for "**index exp**ression"; a PICK/BASIC expression which evaluates to a number to correspond with the numeric position of a statement label in an "ON..GOTO" or "ON..GOSUB" statement.

item Synonym for "record" in the PICK world. Differs from a traditional record in that an item in a PICK system may contain fields or attributes that are not physically located in the item. Therefore, an item is a collection of logically related attributes. Items are stored in groups in a PICK system; a set of logically related groups constitutes a PICK file.

item-id Abbreviation for **Item-Id**entifier. The key or unique identifier to an item in a file. May be any combination of alphanumeric characters, with no practical length restrictions. The use of certain characters should be avoided in constructing item-ids. These characters include: quotes (' or "), backslashes (\), spaces ( ),parentheses, (( )), "up-arrows" (^), and NEVER, EVER, ANY CONTROL CHARACTERS!

itemname Item-id or key. Refers to a single item.

itemlist (ACCESS form) The specific list of items to affect by an ACCESS process, such as a SORT, LIST, COUNT, SELECT, etc. Unless otherwise instructed, ACCESS will affect all items in a file. May be presented in any of the following formats:

1) A single itemname, surrounded by quote marks (") or backslashes (\\)
2) Multiple itemnames, each surrounded by single quotes or backslashes
3) The result of a SELECT, SSELECT, QSELECT, or GET-LIST.

itemlist* (TCL-II form) The specific list of items to affect by any TCL-II process, such as a COPY, ED (EDIT), CATALOG, BASIC, etc. All TCL-II commands must have this parameter indicated, and it may be presented in any of the following formats:

1) A single itemname, surrounded by spaces
2) Multiple itemnames, each surrounded by spaces
3) The result of a SELECT, SSELECT, QSELECT, or GET-LIST.
4) An asterisk (*), which means ALL items currently in the file

K Acronym for **K**ilobytes. 1024 Bytes. Typically used in reference to the amount of RAM memory in a computer.

line# The portnumber of a particular process. Typically used with commands in which a process may be affected by its portnumber, such as LOGON, LOGOFF, and MSG. The line# for a process may be displayed with the WHO, WHAT, WHERE, or LISTU commands.

linkage The reserved area of each data frame used to define the forward and/or backward pointers to the attached (linked) overflow frames. Usually the first twelve bytes of a 512-byte PICK data frame are reserved for linkage information, and the remaining 500 bytes are available for the storage of data. See also: frame.

listname The item-id of a list of items, as stored in the POINTER-FILE, or an optionally specified filename. These lists are created with the SAVE-LIST, COPY-LIST, or EDIT-LIST verbs. Also used with the GET-LIST and DELETE-LIST commands.

literal An alphanumeric string of characters enclosed within quotes, or a number with or without quotes as used in a PICK/BASIC program.

MD Acronym for **M**aster **D**ictionary. The primary vocabulary file for each account. The MD contains verbs, file pointers, PROCs, ACCESS attribute definition items, and various modifiers and connectives. The items placed into each new account MD by the CREATE-ACCOUNT process reside in the NEWAC file in the SYSPROG account.

megabyte One million bytes. Typically used in reference to the amount of (disk) storage available on a computer, before RAM memory got large enough to be measured in megabytes.

modlist Acronym for "**mod**ifier **list**". The list of modifiers used to perform special functions on output of an ACCESS report, such as ID-SUPP, DET-SUPP, LPTR, etc. See the Modifier section of ACCESS for more information.

modulo The number of groups in a file. Defined during the file creation process.

monitor The PICK Operating System software component that controls all input, output, and process scheduling.

NEWACfile The file which contains the verbs, PROCs, and miscellaneous items to be placed into accounts created by CREATE-ACCOUNT.

numexp Acronym for "**num**eric **exp**ression"; a PICK/BASIC expression that evaluates to a number.

outlist Acronym for "**out**put **list**". The names of the Attribute-Defining-Items to output in an ACCESS report.

options Options are typically single-character designators that appear at the end of a command line to alter the normal effect of a particular command. Almost without exception, options are enclosed in parentheses, although the right parenthesis is normally optional. Standard options are discussed at the beginning of each section of this guide. Options that are unique to a command are discussed with the command.

overflow (or overflow table) The list of the available frames on disk that are not being used to store information. Displayed with the POVF command.

parnum Acronym for "**par**ameter **num**ber". Typically used as a reference to one of the locations in the PROC Primary Input Buffer. Alternately may mean whichever input buffer location is active at the time of the instruction.

PCB Acronym for **P**rimary **C**ontrol **B**lock. The first frame of each port/process' workspace. Contains the process' related accumulators, registers, and counters. See the WHERE instruction in the TCL section.

PIB Acronym for **P**rocess **I**dentification **B**lock. Used by the monitor as a scratchpad for process scheduling.

pointer Refers to the "line pointer" counter of the current line number in the editor item.

POINTER-FILE file The file used by default to store lists created with the SELECT, SSELECT, QSELECT, and GET-LIST command. Note: on the PC-AT implementation, each new account is given a Q-pointer into a shared POINTER-FILE in the SYSPROG account.

Primary Input Buffer An area through which data is sometimes capable of being passed from a terminal to the operating system. Typically addressed by the PROC language.

PROCLIB file The file that contains PROCs that are available to all accounts.

PSYM file The file that contains tokens used by the virtual debugger. See also: SET-SYM.

Q-pointer A type of file pointer definition that allows an account to access files defined in a different account.

segment mark The reserved character used to delimit items within a frame on disk. For example:

Hexadecimal Value - FF
Decimal Value - 255
ASCII Value - _

sellist Acronym for "**sel**ection criteria **list**". The selection criteria to limit data being accessed, normally composed of one or more "WITH" clauses in an ACCESS sentence. Unless otherwise instructed, ACCESS will affect all items in a file.

separation The number of frames per group, typically used in the CREATE-FILE command. Normally, separation is "1" because the PICK system automatically links as many frames together as it needs to store data in a group.

seqlist Acronym for "**seq**uence **list**". The collation, or sort, sequence of a report, as defined by one or more "BY" modifiers in an ACCESS sentence. The "seqlist" parameter is only available with ACCESS verbs that sort.

statement A PICK/BASIC command statement.

STAT-FILE file The file used to hold file statistics generated during an ACCOUNT-SAVE or FILE-SAVE.

strexp Acronym for "**str**ing **exp**ression"; a PICK/BASIC expression which evaluates to a string of alphabetic and/or numeric characters.

subvalexp Acronym for "**subva**lue mark count **exp**ression"; a PICK/BASIC expression which yields a number to be used as a subvalue mark count (SVMC) reference.

subvalue A subportion of a value, within an attribute. Delimited by a subvalue mark:

Hexadecimal Value - FC
Decimal Value - 252
ASCII Value - \

SYSPROG-PL file A file that contains miscellaneous PICK/BASIC programs and PROCs and are usually limited to being accessed from the SYSPROG account only.

SYSTEM file The primary file on the R83 PICK system. This file defines all accounts and several system-level files that are accessible to all accounts.

SYSTEM-ERRORS file The file that contains information on hardware-related problems.

TCL Acronym for **T**erminal **C**ontrol **L**anguage. The point from which all operations begin. Indicated with a " " prompt character. In some versions of PICK, there is now support for multiple levels of TCL. Each subsequent level adds an additional prompt character to remind the user where they are. For example, the second level of TCL uses ">" as the prompt character.

timeslice The number of milliseconds allowed to each process upon activation by the PICK Monitor software.

valexp Acronym for "**val**ue mark count **exp**ression"; a PICK/BASIC expression which yields a number to be used as a value mark count (VMC) reference.

value A subportion of an attribute, delimited by a value mark.

Hexadecimal Value - FD
Decimal Value - 253
ASCII Value - <control>]

variable A symbol whose alphanumeric value changes from one repetition of a program to the next in a PICK/BASIC program.

Index

A

B

C

G

H

I

S

T

900	Compusheet+ Introductory Seminar
900e	Compusheet+ Hands-on Workshop
901	Compusheet+ Advanced Seminar
920	Introduction to JET/Word Processing
921	Advanced JET/Word Processing
940	Via-Duct Workshop
945	Via-Vision Workshop
946	Advanced Via-Vision Workshop

In addition to the above Pick and Unix courses, JES offers 15 additional UNIX courses that can be customized to your specific needs.

All JES courses are offered year-round across the United States, Canada, Australia, and soon in Europe and South America. In addition to the public seminar schedule, JES can conduct any of the above classes at your facilities. Please call (714) 553-8200 for a current schedule and course catalog.